the
empathy
advantage

LEADING THE EMPOWERED WORKFORCE

the empathy advantage

HEATHER E. McGOWAN
CHRIS SHIPLEY

Foreword by Denise Williams, Chief People Officer, FIS

WILEY

Published by John Wiley & Sons, Inc., Hoboken, New Jersey.
Published simultaneously in Canada.

For general information on our other products and services or for technical support, please contact our Customer Care Department within the United States at (800) 762-2974, outside the United States at (317) 572-3993 or fax (317) 572-4002.

If you believe you've found a mistake in this book, please bring it to our attention by emailing our reader support team at wileysupport@wiley.com with the subject line "Possible Book Errata Submission."

Wiley also publishes its books in a variety of electronic formats. Some content that appears in print may not be available in electronic formats. For more information about Wiley products, visit our web site at www.wiley.com.

Library of Congress Cataloging-in-Publication Data is Available:

ISBN 9781394155514 (paperback)
ISBN 9781394155521 (ePub)
ISBN 9781394155538 (ePDF)

Cover Design: Wiley
Cover Image: © fixer00/Shutterstock

SKY10041777_012423

For my mother, brother, and father. Their collective empathy while navigating each other with grace through Alzheimer's, terminal cancer, and aging is a rare act of love. —Heather

For those who, during the dark days of the Covid-19 pandemic, opted for empathy and compassion in the face of fear and uncertainty, and especially for Spencer Toder, who is perhaps the most empathic person I've ever known. —Chris

CONTENTS

Foreword: Embrace The Forever-Changed Workforce   *xv*

Acknowledgments   *xix*

Introduction: Discover The New Normal of Work   *1*
Everything Is Different Now   2
Covid as Change Agent   3
A New Bargain   4
   Sidebar: The Great Resignation: A Long Time Coming   6
Not Your Grandparents' Workforce   7
What's a Leader to Do?   9
Notes   10

Part I: Rethink Your Workforce   13
Notes   15

1   *Meet Your New Workforce*   *17*
A Workforce Without a Majority   18
Meet the Pan-Generational Workforce   19
   Sidebar: Managing the Multigenerational Workforce   20
Women Hold Up Half the Workforce   21
The LGBTQ+ Workforce   24
   Sidebar: Navigating Gender: From Fixed to Fluid   25
The Case for a Multidimensional and Diverse Workforce   27

Generational Empathy   28
    Sidebar: Meet Generation Z   29
Notes   30

2 *Understand Your Workers' New Habits*   **35**
We Are No Longer Who We Were   36
    Sidebar: The Pandemic Compressed Time   37
The Empowered Worker: Your Most Valuable New Asset   40
    Sidebar: Where Work Takes Place Today   41
    Sidebar: The Center Shifts   45
    Sidebar: The Great Relocation   46
The Through Line: Creating Life/Work Integration   50
    Sidebar: The Rise of Bleisure   51
Notes   53

3 *Grok the Empowered Mindset*   **57**
Rebalancing Work and Life   59
A New Approach to Work   60
    Sidebar: The Hierarchy of Work Engagement   62
Work That Is Worth It   63
    Sidebar: Origins of the Great Resentment   64
Healing Our Whole Selves: Mental Health and Burnout Are Real   66
    Sidebar: How to Spot Burnout   67
Relationships Matter   68
Humans Are Your Greatest Source of Value   69
    Sidebar: History Rhymes: Our Opportunity Is Now   70
Changing the Goal   71
The Empathy Advantage   72
Notes   72
    Profile: Aqueduct Technologies: Really Great Ideas, Really
    Happy Employees   75

Part II: Rethink Your Organization   77

4 *Upgrade Your Operating Models*   **81**
What Are We Leaving Behind?   82
    Sidebar: The Rise of the Human Value Era   83

What Are We Moving Toward?   85
   Sidebar: Lead Differently in Complexity   86
More Frequent Disruptions   87
Listen Carefully: Change Is the Norm   89
Forging a New Path to the Future of Work   89
Understand the Relationship Between the Individual and Organization   90
Rethink Work and Learning   91
   Sidebar: The Skills Gap May Never Close   92
Recalibrate Your Metrics: Be Like Bhutan   93
It's Time to Finally Address Burnout   95
Benefits for Whose Benefit?   96
Flexibility Is Key to Empathetic Leadership   98
How We Lead Without Maps: Focus on Your People   98
Notes   99
   Profile: Mercy: Leadership Through Community   101

5   *Create the Conditions to Thrive*   **103**
Rethinking Jobs   104
Hire for Culture, Train for Specific Skills   106
   Sidebar: Rethinking Work and Jobs   107
Reporting for (Tour of) Duty   108
Where Work Gets Done   109
Curating the Return to Office   111
Creating the Conditions to Thrive   113
   Sidebar: Understanding DEI . . . and B   116
Unleash the Power of Belonging   117
   Sidebar: The Importance of Belonging   118
Knitting a Psychological Safety Net   119
Creating the Conditions to Learn at Scale   120
Social Capital Creates Collective Intelligence   121
Organizing to Collaborate   122
   Sidebar: Peers as Collaborators   123
Finding Joy in Work   124
Notes   125

6   *Enable Your Empowered Workforce*   **129**
Culture: The Operating Instructions for Your Organization   130
Recognizing Toxic Culture   131

Building Mindful Culture   131
  Sidebar: Nurturing Culture Through Dialogue   132
Living Your Values   133
  Sidebar: Beliefs + Behaviors + Benefits = Culture   135
Trust: The Cornerstone of Healthy Culture   136
Finding Purpose at Work   137
  Sidebar: The Three Faces of Purpose   138
Purpose: Your Most Enduring Competitive Advantage   140
  Sidebar: The Great Reset Opportunity: Why We Work   142
The Trouble with Purpose   144
Notes   145
  Profile: The Canteen: Becoming a Place of Purpose and Belonging 147

Part III: Rethinking Your Leadership   149
Notes   151

7   Pilot Your Expedition Team   153
What Is an Expedition?   154
What to Leave at Base Camp   154
  Sidebar: Understand Your Expedition Team   155
Continued Uncertainty Means Continual Expeditions   157
  Sidebar: Navigating Rising Global Uncertainty   158
Prepare to Cut a Different Path   159
Care for Your Expedition Team   162
  Sidebar: Focus on the Fundamentals   164
Create Enthusiasm Around the Expedition   165
Yes, You Are a Career Coach Now   166
Take That First Step   167
Notes   168

8   Embrace Your Superpowers   171
The Power of Vulnerability and Not Knowing   172
The Power of Awareness   173
The Power of Candor   174
  Sidebar: The Four Leadership Shifts   176
The Power of Listening   177
  Sidebar: Mindset Shift: You Work for Talent   180

The Power of Being Human   181
   Sidebar: Behavioral Shift: Change in Leadership Profile   182
Become the Resilient Leader   183
Notes   184
   Profile: sparks & honey: Building a Practice of Gratitude   185

9   *Emerge the Empathic Leader*   **187**
The Pandemic Was a Quiet Teacher   189
   Sidebar: The Cumulative Shifts Between Individuals and Organizations   190
Understanding Empathy   192
Empathy Is Good Business   194
Empathy, Trust, and Compassion: The Trifecta of Superior Leadership   195
The Power of Listening   197
Welcome to Tomorrow: Leading in Uncertainty   198
Notes   198

About the Authors   ***201***

Praise for* The Adaptation Advantage**   ***203

Index   ***205***

FOREWORD:
EMBRACE THE FOREVER-
CHANGED WORKFORCE

Why, where, and how we work has changed forever. The world of work is almost unrecognizable. This is unchartered territory for many of us. Throw in five generations of people working together who have different backgrounds, different purposes, different expectations, different reasons for working; it's increasingly clear that work isn't returning to "the way it was." Leaders who resist this will struggle the most.

As Chief People Officer for a Fortune 500 fintech company with 65,000+ colleagues globally, it's my job to stay on top of people trends and labor markets and to guide the company with our workforce top of mind. It's my job to anticipate and deliver what we need to cultivate a culture of excellence, attract and develop top talent, and protect our employees' well-being at a time of unprecedented stresses. This is not an easy feat in a "normal" world of work, and we're experiencing anything but.

Like you, I live it every single day – the uncertainty, the rapid change, the disruption. Never in my wildest dreams did I ever think I'd see the day when our entire company would shift to remote work and then face the challenge of getting them to come back to the office. Never did I think the war for talent would be this extreme. Never did I think the meaning of leadership would change so drastically. Yet here we are.

When FIS hosted its annual in-person gathering of its top leaders after two years of virtual working, we needed a dynamic speaker who could give us an honest and almost hard-to-believe view into the changing world of leadership and the future of work – and have the data to back it. Jaws dropped when Heather McGowan presented startling real-life examples of the world we work in today. She shared data that made our leaders sit up and take notice.

The pandemic has caused workplace and worker trends to accelerate. The balance of power has shifted right before our eyes. But you already know these things as leaders. You're operating under extreme circumstances. You're dodging the curve balls. You're planning for the next shoe to drop. You're ready to make a change and lead into the future.

Heather has teamed up again with Chris Shipley to document these seismic shifts and in this book connects so many dots about the new workforce that is evolved, empowered, and exhausted. *The Empathy Advantage: Leading the Empowered Workforce* is as close to a "leading in this new work era playbook" as you'll get. In it you will find real solutions for addressing what no leader has likely experienced before. And it all starts with one behavior: empathy.

People are coping with years' worth of grief, trauma, stress, anxiety, burnout, uncertainty, change fatigue, exhaustion. Mental acuity is harder to achieve when you're dealing with all these emotional roadblocks. Empathy is the new must-have leadership trait – and it doesn't come naturally for everyone.

Over four decades, I have learned that leadership is not a position or title. It's a way of thinking, acting, and behaving. We need to work harder to understand what it might be like to walk a mile in someone else's shoes. And then we have to be flexible enough to change and to make ourselves uncomfortable if that's what it takes to bring out the best in our people.

People have choices. Many, many choices. We're seeing droves of people call it quits just because they can. We're seeing people making drastic career changes because they can. We're seeing people taking pay cuts to work for companies with a higher purpose and aligned values because they can. Nothing is holding them back.

There's a reason as FIS's Chief People Officer, we talk about "The FIS People Strategy." It's every bit as vital to business success as a product or operations strategy. Leaders need to double down on purpose and human-centric leadership. We need to develop new ways to put people first and keep them there, so they return the favor ten-fold in their performance. Building a high-performing team doesn't happen overnight. It starts with a shared sense of purpose – teams want belonging and to feel connected to a unified purpose.

The most successful leaders will be those who embrace the forever-changed workforce and become the adopters of the new reality where talent demands empathy. Workers have broken out of the box. It's time leaders break out of the box too. We will never work again the way we did before. Embrace the change. Shift your mindset. Get comfortable with being uncomfortable. Show your people you care – that you're human. The results will be exponentially better when it's a two-way street.

Organizations that do not make efforts to adapt to the changing workforce are at risk of losing talent, which is insanely hard to find and retain these days, and opportunities for growth. And you know what happens without growth.

I keep coming back to something Heather told our leaders. She said that even with all that's going on in the world, if we focus on the fundamentals, we'll be OK.

—Denise Williams
Chief People Officer, FIS

ACKNOWLEDGMENTS

It is Labor Day 2022, which seems an apt occasion to acknowledge the work of so many people that has gone into this book. Writing a book is usually a labor of love, but on some days it's just a heavy lift. We are eternally grateful to our wives, family, and friends who encouraged us on both the great days and the days that were a bit more of a slog. Pat Coryell, the Gulfport Gang, P-town Pals, her Roslindale Buddies, and her family were firmly in Heather's corner and have been extremely helpful in an extraordinary time. Nancy Latta, The Bubs, The Boyz, The Dees, The CKathys, The Sunderlanders, The Sonomans, and The Belmont Girls provided just enough goading to keep Chris pushing on. And, of course, Zippy and Koa kept watch over the entire process. We could not have done this without so much support.

We are both graced with amazing professional networks that serve as adjunct researchers and scouts as we do our work. Heather is grateful to her speaking agents and event managers, her Impact Eleven partners and community, the reliable and dogged researcher Kath Cote, and a special shout-out to Melissa Kang, "Manage-her" extraordinaire, who made sure Heather completed this book against the backdrop of considerable challenges. Chris has been quietly encouraged and cheered on by the writers and thinkers of Silicon Guild, especially Peter Eagle Sims and Leslie Blodgett. And she is especially grateful to her colleagues at Constituent Connection and C/R Strategy Partners for giving her the time and space to write away the summer.

We are grateful to the business leaders who gave us insights into their organizations and provide outstanding examples of leadership in this new era. Denise Williams provided beautiful context in her foreword. Manak Ahluwalia, Cynthia Bentzen-Mercer, Terry Young, Kristin Cohen, Annalie Killian, and Rob Anderson all pulled back the curtain on their businesses to reveal modern leadership.

We hope this book will also trigger your curiosity and encourage you to dig deeper into the work of Laura Spinney, Anthony Klotz, Margaret Heffernan, Michael Leiter, Mark Crowley, Roger Martin, Jamil Zaki, Roger Hurni, Peter Sheahan, Dave Gray, David Allison, Liz Weaver, Simon Wardley, Ocean Tomo, Laura Park, Joshua Acosta, Alison Levine, Cassandra Worthy, Peter Sheahan, and the many other business leaders who have shared their ideas, concerns, feedback, and encouragement as we developed this book. We learned so much from each of you and have so much gratitude for your generosity of knowledge, insight, and time.

Once again, the people at Wiley were extraordinary collaborators. Richard Narramore and Jessica Filippo guided the process. Kelly Talbot honed our narrative with care, insight, and wit; we are grateful for his fine editor's eye. Donna J. Weinson made certain every word was perfect and Deborah Schindlar drove production of the beautiful book you are holding. We are grateful for them and the many others who, behind the scenes, make this book possible.

These pages are filled with concise and engaging graphics, in large measure the work of infographics designer Jericho Rivera at https://craftyflux.com

Finally, we are grateful for our writing partnership. The summer of 2022 was marked by many challenges, not the least of which was producing a manuscript in record time. This collaboration, rooted in friendship and – it must be said – *empathy*, is the rare partnership that could get it done.

INTRODUCTION: DISCOVER THE NEW NORMAL OF WORK

On a balmy early summer's evening in Calgary, Alberta, Canada, 16 business leaders gathered for dinner to talk about their challenges attracting and retaining great workers. They represented every type and stage of business. Mid-career entrepreneurs to late-career executives. Advanced technology and financial services companies. Civil servants and academic researchers. No matter the specific work, they shared the same concern with Chris: their workforce is caught up in an eddy of change; how might they possibly lead it?

Halfway around the world in Hamburg, Germany, the executive ranks of a global maritime shipping company huddled in rapt attention to hear Heather explain how and why their post-pandemic workforce was so transformed. They, too, were wrestling with the seemingly overnight shifts that were affecting every aspect of their business and especially their leadership. How might they, too, adapt to remain effective leaders for their evolving and now empowered workforce?

In both rooms, the feeling of stress and uncertainty was palpable, as it is in boardrooms, executive suites, and management meetings across the globe. We know, because we have had a privileged seat at those tables, talking with, learning from, and hearing the very real concerns of leaders at every level who sense that the post-Covid world of work has changed dramatically from its pre-pandemic form. They are not sure what to do about it.

Well, here's the deal: that uncertainty is real. So, friend, breathe deeply, roll your shoulders, take another deep breath, and let yourself get comfortable being uncomfortable. Because that professional anxiety? It's normal. You are not alone. And you are going to be okay.

Everything Is Different Now

Make no mistake, everything is different as the world emerges from the trauma and disruption that came in the first giant waves of the Covid-19 pandemic. When we closed the doors of our offices in March 2020, we could not have guessed what the world of work would look like as we began to open them again in the spring of 2022.

This was inevitable. Plagues reorder society. They are an existential crisis from which survivors emerge fundamentally changed. In the 1300s, the Bubonic Plague gave way to the Renaissance. The 1918 influenza pandemic sparked the Roaring Twenties. Covid-19 has given us the Great Resignation, a reckoning that started in America, catalyzing the most significant and rapid economic transformation of the workforce since the rise of the first Industrial Revolution.

Our current moment is remarkably different from the last pandemic almost exactly 100 years ago. Today, computerized technology, rather than electricity, is the disruptive force. Now, gender has become fluid rather than fixed and binary; then, women were just beginning to become full participants in society. Social media bubbles and disinformation, rather than radio, are driving consumerism and both social cohesion and division. A five-day, 40-hour work week was the victory of labor unions and forward-thinking industrialists; now all around the globe we are experimenting with a shortened four-day work week.

Yet, some things are eerily similar. The measure of income inequality – the Gini Coefficient, where 1 is absolute inequality and 0 is absolute equality – is near par today as in the 1920s. Before the pandemic, US immigration levels were at the highest level since the 1920s, although these rates have declined dramatically due in part to policy and in part to Covid travel restrictions. Both the 1920 and 2020 economies boomed, although rising inflation, global conflict, and pandemic-induced supply chain failures have brought the longest bull market to a painful stop. And among the most concerning similarities, we are seeing the resurrection of authoritarianism that is threatening democracies worldwide.

Collectively, these changes demand that we adapt, a reality that elicits fear in some, contemplation in others, and a rethinking of nearly everything for everyone.

The pandemic "changes us in ways we didn't expect and may not be thoroughly conscious of," Laura Spinney, author of *Pale Rider*, told us during a conversation in the summer of 2022. Her book explores the Spanish Flu pandemic 100 years ago that dramatically changed economic and social structures around the world. Now, she theorizes that we are primed to forget the impact of the pandemic.

"I have spent a lot of time wondering why we do not pay more attention to the 1918 flu, and I think there are lots of reasons, but my latest theory is that when we have a war, we send a subsection of our population off to war and they experience something most of us do not," she said. "We seek more documentation of those experiences which are not shared. We all lived through the pandemic and so know what it's like. We don't want to be reminded of it. We've just gone through it. We want to forget it. That is why I think we forget pandemics but remember wars."

Yet with the pandemic still very fresh in our memories, it is critical that we understand its impacts on every aspect of our lives, especially our work lives, the way we organize work, and the way we lead others. That is what we will explore in these pages. Because, in short, the pandemic may not be the cause of so much change, but it certainly brought so much of it into very sharp focus.

Covid as Change Agent

Overnight, millions of workers were sent home: many to work from home, some to no work at all. Businesses embraced the digital transformations that they had long resisted. In fact, McKinsey reports we leapt forward five years in our digital transformation in those first 60 days we worked from home. Why? Because tools like Zoom, seemingly new technologies, were actually a decade or more old. We changed our behaviors and our policies about everything, from work from home to remote jury duty to telehealth visits. But to be clear: digital transformation is simply human transformation – we adapt to the tools that have long been at our disposal. Workers carved home offices out of bedrooms, kitchens, attics, and anywhere else they could get a decent internet connection and a little bit of quiet. "You're on mute," became the catch phrase for a remote workforce that juggled work and caregiving in a context that was at once forgiving and fear-inducing.

Work, caregiving, educating, and self-care tangled into a hairball of demands that forced many workers to reevaluate the meaning of their work and the meaning of their lives. These are just the outward and immediate expressions of trends that have been building for years. Covid simply allowed them to collide and accelerate.

Writing in March 2020, we predicted that Covid-19 would be the greatest catalyst to business transformation in a generation, a prediction that proved to be a gross underestimation. In the few years prior to 2020, every major business consulting firm viewed digital transformation as a decades-long endeavor. That was before Covid, when the pace of change could reasonably be expected to be more leisurely. We all know what happened next.

The pace of digital transformation more than doubled.[1] Business leaders who fought the idea of remote workers suddenly approved requisitions for corporate Zoom accounts and other virtual workplace tools. People moved and families reconfigured to provide support for one another, while physicians and frontline health-care workers administered treatments and researchers burned the midnight oil to develop a lifesaving vaccine 75% faster than any previous vaccine had ever been created.

Amid all that transformation – digital and day-to-day life – we discovered a new way of being that led, inevitably, to a new way of working.

A New Bargain

We used to trade loyalty to our employers for the security they provided: a paycheck, pension, health care, job training, maybe some other perks and benefits. There was a time when that was a reasonable bargain. Then, in 1970, the economist Milton Friedman published an essay in the *New York Times* arguing that the sole purpose of a company was to make money for its shareholders by ensuring ever-increasing profits.[2] The article ushered in the so-called Shareholder Value Era and relegated workers to expense lines in corporate balance sheets.

Workers became both interchangeable and disposable, and the grand bargain between employee and employer didn't seem so grand anymore. But because the supply of workers was greater than demand for them, power remained with the employer, and over time employers chipped away at their side of the deal. Pensions gave way to employee-driven retirement plans. Full-time jobs converted to pay-for-performance contract positions. Corporate mergers triggered layoffs, offshoring, and outsourcing that further eroded worker security.

Then, in August 2019, the Business Roundtable put a stake in the heart of the Shareholder Value Era with its "Statement on the Purpose of a Corporation."[3] That purpose, according to the statement signed onto by 181 of the country's leading CEOs, was to promote "an economy that serves all Americans." With the release of a press statement, the scales began to tip back toward workers.

While those CEOs were wrestling with corporate purpose, technology was giving a leg up to workers who wanted more autonomy. Over the past decade, platforms like UpWork, TaskRabbit, Uber, and Lyft gave workers the freedom to choose where, when, and how they work. Marketplace apps like Etsy and payment tools like Square lowered the bar for artisans and others to take their products to market. Applications for new businesses have risen steadily over the past decade then surged in 2020 and 2021, reaching an all-time high at the height of the pandemic.[4] If workers couldn't find satisfaction working for someone else, they'd find it working for themselves.

As workers steadily marched toward greater autonomy, they also found greater agency. Employee turnover has increased steadily over the last decade and is even more pronounced now, rising from 1.4% a month in 2019 to 2.5% now. The market research firm Gartner predicts total annual turnover will increase from pre-pandemic levels of 20% to reach 24% for the foreseeable future.[5] That's hardly surprising. The existential crisis that is Covid-19 created a new calculus as we evaluated whether the friction of work is worth the reward. Was the employer-employee bargain a bargain after all?

In a massive study of 30,000 people in 31 countries, Microsoft's latest Work Trends Index[6] found that many of the things workers simply accepted in 2019, like the daily commute or the cost of childcare, were no longer worth it. The push for productivity is driving workers to exhaustion. Leaders are out of touch with their employees. Gen Z workers are at risk of burnout.

In short, the workforce is exhausted and far less tethered to their employers than ever before. Nearly three years of work from home employment has weakened the ties that bind employees to their workplaces. When Zoom, Google Meet, or Microsoft Teams is your conference room, the switching costs from one employer to another are extremely low. Work from home, it turns out, has given rise to a sudden, massive, global workforce able to work from anywhere.

No wonder, then, that the so-called Great Resignation is on the march. A record number of employees voluntarily quit their jobs in 2021, over 47 million Americans.[7] While the pandemic puts these numbers in strong relief, the Great Resignation was underway well before Covid-19 shut down offices. In fact, the share of workers voluntarily leaving jobs has nearly doubled since 2009.[8] (See "The Great Resignation: A Long Time Coming.")

The Great Resignation: A Long Time Coming

The timing seems impeccable. A virulent wave of disease washes over the world. Millions die. Many more become sick. The world economy grinds to a crawl. In a matter of days, tens of millions of workers are sent home from their jobs.

If not the timing, then the circumstances. Months of uncertainty dragged on, leaving workers at home to juggle work, family, and fear. Too much for too long had become too much, indeed. If this is what life would continue to look like, why work? Or why work at this particular job?

And thus – the Great Resignation.

By the spring of 2021, more than 4 million people, on average, were leaving their jobs each month. Some ventured out to find new work. Others took hard-earned retirement. Many, many more just took a break.

It's a compelling and easy narrative. It's just not true. The Great Resignation is rooted in something much deeper than an exhausted and burned-out workforce, and it wasn't triggered – as some talk show wags would have us believe – in an entitled workforce happier to receive paycheck replacement benefits than rejoin the workforce. It's not even rooted in an existential crisis that forced a reckoning for everyone.

In the United States, voluntary "quits" rates, as the US Department of Labor calls them, were on a steady upward march for more than a decade before the pandemic. In fact, the uncertainty of the pandemic actually caused quits to dip in mid-2020, until they resumed their upward trajectory.

Certainly, people reevaluated where work fits within the larger fabric of their lives. Paycheck replacement payments may have given workers the opportunity to take a time-out or even re-skill for different jobs, but the pandemic was hardly more than a lens that brought into focus a trend that had been unfolding for more than a decade.

Addressing this trend for the *Harvard Business Review*, researchers Joseph Fuller and William Kerr posit that the Great Resignation may have been "exacerbated by the pandemic," but was largely the result of changing attitudes toward work. "We call these factors the Five Rs: retirement, relocation, reconsideration, reshuffling, and reluctance. Workers are retiring in greater numbers but aren't relocating in large numbers; they're reconsidering their work-life balance and care roles; they're making localized switches among industries, or reshuffling, rather than exiting the labor market entirely; and, because of pandemic-related fears, they're demonstrating a reluctance to return to in-person jobs."[9]

These factors, though, may just be the outward signs of a fundamental change in worker attitudes – a change that smart leaders would do well to note.

The shift to work from home – and the autonomy and trust that came with it – allowed workers to find their agency. That agency has flipped the employer-employee dynamic, giving new psychological power to workers who now know better what they want, how they want to work, and what they will accept as compensation for that work.

This flip is exactly what was needed to usher in a new economic era – one that puts people at the center, where they are empowered to participate fully in the organization and where the organization nurtures its human resources as an investment in its own operational and economic success. In this dynamic, workers and employers are collaborators mutually invested in organizational success.

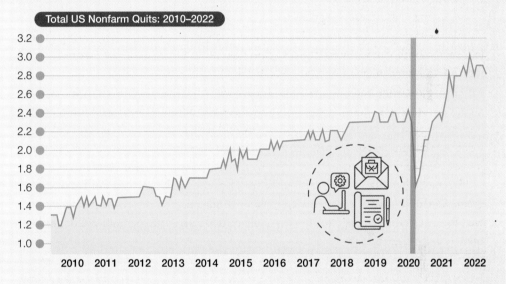

Figure I.1 The Great Resignation: A Long Time Coming

Source: US Bureau of Labor Statistics.

Not Your Grandparents' Workforce

So what's been happening? Again, a number of trends converge. Workers today look a whole lot different from the sitcom working stiffs of 1970s and 1980s television. Demographic shifts – from lower fertility rates to an aging workforce to the recent decline in immigration – are contributing to the greatest labor shortage since World War II. Not only do we have fewer workers, but they look a lot different, too.

For decades, the factory default setting for an American worker was white and male, his life made easier by having a wife to care for his home and children. That stereotype is long gone.

While still a majority, the white population decreased by nearly 9% from the 2010 to 2020 US Census, while the multiracial population increased by 275% and now represents 33.8 million people in the United States. In fact, nearly all racial and ethnic groups – other than white – saw population gains in the decade between the census counts.[10]

There is no racial majority in the 18 and younger cohort, the very people who are filling jobs today and will continue to fill jobs in the future.[11] The diverse workforce is not coming; it is here. Further, in the 100 years from 1920 to 2020, human lifespans doubled.[12] With greater longevity comes longer working lives, so we now have a workforce not only diverse in terms of race, but also in terms of age.

Of course, women have made meaningful gains in the workforce, but gendering the workforce has become complicated, too. Our social understanding of gender has shifted from one that was fixed and binary to one that is increasingly gender fluid. Cases in point: US passports now allow an "unspecified or another gender identity (X)" marker[13] and a growing number of US states and countries around the world recognize nonbinary or third-gender classifications.[14]

If this is a workforce that looks different from *Father Knows Best*–era stereotypes, it's also one that *thinks* differently. Even before the pandemic created an existential crisis for many workers, people valued the human relationships of the workplace and the meaning of the work. Gallup pinned employee engagement, a measure of workers' enthusiasm for their employers, at 20% in 2021.[15] That's four of five employees who *aren't engaged* in their work.

What's going on? Certainly, the pandemic gave workers a chance to really think about the place of work in their lives. Some 65% of workers said the pandemic made them rethink the role of work in their lives, while 52% said it made them question the purpose of their job.[16] Sit with that. More than *half* of all people showing up for work are wondering if their work fulfills something bigger in their lives.

These are just a few of the trend lines that are shaping the complexion of the global workforce, yet one thing is undeniable: these changes have unfolded over decades and there is no going back. And let's be perfectly clear: as business leaders wrestle with "return to office" policies, where work happens is not their biggest problem. Even if every worker went back to the office, they would still be burned out and disengaged. The pandemic merely brought burnout and high rates of mental distress to light. These issues have plagued workers for decades, according to research firms that track employee engagement. The picture is bleak. Gallup's 2022 Global Engagement Survey found that just 21% of employees say they are engaged at work and only a third said they were thriving in their overall well-being.[17]

What's a Leader to Do?

That's the kind of question that might leave you wanting to quit, too.

Don't.

Consider, instead, that you are in great company. Every leader at every level – from the C-Suite to frontline managers – is wrestling with this same challenge. The tables have turned. Workers are more empowered not simply because of workforce shortages, but because workplace attitudes are dramatically different now. If the workforce no longer looks the same or acts the same, then why would it make sense to lead it the same way we have over the last 50 years?

It doesn't.

And that's why you are holding this book at this very moment. Across these next chapters, we'll dive deeper into the psyche of the empowered workforce to give you a clear understanding of what motivates – and demoralizes – today's workers. Then we'll outline the guiding principles around which to organize your workplace and work teams. And finally, we'll look at the evolution of a leader from task master to enabling catalyst.

By embracing, rather than fighting, the workplace trends that have forever changed the employee-employer relationship, you *can* find real joy and purpose for yourself and for the people who work not *for* you, but *with* you to achieve great things together.

That engaged and empowered workforce, after all, is the cornerstone of every thriving business.

Which takes us back to Hamburg, Germany.

After speaking to the leadership team for the shipping company, Heather headed to the airport for the flight home. Her flight delay meant she'd miss her connection, and thus began the extensive customer service negotiations to find a reasonably convenient way home as time and again alternate flights were delayed because of staff shortages. It's a scene that plays out at airports around the world. Workforce shortages lead to flight delays and cancellations. Flight delays and cancellations lead to customer dissatisfaction. Customer dissatisfaction leads to employee stress. Employee stress leads to workforce shortages, and the whole ugly cycle begins again, leaving airport check-in lobbies packed with angry, frustrated passengers and stressed, burned-out airline agents. It is a not-on-brand scene at the Hamburg airport and repeated around the world.

It's time for a new path forward to break the cycle and make work meaningful, truly meaningful, for every worker.

This is our call to action, the chance to make the once-in-a-lifetime changes that create meaningful work for more people, structure working environments to be most engaging, and ultimately to unleash our human potential.

Notes

1. Accenture, 2020, "Is It Time for a Course Correction? COVID-19: What to Do Now, What to Do Next," Accenture, available at https://www.accenture .com/content/dam/accenture/final/a-com-migration/custom/_acnmedia/ thought-leadership-assets/pdf-3/Accenture-COVID-19-3-Course-Correction-Steps-for-Enterprise-Recovery-v2.pdf.

2. Friedman, Milton, 1970, "A Friedman Doctrine – The Social Responsibility of Business Is to Increase Its Profits," *New York Times*, September 13.

3. Business Roundtable, 2019, "Statement of the Purpose of a Corporation," August 19, available at https://www.businessroundtable.org/business-roundtable-redefines-the-purpose-of-a-corporation-to-promote-an-economy-that-serves-all-americans.

4. United States Census Bureau Business Formation Statistics, July 2022, available at https://www.census.gov/econ/bfs/index.html

5. Gartner, 2022, "Gartner Says U.S. Total Annual Employee Turnover Will Likely Jump by Nearly 20% from the Pre-pandemic Annual Average," April 28, available at https://www.gartner.com/en/newsroom/04-28-2022-gartner-says-us-total-annual-employee-turnover-will-likely-jump-by-nearly-twenty-percent-from-the-prepandemic-annual-average.

6. Microsoft, 2021, "The Work Trend Index," March 22, available at https://www .microsoft.com/en-us/worklab/work-trend-index/. Courtesy of Microsoft, Inc.

7. U.S. Bureau of Labor Statistics, 2022, "Job Opening and Labor Turnover" April, available at https://www.bls.gov/news.release/jolts.nr0.htm

8. Fuller, Joseph and Kerr, William, 2022, "The Great Resignation Didn't Start with the Pandemic," *Harvard Business Review,* March 23, available at https:// hbr.org/2022/03/the-great-resignation-didnt-start-with-the-pandemic.

9. Fuller and Kerr, "The Great Resignation Didn't Start with the Pandemic."

10. Jones, Nicholas, Marks, Rachel, Ramirez, Roberto, and Rios-Vargas, Merarys, 2021, "2020 Census Illuminates Racial and Ethnic Composition of the Country," US Census Bureau, August 12, available at https://www.census .gov/library/stories/2021/08/2020-united-states-population-more-racially- ethnically-diverse-than-2010.html.

11. Hall, Madison, 2021, "A Key Change in the Census Showed the US Is Diversifying Across All Age Groups: Here's Why That Matters," *Business Insider*, August 20, available at https://www.businessinsider.nl/a-key-change- in-the-census-showed-the-us-is-diversifying-across-all-age-groups-heres-why- that-matters/.

12. Johnson, Stephen, 2021, "How Humanity Gave Itself an Extra Life," *New York Times*, April 27.

13. US Department of State – Bureau of Consular Affairs, 2022, "Selecting Your Gender Marker," July, available at https://travel.state.gov/content/travel/en/ passports/need-passport/selecting-your-gender-marker.html.

14. Wikipedia, 2022, "Legal Recognition of Non-binary Gender," October 25, available at https://en.wikipedia.org/wiki/Legal_recognition_of_non- binary_gender.

15. Gallup, 2020, "The State of the Global Workplace 2021," Gallup, available at https://www.gallup.com/workplace/349484/state-of-the-global- workplace.aspx.

16. Gartner, 2022, "Gartner 2021 Hybrid and Return to Work Survey," Gartner, Inc., January 13, available at https://www.gartner.com/en/articles/ employees-seek-personal-value-and-purpose-at-work-be-prepared-to-deliver.

17. Gallup, "The State of the Global Workplace 2021."

Part I
Rethink Your Workforce

It was bound to happen. Fifty years of the Friedman Doctrine – economist Milton Friedman's 1970 proposition that the sole purpose of a corporation was to return profits to its shareholders – had drained the workforce dry.

By 2019, the US federal hourly minimum wage had been stuck at $7.25 for a decade. Had the minimum wage kept pace with inflation, hourly workers would be making $24 an hour. Had wages kept pace with productivity, the hourly rate would be $26. But wages didn't keep pace. Working a 40-hour week at minimum wage in 2019 didn't earn enough pay to peek above the federal poverty line, and it certainly wouldn't afford reasonable living accommodations.

Salaried workers didn't fare much better. The average full-time employee across any salary level was working nearly 9 hours a day.[1] In exchange, workers took home a median income of $69,560 that year.[2]

Meanwhile, corporate profits surged to more than $2.3 *trillion dollars*.[3]

Americans were working longer and harder and getting less for it. The Gini Coefficient – a measure of income inequality where 0 represents perfect equality and 1 perfect inequality – climbed to .484,[4] continuing the upward trend it had been on since the early 1990s[5] to reach the highest level of income inequality since the 1920s.

The Covid-19 pandemic was simply the last straw. By March 25, 2020, more than 3 billion people across 70 countries were sent home from work[6]. A weary workforce had to juggle their now work-from-home jobs with caregiving responsibilities that often included their children's remote learning, all the while adopting unfamiliar health protocols to prevent infection by a virulent disease. Overnight, businesses transformed into virtual organizations. Those that couldn't were shuttered completely. Streets and neighborhoods were eerily quiet as offices, shops, bars, restaurants, and anything deemed not essential temporarily closed. Restaurants that could pivot to takeout, did. Transportation systems ground to a halt; what vehicles that were in motion were transporting essential workers to hospitals, pharmacies, grocery stores, and other critical businesses. By April 7, 2020, according to a BBC report, "81% of the global workforce of 3.3 billion people had their workplace fully or partly closed."[7] Those jobs that survived were forever changed.

The workers, your workers, adapted superbly and rose to the challenge of maintaining business continuity amid the chaos that was the uncertainty of Covid-19. As with any emerging novel outbreak, we did not know what we did not know, so we acted on instincts and best current advice. The idea that we needed to isolate in our homes came from past pandemics and that period at home extended beyond anyone's expectation, causing a convergence in our professional and personal lives that is not easily undone.

Psychiatrists say it takes 66 days to form a habit. In the three years since the World Health Organization declared a global pandemic on March 11, 2020, we have had plenty of time to form new habits. Our once separate personal and professional lives have merged. "The Pandemic merged our understanding of value, both professionally and personally and it is unlikely we ever separate them again," Babson College President and Jiffy Lube Cofounder Steve Spinelli told us. "We want to fully integrate all spheres of our lives."

In education, academics and student life are now intertwined, he said, noting that the separation never made sense when you consider "the complex interplay of the personal and professional development of an individual."

In the workplace, he added, people will no longer have discontinuous personal and professional selves, "and we should not want them to. Humans create their best value when they tap into their skills, passions, values, and authentic drive for self-expression," he said.

In other words, the pandemic was merely a fast-acting catalyst for changes that had been afoot for a decade or longer. Shifting demographics, social norms, and generational experiences have permanently reshaped the workforce in ways larger than any one seismic event. Our workforce is now an amalgam of age, experience, and attitudes. The arrival of Gen Z into the workforce permanently fixes this new composition. Indeed, by 2030, Gen Z will fill 30% of the global workforce. They are the most diverse, well educated, authentic, and socially engaged generation, and they would rather not work than work in jobs and organizations and systems that don't reflect and respect their values and interests.

And there you are, smack in the middle of these converging trends, trying to figure out what this means for the people you lead and the organization you support. Everything has changed, yet the pressure to build and support a thriving business remains the same. It's no wonder that business leaders are facing a crisis of their own.

But here's the thing: what you are feeling is real. It is understandable. It is okay. And now is your opportunity to step into all this change and become the leader that you know you can be.

It starts with knowing and understanding the people you hope to lead. So, let's start there.

Key Takeaways:

- The Global Workforce has taken on an entirely new look across every vector, driven by demographic, cultural, and generational shifts.

- The arrival of Gen Z workers makes these shifts permanent and demands that employers adapt and embrace their authentic and whole selves.

- The pandemic upended how, when, and where work is done. Work has been reframed into the context of the whole person merging their personal and professional lives.

Notes

1. U.S. Bureau of Labor Statistics.

2. U.S. Census Bureau.

3. "Corporate Profits in the United States from 200 to 2020." Statista, September 2021.

4. Semega, Jessica, Kollar, Melissa, Shrider, Emily A., and Creamer, John, 2020, "Income and Poverty in the United States," U.S. Census Bureau, September.

5. "U.S. Household Income Distribution from 1990 to 2020," Statista, September 2021.

6. "More Than 3 Billion Told to Stay Home Worldwide over Virus," Medical Express, March 25, 2020, available at https://medicalxpress.com/news/2020-03-billion-told-home-worldwide-virus.html.

7. "Coronavirus: Four out of Five People's Jobs Hit by Pandemic," BBC, April 7, 2020, available at https://www.bbc.com/news/business-52199888.

1 Meet Your New Workforce

Fifty years ago, television depicted the working family in simplistic form. Each morning, a straight white male kissed his dutiful wife as she handed him his briefcase and sent him off to work at an office job, surrounded by other white men, occasionally interrupted by the single Gal Friday. Meanwhile, Mom stayed home to care for the house and raise the couple's precocious children, helped from time to time by a housekeeper or handy man, often the only characters of color seen on television.

That classic television script persisted well beyond the years when women joined the workforce. Over time, the media slowly integrated racial and cultural diversity into its prime time programming, but the male business boss remained the go-to script. Media reflected the stereotypes, world view, and likenesses of the people who held power and sway. The workforce the media depicted in that era put the "white" in white-collar jobs. Women in the workforce were an anomaly. The roles depicting blue-collar service and domestic workers tended to go to people of color. Even as we watched, laughed, and took some familiar comfort in these depictions, we had more than a hunch that television didn't reflect our reality.

In fact, reality was quite drastically different. Women were 34% of the workforce in 1950, a number that rose to 38% in 1960, 43% in 1970, and sits at 47% today where it is expected to remain.[1] Unfortunately, the Bureau of Labor Statistics didn't document data on nonwhite workers until the 1980s.[2] Still, many assumed – and built social structures around – a factory default setting of a straight white male worker supported by a caregiving wife. There's nothing quite like a pandemic to finally blow up that assumption once and for all.

The diverse workforce is not coming; it is here. That, no doubt, becomes more and more obvious every time you hold a team meeting. The faces around the table – or in the Zoom video windows – probably don't look much like you or each other. That demographic diversity can be challenging when it contradicts your comfortable norms and usual assumptions. If there's no factory default setting for the workforce, then there's certainly not one for leadership, either.

It was never safe to assume that workers who looked like you shared your motivations and experiences. Now, those assumptions are an occupational liability. Our workforce is a mélange of life experiences and rich perspectives that can make our work more enriching and more valuable. Our workforce, and now its leadership, is starting to look like the markets we serve. To tap that value, you're going to have to see – *really see* – the new workforce. Let's take a closer look at today's workforce.

A Workforce Without a Majority

At first blush, the workforce, in the United States, still looks pretty white, but trend lines make it clear that we are on the cusp of change. The US population is more racially and ethnically diverse than at any time in our country's history, data from the 2020 US Census shows,[3] yet 78% of the workforce is white, according to the US Bureau of Labor Statistics. That white majority will ebb come 2045 when whites will make up less than 50% of the workforce, Hispanics nearly 25%, Blacks 13%, nearly 8% Asian, and almost 4% will be multiracial.[4]

So, what's driving the big change, you might ask? There is no racial majority in the 18 and younger cohort,[5] the very people who are filling jobs today and will continue to fill jobs in the future. Within 10 years, in fact, Gen Z workers (those born in or after 1997) will fill 30% of the workforce. This racial reordering has given rise to the "People of the Global Majority,"[6] a reference to the global market that now comprises more Black, Indigenous, and people of color (BIPOC) than whites.

Meet the Pan-Generational Workforce

The influx of young workers came as some Boomers (born between 1946 and 1964) were staying in the workforce longer. After a pandemic-driven uptick in retirements in 2020,[7] some Boomers came back to the workforce. Some, spurred by the existential crisis of the pandemic, retired early. Others pushed off retirement for the economic stability that comes with work. And many of these older workers simply want to remain productive longer. And why not? Lifespans have doubled in the hundred years from 1920 to 2020.[8]

Curiously, these bookends of the pan-generational workforce have rather similar demands of their workplaces. Among Gen Z workers, 40% say "flexibility and adaptability" are critical to their organization.[9] At the other end of the age spectrum, Boomers are also seeking a flexible work schedule (79%) or reduced hours (57%).[10] Providing that flexibility to older employees is critical to maintaining and passing down institutional knowledge. Employers are inviting retired employees back to work as knowledge experts (21%), mentors to younger employees (16%), or to handle critical client relationships (14%).[11]

These are just a few of the benefits of a blended workforce. In the world of work that requires continuous learning and adaptation, an age-diverse workforce has a distinct advantage over a singularly young or singularly older workforce because our brains develop different capacities at different ages. A 2015 research study by Dr. Laura T. Germine of Massachusetts General Hospital and Dr. Joshua K. Hartshorne at MIT found a range of cognitive peaks across the lifespan.[12] Fluid intelligence – the ability to respond quickly – peaks earlier in life and crystallized intelligence – the accumulation of facts and knowledge – peaks later. Things like vocabulary and ability to read emotions peak in the 40s and 50s. A pan-generational – or age-diverse – workforce, then, enables all employees to benefit from these developmental peaks. (See "Managing the Multigenerational Workforce.")

To be clear, however, the pan-generational workforce isn't exactly pan-global. In some parts of the world, aging societies are facing labor shortages as birth rates plummet. Elsewhere, youth booms are leading to labor surpluses. This uneven distribution of talent begs for a location-independent workforce to meet labor needs around the world.

Managing the Multigenerational Workforce

We are shaped, undoubtedly, by the historical and cultural context of our upbringing, a thought that ought to stay top of mind when the urge strikes to whisper under our breath, "Okay, Boomer," "kids today," or simply "Gen Z!" With four generations actively participating in today's workforce, mindfulness of generational context is essential for empathetic leadership.

Born into a period of high public investment, Boomers pushed against their parents' WW2-born conformity to experiment with a sexual revolution and to march for civil rights. For many, if not most, work was an escalator to status and reward; the ultimate achievement was a comfortable retirement.

Generation X was born into global chaos. In the years between 1965 and 1981, the Berlin Wall came down, a global energy crisis and rampant inflation reframed consumerism, and corporate profiteering shut factories and sent jobs offshore. Watching waves of layoffs, Gen X learned to never fully trust the stability of their jobs, yet remained constantly connected to work via email and mobile phones.

The social contract most at risk for Millennials, those born between 1982 and 1996, was the marriage license. Divorce was the norm and parents held their fractured families together by focusing on their children. Accustomed to being the center of attention, Millennials are more likely to expect the job to bend toward them and use their work as an expression of their values.

Born into a post-9/11 world (between 1997 and 2012), Generation Z does not know a time without global conflict or a time without smartphones. They are entrepreneurial, purpose driven, and firm in their desire to improve the world. They have also been disproportionately impacted, economically and emotionally, by the coronavirus pandemic.

Quickly, then, it becomes clear that a one-size-fits-all approach to leadership is not effective among so many differing experiences. On the flip side, however, these different perspectives make for a dynamic, learning-centric workforce.

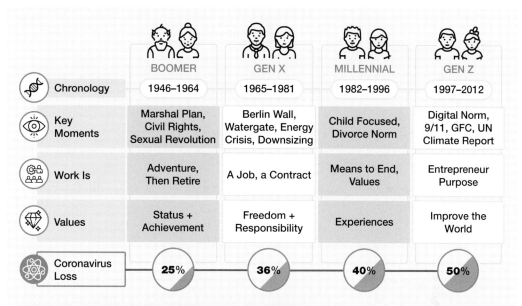

Figure 1.1 **Managing the Multigenerational Workforce**

Data Sources: Kansas Exchange: Boomers, Gen X, Gen Y, Gen Z Explained; Pew Research: What We Know About Gen Z So Far (2021), Catalyst.

Women Hold Up Half the Workforce

Cutting across race, ethnicity, and age is gender, and it is here that we see some of the most profound changes in the composition of the workforce.

Faced with labor shortages in 1950s China, Mao Zedong famously noted that "women hold up half the sky," spurring women to enter the workforce on equal footing with men. Since the 1970s, nearly all the gains to the US middle class have come from women entering the workforce.[13] And by the first quarter of 2019, women became the larger share of the university-educated workforce for the first time in history.[14] "In the next few years, two women will earn a college degree for every man, if the trend continues," Douglas Shapiro, executive director of the research center at the National Student Clearinghouse, told the *Wall Street Journal*.[15] In fact, more women than men have earned bachelor's degrees since 1982, master's degrees since 1986, and doctoral degrees since 2006.[16] That is a robust talent pipeline of 13 million more university-educated women than university-educated men over the last few decades.

Adding well-educated women to the workforce has significant and universal benefits, especially now as we tackle thorny challenges from climate change to income inequality to navigating the Covid-19 pandemic. This challenging future requires a different style of working, one that is less about individuals executing tasks in isolation and more about collaborative exploration. The collective intelligence needed to tackle complex challenges especially requires the input of women. In the cross-disciplinary paper titled "Quantifying Collective Intelligence in Human Groups," coauthor Anita Williams Woolley spoke to the advantages of women's participation in workgroups: "Having more women in the group raises collective intelligence, and in the supplement, we specifically compare face-to-face and online collaborators and find few differences in the elements that lead to collective intelligence."[17]

Yet despite the dramatic increase in the population of university-educated women and the clear benefit they bring to much-needed collective intelligence, women continue to be underrepresented in the higher echelons of corporate America. At the largest (by market capitalization) and arguably most influential companies in the United States – technology companies including Apple, Amazon, Facebook, Alphabet (Google), and Microsoft – employee gender in 2020 skewed more than 72% male.[18] Across the S&P 500, women account for only 7.8% of CEO roles.

Yet even as women prove valuable in the workforce, we are losing their contribution, largely due to the burden of caregiving and the lack of childcare infrastructure in the United States. We lost nearly three million women from the workforce at the height of the pandemic[19] and 1.5 million women have yet to return to work.[20] Many of those women are moms or otherwise have caregiving responsibilities for their families. Prior to the pandemic, 70% of working moms participated in the labor force, according to data from the US Department of Labor. In fact, the Massachusetts Taxpayers Foundation, a nonpartisan public policy organization, found that due to inadequate childcare infrastructure the state loses $2.7 billion dollars a year, a hefty combination of $812 million in lost productivity from higher turnover costs, $1.7 billion in lost wages from employees who miss work and reduce their hours, and $188 million in lost employment tax income.[21]

And make no mistake, those working caregivers have their hands full. The folks at grape juice giant Welch Foods commissioned a study that found that moms (usually) spend 98 hours a week in caregiving. That's the equivalent of *more than two jobs* before she even clocks in for work.[22] Women (and sometimes men) have been juggling these dual responsibilities with varying degrees of success. The pandemic gave employers a clearer view of that balancing act when Zoom opened a window into workers' homes. Now able to see that caregiving responsibilities are the norm and not the exception for women at work, smart businesses can follow the lead of the really great companies that have made caregiving support – from on-site daycare to flexible work hours for caregiving employees – a part of their organizations.

Clearly, addressing the lack of childcare infrastructure in the United States is a valuable and, ultimately, profitable problem to solve. In a *Washington Post* article titled "Putting Parents First Could be the Secret to a Successful Return-To-Office," parenting columnist Alyssa Rosenberg argues that offering on-site childcare may be the one perk that could motivate parents to return to the office. She cites as examples Goldman Sachs and Patagonia, which both offer on-site childcare and report lower rates of employee turnover amidst the Great Resignation, turnover that can cost twice the annual worker salary.[23]

Our ability to address this challenge will determine our ability to meet what many predict will be an ongoing labor shortage. The rise of women in the workforce has been met with a decline in male labor force participation, and not just as a matter of averages. Men are dropping out of the labor market and more than half of unemployed men in their 30s have criminal records.[24] Most likely, these men aren't hardened criminals. The blot on many a young man's record is conviction for possession of even a small amount of marijuana. Recognizing the albatross that is a federal marijuana conviction, President Joe Biden pardoned all federal offenses of simple possession of marijuana, then took the further step of urging state governors to do the same for state marijuana possession crimes.[25] Even as more than half of the United States have eased marijuana laws, only a small handful of states enable those previously convicted of cannabis-related crimes to petition to have their records cleared.

Overall, participation by men in the labor force has declined by 10% over the last 50 years, due in large part to our failure to provide pathways for men from manual to cognitive labor as our economy shifted from a manufacturing to a knowledge base. Looking forward, the picture is even more bleak. Women now outnumber men in university populations, earning more degrees than men in every category. We need both women and men, albeit barred by different obstacles, to participate more fully and more flexibly in the workforce to address the growing worker shortages.

Simply put, given the labor force shortages that show no signs of abating, we need to find ways to engage everyone in the workforce. In the United States, we need to figure out how to construct a caregiving infrastructure – a concept that has eluded us even though it has been bridged by nearly all our peers in the developed world. We need to expunge the records for minor offenses that are barring some men from engaging in the workforce. We need more pathways to skills training beyond two- and four-year programs that are inaccessible to some men and women while finding ways to engage more men into and through higher education to help them transition to the workforce we need.

The LGBTQ+ Workforce

Perhaps the most rapidly transforming demographic marker in the workforce is gender and sexual identity. Once firmly defined as fixed and binary, gender and sexual orientation are increasingly understood to be fluid and to exist on a continuum. For example, 17% of Generation Z in the United States report being part of the LGBTQ+ community[26] and of that group, 25% report that they expect to change their gender identity in their lifetime.[27] The number of those who identify as something other than cisgender – where one's personal identity and gender correspond with their sex as assigned at birth – and heterosexual is nearly doubling every generation. (See "Navigating Gender: From Fixed to Fluid.")

There is no doubt that changing attitudes about gender have sparked culture wars in pockets of the United States and around the world, making it dangerous, still, to be gay, nonbinary, or transgender. But increasingly, acceptance is being codified in law. The US Department of State now allows passports applicants to select "X" as a nonbinary gender distinction[28] and currently 21 US states and the District of Columbia legally recognize nonbinary gender designations, up from 11 states in 2019, as do more than 20 countries around the world.[29]

Navigating Gender: From Fixed to Fluid

On January 11, 2003, Alex MacFarlane, an Australian from Perth, got the passport they had been pursuing. Biologically intersex, MacFarlane believed that neither M nor F was an accurate representation of their sex. The sex designation in MacFarlane's passport now reads X. Twenty years on, and with our understanding of gender as far more fluid than binary, 21 US states and the District of Columbia allow a third designation. As of April 2022, the third option was made available on all United States passports, and 15 other countries from Argentina to Australia to India offer the third distinction.

In short order, gender went from fixed and binary to fluid. Globally, the rates of people identifying as either nonbinary gender or as members of the LGBTQ+ community are doubling with every passing generation.

In a June 2020 6–3 ruling, the US Supreme Court found that federal law bans employment discrimination based on sexual orientation and gender identity under Title VII of the Civil Rights Act, which made it illegal for employers to discriminate in employment because of a person's sex.[33]

Even with legal protections, nonbinary, gay, and transgender workers need the empathetic support of their employers, even as they themselves adjust to a New Now. Fixed gender markers are a thing of the past. It's time to end the so-called "pink tax" that puts higher prices on products and services such as razors and dry cleaning when they are marketed and sold to women. All-gender bathrooms have supplemented or even replaced men's and women's restrooms. Using preferred pronouns is a sign of acceptance and inclusion. (Pro tip: use "they" as the default in your communications and you'll have everyone covered.)

(Continued)

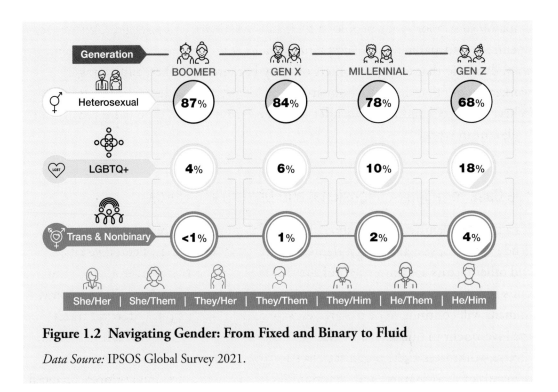

Figure 1.2 Navigating Gender: From Fixed and Binary to Fluid

Data Source: IPSOS Global Survey 2021.

Despite dramatic shifts in social acceptance, including full marriage equality in the United States in 2015, still 46% of LGBTQ+ people say that they are closeted at work, according to the Human Rights Campaign, a number only marginally better than the 50% of people who in 2008 said they were closeted at work.[30] This lack of disclosure – and the further complexity of intersectionality – makes it challenging to collect meaningful statistics on LGBTQ+ workers.

Still, the speed at which gender norms have changed in the United States and around the world has been unmatched by virtually any other shifting societal norm. About 1.6% of all adults identify with a gender other than the one they were assigned at birth, according to Pew Research Center, and 5% of Americans ages 18 to 29 – your current and future workforce – identify with a gender other than the one that was assigned at birth.[31] The decision to be open about one's changing gender identity, for example, is fraught with risk.

You might be wondering, then, how shifting norms (with or without legal protections) will affect the workplace and allow your LGBTQ+ colleagues to contribute most fully to a collaborative team. Now is the time to lean into your empathy to support your people in their full experience and struggles. Awareness, openness, transparency, and acceptance go a long way to create a workplace and team dynamic that engages workers of every background. That, and younger workers, more than half of whom are in the Gen Z and Millennial cohorts, believe that fixed and binary gender markers – from pronouns to bathrooms – are irrelevant in work.[32]

The Case for a Multidimensional and Diverse Workforce

It's a simple, identifying trait: about 1–2% of all people have red hair. Hair color, gender identity, sexual identity, right- and left-hand dominance, neurodiversity, and other factors are simply part of the rich fabric that makes your workforce and our society so interesting and capable. As we drive deeper into the digital economy, humans will continue to be the greatest source of value creation. Little optimizes the investment in humans more than diversity in the workforce. Multidimensional, diverse workforces make organizations stronger and better equipped to meet the demands of their markets and communities by every measure: innovation,[34] financial returns,[35] and employee engagement.[36]

As leaders seek to build value of all kinds (not just financial), we need to do a better job of tapping into a diverse workforce and creating the conditions for people to thrive. Diversity doesn't mean simply adding more women, more people of color, more LGBTQ+ people to our employment rolls. We need more than a checkbox diversity. We need to fundamentally shift organizational structures and cultures to fully embrace and capture the benefits of the diverse perspectives. As Liz Fosslien, Head of Content and Communications at human resource company Humu, posted on LinkedIn, "Diversity is having a seat at the table, inclusion is having a voice, and belonging is having that voice be heard. A sense of belonging is not the same as feeling similar to everyone else. Instead, it's when you feel safe and valued for embracing what makes you different."[37] Belonging, then, is critical to unlocking the power of diversity. We must create work environments, structures, processes, recruitment strategies, retention plans, and talent mobility that shatter old stereotypes to build workforce structures that maximize *all* human potential. Smart leaders embrace these shifts and adapt their leadership style not just to accommodate them, but to celebrate the perspectives and experiences they bring to every workday.

Generational Empathy

We must embrace our diverse workforce in the context of each of our workers' experiences. The Gen Z worker entering the workforce today, for example, comes with a dramatically different set of life experiences than a Gen Xer. For all practical purposes, Gen Z workers have never known a world without conflict, coming of age in a post-9/11 fight against global terrorism. They've also never known a world without readily available mobile internet, where any question or curiosity is quickly met with a flood of information, media, and social commentary.

The result of this continuous, high-impact change is a Gen Z worker who appreciates the fragility of life because they have grown up in near-continuous trauma. (See "Meet Generation Z.") This generation struggles with stress and depression at higher rates than previous generations.[38] The effect is a young workforce that wants more purpose and less workplace politics, a young workforce that has agency and little patience for command-and-control leadership. They have seen existential challenges, from climate change to educational debt to gun safety, merely kicked down the road by other generations and left for them to solve.

Contrast that with the Boomer generation that came of age in the Age of Aquarius and the *Encyclopedia Britannica*. These people came into the workforce in the era of 1980s Wall Street "Greed is Good" and "Me Generation" thinking. Work, as much as any other factor, was intrinsic to personal identity and value.

Generation X, a cohort of latchkey kids who were more likely than those in prior generations to witness their parents' divorce and watch them lose jobs amid a wave of offshoring, lost trust in institutions, something that has only grown with each subsequent generation. Gen Xers entered the workforce when mobile phones, email, and internet were standard workplace tools; they are the first "always on" generation.

One generational experience is not *better* than another; it's just different. And that difference suggests that in order to lead well, we must adapt to and embrace those differences. We are not moving fast enough to leverage this diversity. Researchers at McKinsey have been tracking the impact of diversity in the workforce since 2014, gathering data from more than 1,000 large companies across 15 countries. Without question, the research shows that "the most diverse companies are now more likely than ever to outperform less diverse peers on profitability."[39]

Meet Generation Z

By 2030, Generation Z – those born between 1997 and 2012 – will fill more than 30% of all jobs, and the experiences of their still young lives will make an indelible mark on the workplace.

At every stage of their lives, Gen Z has met with trauma and uncertainty. They learned to walk in the shadow of 9/11, headed to middle school amid a global financial meltdown, came of age as the United Nations declared a climate crisis, and graduated to virtual *Pomp and Circumstance* as the Covid-19 pandemic cast a cloud over their early careers. Active shooter drills were as much a part of their curriculum as reading, writing, and arithmetic, and they have *never* known a world that was not, somewhere, at war. Likely it is because of these experiences that Gen Z also exhibits higher instances of mental illness, especially anxiety and depression, than any prior generation.

Nevertheless, they are perhaps the most resilient, racially diverse, and well-educated generation we have known. Living in an eddy of change, Generation Z survives – and even thrives – with an agency not often seen in young workers. They are unwilling to compromise their values for a paycheck, and they have a burning desire to improve the world that was handed to them.

Given these life experiences, Gen Z isn't one to coddle, or even harness. Rather, channel your empathy, provide direction, channel their passion, and get out of the way.

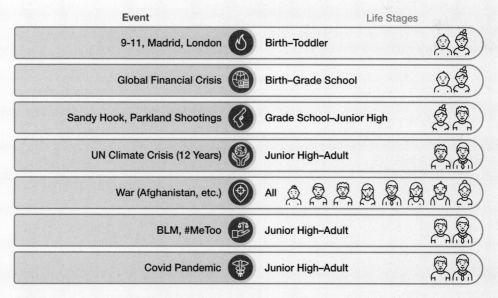

Figure 1.3 Meet Generation Z

Nonetheless, the report also bemoans the "slow progress" of companies toward building diverse and inclusive workforces. This, though, is changing rapidly, too. Indicators including the Fortune 500 Measure Up[40] and the Edelman Trust Barometer[41] point to changing sentiment among investors who now demand diversity not as an HR strategy, but as an essential business driver.

Your experiences, identity, beliefs, and perspectives may or may not be shared with your workforce. To be sure, there is opportunity in honing your ability to empathize and learn from those who are different from you and from your wildly diverse customer base. The more you can make the inside of your company look like the markets you serve, the better positioned you will be.

The New Now of work is reshaping every aspect of the global workforce, and it requires organizations and employees alike to rethink every aspect of work from the demographic composition of the labor force to how we measure the meaning and outcomes of jobs. What's changing? Simply everything.

Let's keep going, then.

Notes

1. Toossi, Mitra, 2002, "A Century of Change: The U.S. Labor Force, 1950–2050," Office of Occupational Statistics and Employment Projections, Bureau of Labor Statistics, May, available at https://www.bls.gov/opub/mlr/2002/05/art2full.pdf.

2. Chao, Elaine L., 2001, "Report on the American Workforce," US Department of Labor, available at https://www.bls.gov/cps/counting-minorities-report-on-the-american-workforce-2001.pdf.

3. Jensen, Eric, Jones, Nicholas, Rabe, Megan Pratt, Beverly, Medina, Lauren, Orozco, Kimberly, and Spell, Lindsay, 2021, "The Chance That Two People Chosen at Random Are of Different Race or Ethnicity Groups Has Increased Since 2010," US Census Bureau, August 12, available at https://www.census.gov/library/stories/2021/08/2020-united-states-population-more-racially-ethnically-diverse-than-2010.html.

4. Frey, William H., 2018, "US Will Become 'Minority White' in 2045, Census Projects," Brookings, March 14, available at https://www.brookings.edu/blog/the-avenue/2018/03/14/the-us-will-become-minority-white-in-2045-census-projects/.

5. Hall, Madison, 2021, "A Key Change in the Census Showed the US Is Diversifying Across All Age Groups. Here's Why That Matters," Business Insider, August 20, available at https://www.businessinsider.nl/a-key-change-in-the-census-showed-the-us-is-diversifying-across-all-age-groups-heres-why-that-matters/.

6. "About PGM ONE: People of the Global Majority in the Outdoors, Nature, and Environment," n.d., PGM ONE/Earth Island Institute, available at https://www.pgmone.org/about (access date: July, 2022).

7. Fry, Richard, 2020, "The Pace of Boomer Retirements Has Accelerated in the Past Year," Pew Research Center, November 9, available at https://www.pewresearch.org/fact-tank/2020/11/09/the-pace-of-boomer-retirements-has-accelerated-in-the-past-year/.

8. Johnson, Stephen, 2021, "How Humanity Gave Itself an Extra Life," *New York Times Magazine*, April 27.

9. Parmelee, Michele, 2021, "Millennials, Gen Zs Prioritize Flexibility," Deloitte – *Wall Street Journal*, August 3, available at https://deloitte.wsj.com/articles/millennials-gen-zs-prioritize-flexibility-01628013560.

10. "Semi-Retirement Could Help Ease Labour Shortages but Employers Slow to Adapt," Express Employment Professionals and The Harris Poll, January 12, 2022, available at https://www.globenewswire.com/en/news-release/2022/01/12/2365712/0/en/Older-Workers-Want-to-Stay-in-Workforce-But-Most-Employers-Don-t-Offer-Semi-Retirement.html.

11. Ibid.

12. Hartshorne, Joshua K. and Germine, Laura T., 2015, "When Does Cognitive Functioning Peak? The Asynchronous Rise and Fall of Different Cognitive Abilities Across the Life Span," *Sage Journals*, March 13, available at https://journals.sagepub.com/doi/abs/10.1177/0956797614567339.

13. Sawhill, Isabel V. and Guyot, Katherine, 2020, "Women's Work Boosts Middle-Class Incomes but Creates a Family Time Squeeze That Needs to Be Eased," Brookings, May, available at https://www.brookings.edu/essay/womens-work-boosts-middle-class-incomes-but-creates-a-family-time-squeeze-that-needs-to-be-eased.

14. Fry, Richard, 2019, "U.S. Women Near Milestone in the College-Educated Labor Force," Pew Research Center, June 20, available at https://www.pewresearch.org/fact-tank/2019/06/20/u-s-women-near-milestone-in-the-college-educated-labor-force/.

15. Belkin, Douglas, 2021, "A Generation of American Men Give Up on College: 'I Just Feel Lost,'" *Wall Street Journal*, September 6, available at https://www.wsj.com/articles/college-university-fall-higher-education-men-women-enrollment-admissions-back-to-school-11630948233.

16. "Degrees Conferred by Postsecondary Institutions, by Level of Degree and Sex of Student: Selected Years, 1869–70 Through 2030–31," *Digest of Education Statistics*, National Center for Education Statistics, 2021, available at https://nces.ed.gov/programs/digest/d21/tables/dt21_318.10.asp.

17. Riedl, Christoph, Kim, Young Ji, Gupta, Pranav, and Williams Woolley, Anita, 2021, "Quantifying collective intelligence in human groups." Proceedings of the National Academy of Sciences of the United States of America, May 17, available at https://www.pnas.org/doi/10.1073/pnas.2005737118.

18. "Amazon, Apple, Google, & Microsoft – Employee Demographics," Statsocial, December 3, 2020, available at https://www.statsocial.com/employee-demographics-amazon-apple-google-microsoft.

19. Gerullo, Megan, 2021, "Nearly 3 Million U.S. Women Have Dropped Out of the Labor Force in the Past Year," *CBS News*, February 5, available at https://www.cbsnews.com/news/covid-crisis-3-million-women-labor-force/.

20. Riley, Katherine and Stamm, Stephanie, 2021, "Nearly 1.5 Million Mothers Are Still Missing from the Workforce," *Wall Street Journal*, April 27, available at https://www.wsj.com/articles/nearly-1-5-million-mothers-are-still-missing-from-the-workforce-11619472229.

21. "The Untold Cost of Inadequate Childcare," Massachusetts Tax Payer Foundation, April 2022, available at https://www.masstaxpayers.org/sites/default/files/publications/2022-04/The%20Untold%20Cost%20of%20Child%20Care%20Report%20FINAL.pdf.

22. Brodsky, Samantha, 2017, "The Average Mom Reportedly Works the Equivalent of 2 Full-Time Jobs Per Week," *Good Housekeeping*, July 31, available at https://www.goodhousekeeping.com/life/parenting/news/a45318/average-mom-clocks-two-full-time-jobs/.

23. Rosenberg, Alyssa, "Putting Parents First Could Be the Secret to a Successful Return-to-Office," *Washington Post*, August 15, 2022, available at https://www.washingtonpost.com/opinions/2022/08/15/on-site-child-care-back-to-office/.

24. "More than Half of Unemployed Young Men Have Criminal Records; Finding Suggested New Approach Needed to Aid the Unemployed," Rand Corporation, February 19, 2022, available at https://www.rand.org/news/press/2022/02/18.html.

25. The White House, 2022, "Statement from President Biden on Marijuana Reform," October 6, available at https://www.whitehouse.gov/briefing-room/statements-releases/2022/10/06/statement-from-president-biden-on-marijuana-reform/.

26. "LGBT+ Pride 2021 Global Survey Points to a Generation Gap Around Gender Identity and Sexual Attraction," Ipsos, June 9, 2021 available at https://www.ipsos.com/en/lgbt-pride-2021-global-survey-points-generation-gap-around-gender-identity-and-sexual-attraction.

27. Kenney, Lisa, 2020, "Companies Can't Ignore Shifting Gender Norms," *Harvard Business Review*, April 8.

28. "Selecting Your Gender Marker," 2022, Bureau of Consular Affairs, US Department of State, available at https://travel.state.gov/content/travel/en/passports/need-passport/selecting-your-gender-marker.html (access date: July, 2022).

29. Wikipedia, 2022, "Legal Recognition of Non-Binary Gender," available at https://en.wikipedia.org/wiki/Legal_recognition_of_non-binary_gender (access date: July, 2022).

30. Turner, Allison, 2018, "HRC REPORT: Statline Data Reveals Half of LGBTQ Employees in the U.S. Remain Closeted at Work," Human Rights Campaign, June 25, available at https://www.hrc.org/news/hrc-report-startling-data-reveals-half-of-lgbtq-employees-in-us-remain-clos.

31. Brown, Anna, 2022, "About 5% of Young Adults in the U.S. Say Their Gender Is Different from Their Sex Assigned at Birth," Pew Research Center, June 7. available at https://www.pewresearch.org/fact-tank/2022/06/07/about-5-of-young-adults-in-the-u-s-say-their-gender-is-different-from-their-sex-assigned-at-birth/.

32. Reynolds, Daniel, 2021, "Study: Half of Gen Z Believes the Gender Binary Is Outdated," *Advocate*, February 24, available at https://www.advocate.com/business/2021/2/24/study-half-gen-z-believes-gender-binary-outdated.

33. Bostock v. Clayton County, Georgia, No. 17–1618, U.S. Supreme Court, June 15, 2020.

34. Eswaran, Vijay, 2019, "The Business Case for Diversity in the Workplace Is Not Overwhelming," The World Economic Forum, April 29, available at https://www.weforum.org/agenda/2019/04/business-case-for-diversity-in-the-workplace/.

35. Gompers, Paul and Kovvali, Silpa, 2018, "The Other Diversity Dividend," *Harvard Business Review*, July–August.

36. "Diversity & Inclusion Can Boost Employee Engagement," Rewardian, September 9, 2020, available at https://blog.rewardian.com/diversity-inclusion.

37. Fosslien, Liz, Linkedin.com, March 2022, available at https://www.linkedin.com/posts/liz-fosslien_diversity-is-having-a-seat-at-the-table-activity-6917946008253472768-IJxk?utm_source=share&utm_medium=member_desktop.

38. Coe, Erica, Cordina, Jenny, Enomoto, Kana, Jacobson, Raelyn, Mei, Sharon, and Seshan, Nikhil, 2022, "Addressing the Unprecedented Behavioral-Health Challenges Facing Generation Z," McKinsey, January 14, available at https://www.mckinsey.com/industries/healthcare-systems-and-services/our-insights/addressing-the-unprecedented-behavioral-health-challenges-facing-generation-z.

39. Dixon-Fyle, Sundiatu, Dolan, Kevin, Hunt, Vivian, and Prince, Sara, 2020, "Diversity Wins: How Inclusion Matters," McKinsey, May 19, available at https://www.mckinsey.com/featured-insights/diversity-and-inclusion/diversity-wins-how-inclusion-matters.

40. "Measure Up Initiative: Fortune and Refinitiv Partnership," *Fortune*, February 2021, available at https://fortune.com/franchise-list-page/measure-up-initiative-fortune-refinitiv-partnership-methodology/.

41. Cydney Roach, 2021, "Employees Now Considered the Most Important Group of Companies' Long-Term Success: What Are the Boardroom Implications?" Edelman, May 20, available at https://www.edelman.com/trust/2021-trust-barometer/spring-update/employees-now-considered.

2 Understand Your Workers' New Habits

Many things conspired over many years to transform the ways in which work gets done, but none more significant than the work itself. Technology increasingly consumed repetitive and sometimes dangerous labor, moving workers off shop floors to work behind computer terminals. Service and support roles relocated to call centers around the world. Knowledge workers were becoming increasingly detached from specific workplaces; a mobile phone and a laptop were the highly portable tools of the trade.

Digital transformation experts of all stripes had mapped a path to full automation that would extend well into the 2030s and beyond. Algorithms were taking over routine, predictable work tasks and advances in artificial cognition began to demonstrate that even more complex tasks such as writing and designing could be augmented with technology.

All of this was unfolding in the first two decades of the twenty-first century. And then, these trend lines passed through the great accelerator that was the COVID-19 pandemic.

The pace of technology adoption and implementation accelerated so quickly that consulting firm McKinsey & Company saw businesses leap forward five years in just the first 60 days after lockdown orders took effect around the world.[1]

We Are No Longer Who We Were

Prior to the pandemic, business and society had experienced a 15-year period of exponential technology-driven growth. Every forward step today was twice the leap of the day before and yet only half the progress of tomorrow. The pandemic only accelerated that change. As the world changed, we evolved, and so did the way we work. The following sections explore these life-shifting transformations.

We Embraced Existing Technology

We started using the tools that were already around us – many of them a decade old or older – including Zoom (2011), Microsoft Teams (2016), WebEx (1995), Google Meet (2017), FaceTime (2013), and Skype (2003). Medical offices embraced telemedicine and consumers adopted every manner of app to stay connected professionally and personally. Small businesses and individuals adopted non-cash payment systems. QR codes finally had a reason to exist at scale. Digital payments on platforms like Venmo, Zelle, and PayPal surged.[2] And we learned how to use all of it.

Given that very few of these technologies were new, this rapid digital transformation was due to a *human transformation*. Technologies relegated to specific use cases became near universal. *We* transformed *ourselves* to enjoy the benefits of these technologies. These benefits were just the tip of the spear. (See "The Pandemic Compressed Time.")

We Learned to Trust

None of these virtual meeting tools – indeed, remote work itself – would have been effective at all, however, if we had not made the collective decision to trust one another, at least at a fundamental level. Dov Siedman, author of *How: Why How We Do Anything Means Everything*, is famous for saying, "Trust is the only human performance enhancing drug." The trust we found in ourselves and one another helped us make it through three years of remote work. Only because we finally trusted our people and each other to work with autonomy were we able to maintain performance and productivity.

The Pandemic Compressed Time

If the pace of change was accelerating before the pandemic (and it was), Covid put change in overdrive.

In 2013, Frey and Osborne modeled the replacement of human work by technology and predicted that about half of work-related tasks would move from human to machine by 2030.[3] Now, the World Economic Forum says we'll reach that threshold within five years.

Pre-pandemic, Accenture estimated that about 20% of business functions had migrated to the cloud, and within 10 years, the migration would be complete. Now, Accenture contends that business is moving at twice the speed and business will be fully cloud based within five years.[4]

McKinsey's measures are even more aggressive, suggesting digital transformation leapt forward five years in the first 60 days of the pandemic.[5] Why? Because business had no choice. When in-person engagement was not an option, we turned to already-available technologies from teleconferencing to telehealth. Zoom became ubiquitous during the pandemic, yet it had been introduced to market more than a decade before its widespread, Covid-induced adoption. The technology was available long before conditions required us to adapt our behaviors to use it. That's why we say that digital transformation is mostly human transformation; it is behavior change more than it is technological innovation. And that behavior change also changes the trajectory of business.

The long march of digital transformation delivers many benefits, yet is not without its disruptive consequences. Economist Joseph Alois Schumpeter, best known for his 1942 book *Capitalism, Socialism, and Democracy*, developed the theory of creative destruction, positing that economic progress depends upon dismantling the status quo and the introduction of new products and processes that make prior solutions obsolete. The consulting firm Innosight tracks the acceleration of "creative destruction" by noting the shrinking lifespan of companies listed on the S&P500. Where these companies perched upon the top of the business world for an average of 30–35 years in the 1970s, today they are lucky to hold that spot for 15–20 years.[6] This march of creative destruction both truncates the lifespans of companies and shortens the useful life of technical skills.

Change always demands that we learn and adapt. The pandemic applied unprecedented pressure that we do that even faster, too.

(Continued)

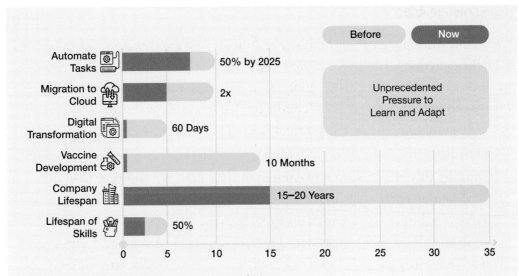

Figure 2.1 The Pandemic Compressed Time

Data Sources: Vaccine: (www.historyofvaccines.org), Digital Transformation (McKinsey), Migration to Cloud (Accenture), Automation of Tasks (World Economic Forum), Company Lifespan (Innosight), Skill Lifespan (IBM)

We Learned to Collaborate at Scale

An urgent crisis can be a catalyst for dramatic behavior change, and few things exemplify this like the development of the Covid vaccine in just 10 months. How did that happen? With the advantage of advanced genomic tools, scientists identified the genetic sequence of the Covid-19 virus in a matter of weeks. Then, they widely shared this discovery by tweeting out the information so that anyone could get to work on a vaccine, in what is no doubt one of the greatest acts of open innovation ever.

More than a dozen biopharmaceutical companies worked round the clock developing and testing vaccine candidates, and by mid-2022 more than 120 vaccines had been developed and nearly 50 were in human trials.[7] Researchers tapped previous innovations in mRNA and vaccine technology and leveraged computational immunology to simulate what the vaccines would do in the body. By radically sharing, these scientists compressed time, developing effective vaccines in less than a year. Until then, no vaccine had been developed in fewer than four years.[8]

We Learned to Adapt

Whether it was embracing new tools or embracing new collaborators, the pandemic, more than anything, required everyone to confront unprecedented change. Amid so much that is horrible about the pandemic, it did provide at least one valuable gift: it taught us to adapt. We can't underestimate that lesson in the future of work. In fact, we believe so deeply in the power of adaptation that we made it the title of our last book.

Consider this: the lifespan of a company – no doubt the company *you* work for – is declining at the very same time the lifespan of those who work in those companies has begun to expand, a positive trend line that dipped a bit during the pandemic. There was a time, not so long ago, when a person could expect to spend a 30- or 40-year career with one company. Now, mergers, acquisitions, new competition, and digital disruption are acting in concert to shorten the average time in business of most companies. Further, as evidenced by the Great Resignation, we're no longer tied to the expectation of long-term tenure at a company or in a role. People are much more free to switch jobs, careers, or industries with marked frequency.[9]

Think, too, about the lifespan of technical and other job-specific skills. IBM estimates that the half-life of a technical skill has dropped in half from five to under three years.[10] New technologies emerge at a faster and faster clip, usually replacing existing tools and processes. To keep pace, we will all need to adapt, a process of learning new skills and unlearning the habits and systems that prevent progress.

What does this compression of time mean? We now, irrefutably, live with an unprecedented demand to learn and adapt as changes reshape our work and our environment. This demand will *never* be met through external pressure. We cannot threaten, reward, or require our employees to learn at the speed and scale necessary to effectively operate in a whirlwind of change. What, then, is a leader to do?

Activate your employees' agency, encourage autonomy, and recognize that your role as leader is not to manage people but to enable them to do their best work.

Said differently, in the modern work environment, the cycle of learning, unlearning, and learning again demands that workers embrace their agency to act and work in ways that make them more creative, more productive, and more fully human. Workplace leaders must risk the vulnerability to admit they don't have all the answers and willingness to discover together with their teams. The honest and fearless embrace of your own vulnerability builds the psychological safety that enables your team to be active, adaptive learners.

We'll address this idea in greater detail in Parts Two and Three, but let's start now by understanding all the ways that workers are claiming their agency and power.

The Empowered Worker: Your Most Valuable New Asset

The factors described in the previous sections, among others, changed so much about where, when, how, and why we work, *and where, when, how, and why we don't.*

Where We Work

Both the work and the technology liberated work from the office long before the pandemic shattered our perceptions and changed our attitudes toward work immeasurably. (See "Where Work Takes Place Today.")

Prior to 2020, about 17% of workdays were taken remotely.[11] In a matter of weeks, Covid changed all that. Even the most reluctant business leaders were forced to embrace remote work at least temporarily. As vaccinations afford a return to office-based work, every industry has struggled to envision a "new normal" workplace. A return to the office setting of pre-2020 seemed unlikely. But it also doesn't seem that the pandemic-era pants-less, work-from-anywhere remote environment would be the sole office of the future, either.

By 2022, many workplaces were settling into a hybrid model that provides flexibility to work remotely all the time for some and for many, some of the time. In KPMG's Global 2021 CEO Outlook, only 37% of surveyed CEOs said most of their employees will work remotely at least two or more days per week, yet 42% said they will seek to hire primarily remote workers in a bid to tap a wider talent pool.[12] In the global competition for the most talented workers, Salesforce is one example of a company that has shifted hiring practices to embrace remote workers. Job openings are clearly categorized as remote and regional regions rather than by specific cities and offices.[13]

Where Work Takes Place Today

In a matter of weeks in the spring of 2020, business leaders who couldn't imagine commanding a remote workforce were suddenly at the helm of one. With offices shuttered and businesses closed, corporate leadership hustled to figure out which work could take place remotely, which had to happen at a corporate facility, and which could straddle both.

Virtual conferencing company Owl Labs dug into that question and found that, globally, 16% of companies were able to operate 100% remotely, 44% of companies required work that must be done on-site, and 40% did work that needed to be done in a hybrid model.

At first blush, we tend to imagine that it is only office or knowledge work that can be done remotely. All you need is a computer and an internet connection. Other, more physical labor is hard to imagine being done remotely. After all, you can't pave a driveway, walk a dog, or polish diamonds in your spare bedroom.

Still, an increasing number of jobs and tasks are finding their way onto remote platforms. For example, drive-through food service may seem an unlikely candidate for remote work. But software created by Bite Ninja offers "cloud labor for restaurants" that can employ remote workers to take drive-through orders. The company conducted pilot programs with Tennessee-based Baby Jacks BBQ and the Texas- and Arizona-based chain ChopShop.

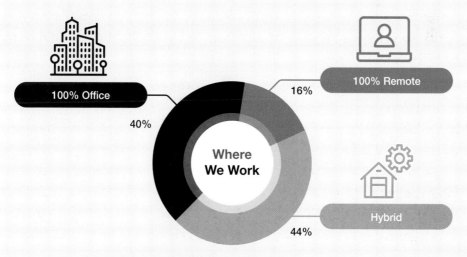

Figure 2.2 Where Work Takes Place Today

Data source: Owl Labs, 2021.

"The pandemic has taught us that it doesn't matter in which city you live," Salesforce CEO Bret Taylor told a reporter at *Welt am Sonntag* in May 2022. "Only the time zone is important in order to communicate and work together in this world."[14]

Still, trend lines are pointing to at least a partial return to the office that seeks to balance the practical benefits of in-person and collaborative office work with the newfound flexibility and autonomy of workers when they have greater say in where and how they engage with the corporate "mothership." In KPMG's annual CEO survey in 2020, nearly 70% of corporations said they planned to downsize and reconfigure office space to adjust for work-from-home policies. A year later, in an embrace of hybrid strategies, only 21% of surveyed CEOs said they had reduced or planned to reduce corporate office space.[15]

While these numbers may suggest that CEOs are flip-flopping on workspace decisions, they signal something much more important: We simply do not yet know. We are still learning about the long-term consequences and advantages of so many decisions taken in the early months of 2020. It is too early to assume that those decisions, our perceptions, or any policy will be permanent.

While the pandemic changed our default assumption about where knowledge work takes place (always in person, always in an office), it has not yet made clear how, when, and why we come together. Some of our work involves asynchronous tasks that are more efficiently done without the burden of a commute. Our current virtual collaborative tools worked well enough when we had no alternatives, yet we're still very much experimenting with virtual and in-real-life collaboration. How can we improve collaboration if we don't share a common time and space? How can we strengthen weak ties and the serendipitous collaborations they afford? How will we build social capital, trade social currency, and enhance our professional networks? How do we build a deep sense of belonging, which research shows is essential to a strong culture and employee engagement?

Now that we know some of the key questions we want to answer, we need to figure out how to create better technology tools, smarter processes and practices, and better office and shared spaces – then use both to best align work into the fabric of people's lives.

No doubt, the pendulum will continue to swing as employers and employees navigate the desirability and necessity of work location. But one thing we do know for sure, however, is this: The knee-jerk desire to return to 2019 or to demand office time will do more to erode the trust and goodwill that was well earned when we both trusted and listened to our people during the pandemic.

Physical office space, however, is only one factor determining where work will happen and how effective it can be. The sudden shift to both remote work and school created a childcare nightmare for many households. Parents – primarily mothers – juggled their office work with their children's learning and development needs, taking on the added role of teacher in the absence of in-person instruction. To fully value human beings, businesses will need to push beyond old notions that work from home is career limiting and instead design human-centric, caregiver-first, flexible work environments that unleash the potential of more of us.

Collaboration from Anywhere?

Much of the debate about where work takes place is based on the argument that in-person interactions are necessary building blocks of social capital and innovation. We simply do not know if that is true. Consider some provocative data. Of the 10 largest population centers, only two are countries: China and India both having residential populations that well exceed 1 billion people. The remaining aggregated communities are digital platforms. A census of social media platforms counts "populations" ranging from over 700 million to almost 3 billion.[16] These virtual environments took hold over the last decade and well before Covid-19 shut down in-person workplaces. Consider, too, that today about 25% of cisgender, heterosexual couples and more than 70% of LGBTQ+ couples meet online.[17] Quickly, it becomes clear that we can and do build social capital and community virtually.

Look further to new and emerging virtual reality and augmented reality technologies from Facebook Horizon Workrooms, Google's Project Starline, and a host of other technology ventures and you'll see that these experiments with the "metaverse" are more than a gimmicky parlor trick; they have the potential to evolve into the next mode of work and collaboration. Surely, we have a lot to learn to best leverage virtual workspaces and modalities – most notably in terms of ethical concerns still to be addressed on social media platforms. We will do so while also rethinking how, why, and when to best use both real-time and face-to-face interactions.

Why Where Matters

As companies wrestle with the operational and logistical considerations of remote, hybrid, and office work, leaders are facing a more complex reality. The pandemic unleashed a sudden, global, work-from-anywhere workforce that fundamentally repositioned work within the larger context of employees' lives. Or, as we like to say, it became much more about where work fits into our lives than where work takes place.

For much of our lives, our jobs were the catalyst for many of our life decisions: where we worked, where our kids went to school, where we built community and a sense of belonging. (See "The Center Shifts.")

In his 2002 book, revised in 2019, *Rise of the Creative Class*, urban studies theorist Richard Florida proposed that a "creative class" of some 40 million people who earned a living in knowledge- and creativity-centric occupations had the freedom to settle in communities that fueled their passion because they could effectively work from anywhere.[18] Now, as rapid digital transformation turns many if not most jobs into "creative class" occupations, that soul-nourishing community is separated from work. Put another way, our lives now come before our livelihoods. Jobs fit into our lives, rather than driving so many of our life decisions. We moved from striving for work-life balance to life-work integration.

This reversal of roles has the additional effect of shifting settlement patterns. (See "The Great Relocation."). Workers may no longer need to settle in urban centers to reap the benefits of urban corporations. Central offices may become places we visit as much as they are places where we work, freeing workers to migrate to affordable small towns and rural communities, move "home" to be closer to family, or pick new areas that cater to favorite activities and lifestyles. Big-city corporate offices might reconfigure, too, shifting from towering office buildings to smaller hub-and-spoke workplaces. It is as exciting as it is challenging to imagine all the possibilities to transform the once-typical work environment to suit a diverse workforce. Yet much like remote and hybrid work itself, we are just beginning to figure out what works for our newly empowered workforce.

The Center Shifts

For too long, we centered our lives on our jobs.

Where we worked determined, in large measure, where we lived, where our kids went to school, and with whom we socialized. Consider it. You take a job in a city, say Boston, and move into a neighborhood or suburb that seems to fit your needs, style, and budget. Often, your spouse takes a job and you make accommodation for commutes and schedules. You settle in and begin a search for a sense of belonging, places of worship, bars, gyms, civic organizations, dog parks, country clubs. Soon, and almost by accident, you've found or created your community as a by-product of your career move.

After nearly three years of pandemic, the center has shifted. We have looked for meaning in our lives and recognized what – and more importantly, who – is most important to us. Now, we want to build our lives around belonging and community. We settle our homes in the places that fulfill our physical and emotional needs, then layer in our jobs, either working remotely or finding work that is more purpose aligned and in the place we want to be.

This is the reordering that many folks are now doing, either because remote work has liberated them from place or because after facing an existential crisis they have determined to build work around their lives rather than building lives around their work.

This shift is likely permanent as more and more people prioritize community in their lives. And, make no mistake, this is good news for leaders who might be inclined to revert to the office-centric work lives on which they built their success. Hybrid and remote work is, in effect, a new work contract that honors the whole person and recognizes that happy and engaged people are the foundation for new value creation.

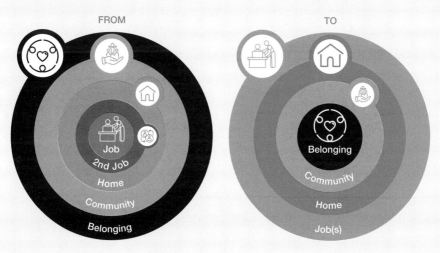

Figure 2.3 The Center Shifts

The Great Relocation

The Great Relocation is well underway.

The onset of the Covid pandemic was an opportunity for many to experiment with new environments. Remote work meant that any location with a broadband internet connection could be "home." Some people used work-from-home to expatriate temporarily and explore foreign environments. Others moved closer to family support systems to tough out lockdowns together.

As the pandemic wore on, though, many people realized the opportunity to make these moves permanent, ditching high-cost urban living for less expensive suburban and even rural communities. In fact, according to research by Owl Labs, more people moved away from large cities than moved toward them, forming what folks are now calling "Zoomtowns" based on the influx of remote workers to more suburban and rural communities.

As remote or hybrid work becomes a reliable option, we expect to see the great migration truly begin, because work no longer ties us to place. Salesforce, for example, is more inclined to hire by time zone rather than office location.[19]

Movement will not just be domestic. Americans are heading to Europe, where Italy, Portugal, Spain, Greece, and France are among the most popular relocation destinations. American interest in moving to Greece is up 40%, real estate giant Sotheby's reports, while Americans now account for 12% of Sotheby's Italian revenue, up from 5% a year ago.[20] Further, an Upwork research report titled "Economist Report: Remote Workers on the Move" predicts that between "14 to 23 million Americans are planning to move as a result of remote work. Combined with those who are moving regardless of remote work, near-term migration rates may be three to four times what they normally are."[21] With a strong dollar and a decade of rising housing prices in the United States, the Great Relocation has begun.

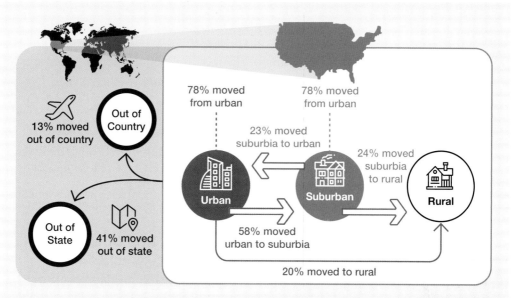

Figure 2.4 The Great Relocation

Data source:: Owl Labs, 2021.

More than 20 years after Robert Putnam wrote *Bowling Alone: The Collapse and Revival of American Community* to document the 50-year decline in social capital in the United States, might this be the moment when we begin again to put community at the center rather than having it as the by-product of our activities? We certainly hope so, and we take heart in Putnam's most recent work, *The Upswing: How America Came Together A Century Ago and How We Can Do it Again* in which he describes the 100-year cycles of the rise and fall of community engagement.

Remote Work Lowers Switching Costs

While physical movement creates opportunity for workers and employers alike, there is another sort of movement that creates a very real downside for employers. Without a physical place to bind your workforce to your organization and to one another, it becomes easier for employees to leave, particularly when the switching cost is little more than a different Zoom link and email address.

Team leaders, then, must work even harder to build meaningful connections with those they lead and among remote teams to create the valuable workplace community that creates contentment and engenders commitment.

When We Work: Where Changes When

Location-flexible work environments are often also time-shifted workplace, and the 9-to-5 workday may well become a thing of the past as newly empowered workers are more able to set their own terms to work around other commitments in their lives. And not a moment too soon.

The eight-hour workday is an artifact of the original assembly line. Watching his production line more than 100 years ago, Henry Ford discovered that workplace accidents happened more frequently after the ninth hour of work. Limit a work shift to eight hours and you have fewer accidents and greater productivity. Thus, the eight-hour workday was born of the realities of manual labor.[22]

Enter the not-so-physical labor of the knowledge economy. We recognize that knowledge work is not yet the majority of the work done today, but if you're holding this book in physical or digital form you are most surely steeped in knowledge-based work, which is our focus. Cognitive labor follows a very different pattern, and productivity is not so easily measured. In a 2016 survey of 1,989 full-time office workers in the United Kingdom, nearly 80% said they were not "productive" throughout the workday. Instead, they said they were productive for an average of just 2 hours and 53 minutes.[23]

We have to ask, though: what does "productivity" mean in the context of knowledge work? These office workers said they used their work hours to scan social media, surf the web, chat with colleagues, and fill their coffee cups. But is that really unproductive? No doubt they underestimate the time spent preparing for meetings, writing reports, answering questions for colleagues, or writing the perfect email – all activities that are, in fact, part of the job.

Thinking up a new product, a new sales strategy, or a new way to engage your team may not look "productive" if you are doing something other than pounding away at your keyboard when you do it. Knowledge creation rarely happens on demand in some easily measured unit of productivity. What looks like goofing off to some eyes might actually be the stroke of genius that saves the fiscal quarter.

The UK study, though, did present one worrisome piece of data. Nearly 20% of these office workers said they spent almost a half hour each workday searching for another job.[24] The survey was commissioned by the digital coupon company Vouchercloud well before the pandemic surfaced attitudes about work. Surveys vary, but some polls suggest that more than two-thirds of today's workers are actively thinking of leaving their current jobs.[25]

All that office time may not be necessary. In fact, it may well be more healthful and spur greater productivity to spend *less time* at work. Researchers in Iceland conducted a massive study with about 1% of the country's workforce. Without taking a cut in pay, these workers cut out 3–5 hours each week. The study found that these workers maintained productivity levels and improved well-being. In fact, the research was such an "overwhelming success" that now nearly 85% of Icelanders work just a four-day work week.[26]

In the summer of 2019, Microsoft instituted a temporary four-day work week for its workforce in Japan. Productivity jumped 40%.[27] Perhaps not surprisingly, 92% of employees said they liked the shorter week, and 25% took less time off during the trial period. Microsoft reaped some unexpected benefits, too. Electricity use dropped by 23% and printing was down 59%.[28] One key factor in the success of this pilot was the integration of time management training and strict protocols around meeting times, lengths, and number of attendees. Perhaps not surprisingly to those of us whose days are filled with meetings, Microsoft found some of the biggest chunks of wasted time were in unnecessary meetings.

Evidence that a shorter work week leads to greater productivity and happier employees continues to mount. A study underway in the United Kingdom as of this writing might provide the big push to move business to this less-is-more strategy for work. A team of academic and nonprofit researchers have joined with 70 employers with more than 3,300 employees to test a four-day work week for a period of six months. These companies span a range of industries, including market, retail, financial services, information technology, and consumer goods, among others. Workers get 100% of their pay while working 80% of their prior schedule, with one catch: they have to maintain 100% of their productivity.[29]

At the midpoint of the study, participating companies report overwhelming that they plan to continue the practice and cited same or higher levels of productivity and higher levels of wellbeing as the reason why.

These experiments, coupled with workers' newfound flexibility to work from anywhere, ought to encourage business leaders to chuck the time clock and trust their teams to get the work done in the hours needed to do the work, rather than hours required to report for duty.

The Through Line: Creating Life/Work Integration

The changing workstyles of today's empowered workers are about more than wanting the flexibility to work where and when they want. Surely, the existential threat created by the Covid-19 pandemic was a driver in reshuffling priorities. Yet the reality is that most workers have wrestled with work/life balance for as long as they have been working, struggling to make room for life amid demanding work Three years of existential contemplation, though, has had its impact. Workers are now making life outside the job a priority, flipping the mantra from work/life balance to life/work integration.

In its 2016 Millennial Survey, Deloitte identified the same demands for flexible work hours (88%) and remote work (75%) that we now tend to attribute to the pandemic.[30] And poll after poll shows that Gen Z workers would rather have purpose in their work than higher pay and other benefits.[31] In fact, 50% of Gen Z workers say it is a "must" that employers not only enable, but respect, a work/life balance.[32]

Workers, then, are questioning where work fits in their lives. Or, perhaps more aptly, how to fit work into their lives. (See "The Rise of Bleisure.")

Why We Work

The key shift here is simple: Once, we worked for survival. Then, we worked for identity and status. The pandemic, which placed new demands on those it didn't throw out of work entirely, has led many workers to rethink why they are working and what – beyond a paycheck and benefits – they hope to get from work. Now, more and more people are working to fulfill a greater purpose.

If we need our workforce to engage deeply, to learn and adapt continuously – and we do, amid so much change – then leaders need to help that workforce connect to their internal motivational drive. That, more than an office or a time clock or any other instruction or incentive, will serve to bind workers to their work and their employers. And as workers shift to more purpose-centric employment, corporations face increasing pressure to put purpose in line with, if not ahead of, profits, and explore the interconnections and interdependencies of worker empowerment to create a truly human-centered workplace.

The Rise of Bleisure

In 2009, writers Jacob Strand and Miriam Rayman, documenting Future Laboratory's biannual Trend Briefing, coined the term "bleisure," a portmanteau that described the convergence of business and leisure travel.[33]

Traveling for business? Tack on a few days to enjoy a brief vacation. Taking a holiday? Why not blend a bit of work and make the whole thing a write-off? While bleisure is nothing new, more and more people are adding pleasure to work travel. So much so that long-term rentals are spiking across the board.

Digital nomads are exploring the far corners of the earth, taking their work with them when they do. Snowbirds – those retired folks in northern United States who decamped to warmer climates for the winter months – are no longer just retired folks. Millennials are picking up second properties in sunnier climates as part of the larger remote, work-from-anywhere trend. Home-share booking platform Airbnb reported that long-term stays of a week or more hit an all-time high in the first quarter of 2022, twice the number in 2019. In fact, one in five nights booked on Airbnb are part of a long-term rental.[34]

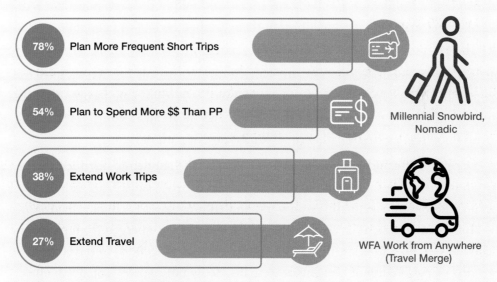

Figure 2.5 The Rise of Bleisure

Data sources: Expedia 2022 Travel Survey; Deloitte 2022 Travel Outlook.

The COVID-19 pandemic, while tragic, forced long-overdue behavior changes and reset mental models around every aspect of work. Perhaps most importantly, though, we've had the opportunity to step back and examine *why* we work. As we generate more and more value through human activities and ingenuity, and as complex challenges demand greater collaboration and leveraged collective intelligence, we stand at the threshold of a tremendous opportunity to rethink work and leadership to unleash more potential, engender deeper engagement, and generate even more business value in the process.

Case in point: Environmental and Social Governance (ESG) has taken on greater importance because investors are demanding it. The "environmental" in ESG refers to climate. The "social" to people. Both have always and inextricably been part of work, and both have both taken a back seat to profits over the past 50 or more years. That's beginning to change.

Scientists have long posited that human activity was the primary source of our changing climate, raising an ever-louder alarm over decades until, in 2018, the UN climate report warned that we had just 12 years left to save the planet. Since then, we've experienced unprecedented wildfires, superstorms, and floods. At the height of the pandemic, Lululemon CEO Calvin McDonald said he'd closed more stores due to hurricanes in the gulf and wildfires in the west than he had to pandemic-related lockdowns.[35]

Why do we mention this? Because behavioral change only begins when we feel the pain of change. In the case of climate, decades of warnings are heard only when unseasonable temperatures blanket the planet, fires burn out of control, torrential storms flood homes, and weather of all kinds leaves a path of destruction.

So what about the people component of ESG? The pandemic provided the existential crisis that let us feel the pain of decades of work-caused stress, burnout, social and economic inequality, overwork, and eroding trust. A climate change in the human environment of work came swiftly. Even as we emerged from pandemic lockdowns in 2022 to again frequent restaurants, bars, and clubs, to travel again on crowded planes, or attend events that were decidedly not socially distanced, office occupancy remained stuck between 35–40%.

Why? We had fundamentally reordered where work fit in our lives. By the start of 2022, employers were struggling with the Great Resignation. Millions of people were opting out of the workforce for myriad reasons. Businesses in every industry had job openings that they could not fill. Many pundits assumed this was a short-term problem promoted by early retirement and general labor shortages. Inflation and need will ultimately bring workers back to fill those jobs, and perhaps it will to some degree. But we think something different, something much bigger than short-term change is happening.

Workers have become empowered. The trust and autonomy mixed with the pressures of juggling work and increasingly complicated lives during the pandemic gave workers new agency to weave work into the broader cloth of their lives. Empowered workers don't give up that agency once they have experienced it. Inflation or even a recession won't change this fundamental shift. The empowered worker is here to stay. And that, friend, is an opportunity to lead differently.

Notes

1. Baig, Aamer, Hall, Bryce, Jenkins, Paul, Lamarre, Eric, and McCarthy, Brian, 2020, "The COVID-19 Recovery Will Be Digital: A Plan for the First 90 Days," McKinsey, May 14, available at https://www.mckinsey.com/capabilities/mckinsey-digital/our-insights/the-covid-19-recovery-will-be-digital-a-plan-for-the-first-90-days.

2. McKee, Jordan, 2021, "State of the Union: Global Digital Payments and Fintech Ecosystem," Discover Digital Network, September, available at https://insights.discoverglobalnetwork.com/digital-commerce/global-digital-payments-fintech-ecosystem.

3. Frey, Carl Benedikt and Osborne, Michael A., 2013, "The Future of Employment: How Susceptible Are Jobs to Computerisation?" September 17, available at https://www.oxfordmartin.ox.ac.uk/downloads/academic/The_Future_of_Employment.pdf.

4. Ikink, Roy, 2021, "20 Cloud Trends for 2021 and Beyond," Accenture, March 4.

5. Baig, "The COVID-19 Recovery Will Be Digital."

6. Viguerie, Patrick S., Calder, Ned, and Hindo, Brian, 2021, "2021 Corporate Longevity Forecast: As S&P 500 Lifespans Continue to Decline, Fast-Shaping 'Hybrid Industries' Create New Risks and Opportunities," Innosight, May, available at. https://www.innosight.com/insight/creative-destruction/.

7. Zimmer, Carl, Corum, Jonathan, Wee, Sui-Lee, and Kristoffersen, Matthew, 2020–ongoing, "Coronavirus Vaccine Tracker," *New York Times*, available at https://www.nytimes.com/interactive/2020/science/coronavirus-vaccine-tracker.html.

8. Ball, Philip, 2020, "The Lightning-fast Quest for COVID Vaccines – and What It Means for Other Diseases," *Nature*, December 18, available at https://www.nature.com/articles/d41586-020-03626-1.

9. Clark, D., 2021, "Average Company Lifespan of S&P 500 Companies 1965–2030," Statista.com, August 27, available at https://www.statista.com/statistics/1259275/average-company-lifespan.

10. Malik, Sonia, 2020, "Skills Transformation for the 2021 Workplace," IBM, December 7, available at https://www.ibm.com/blogs/ibm-training/skills-transformation-2021-workplace/.

11. Sava, Justina Alexandra, 2022, "Remote Work Frequency Before and After COVID-19 in the United States 2020," Statista, February 16, available at https://www.statista.com/statistics/1122987/change-in-remote-work-trends-after-covid-in-usa/.

12. Holt, Jonathan, 2021, "Global CEO Confidence Returns to Pre-pandemic Levels: KPMG Study," KPMG, September 1, available at https://home.kpmg/xx/en/home/media/press-releases/2021/09/global-ceo-confidence-returns-to-pre-pandemic-levels.html.

13. Hetzner, Christiaan, 2022, "Job Vacancies for Salesforce Are Now Listed by Time Zone, Reveals Co-CEO Bret Taylor," *Fortune*, May 9, available at https://fortune.com/2022/05/09/silicon-valley-salesforce-wall-street-recruiting-hiring-talent-employees/.

14. Ibid.

15. Newton, Mel, 2021, "Is Hybrid Working Really the Future of Work," KPMG, September 29, available at https://home.kpmg/uk/en/blogs/home/posts/2021/09/is-hybrid-working-really-the-future-of-work.html.

16. Dixon, S., 2022, "Global Social Networks Ranked by Number of Users 2022," Statista, March 8, available at https://www.statista.com/statistics/272014/global-social-networks-ranked-by-number-of-users/.

17. Buchholz, Katharina, 2020, "How Couples Met," Statista, February 13, available at https://www.statista.com/chart/20822/way-of-meeting-partner-heterosexual-us-couples/.

18. Florida, Richard, 2014, *Rise of the Creative Class*, Basic Books.

19. Hetzner, "Job Vacancies for Salesforce Are Now Listed by Time Zone."

20. Kantor, Alice, 2022, "Americans Who Can't Afford Homes Are Moving to Europe Instead," Bloomberg.com, July 2, available at https://www.bloomberg.com/news/articles/2022-07-20/americans-moving-to-europe-housing-prices-and-strong-dollar-fuel-relocations.

21. "Economist Report: Remote Workers on the Move," Upwork, 2021, available at https://www.upwork.com/press/releases/economist-report-remote-workers-on-the-move.

22. "Ford Factory Workers Get 40-hour Week," History.com, November 13, 2009, available at https://www.history.com/this-day-in-history/ford-factory-workers-get-40-hour-week.

23. "How Many Productive Hours in a Work Day? Just 2 Hours, 23 Minutes . . . ," Vouchercloud, 2016, available at https://www.vouchercloud.com/resources/office-worker-productivity.

24. Ibid.

25. Dean, Grace and Hoff, Madison, 2021, "Nearly Three-quarters of Workers Are Actively Thinking About Quitting Their Job, According to a Recent Survey," Business Insider, October 7, available at https://www.businessinsider.com/great-resignation-labor-shortage-workers-thinking-about-quitting-joblist-report-2021-10.

26. Lau, Virginia and Sigurdardottir, Ragnhildur, 2021, "The Shorter Work Week Really Worked in Iceland. Here's How," Bloomberg, October 14, available at https://www.bloomberg.com/news/articles/2021-10-14/the-shorter-work-week-really-worked-in-iceland-here-s-how.

27. Paul, Kari, 2019, "Microsoft Japan Tested a Four-day Work Week and Productivity Jumped by 40%," *Guardian* (US edition], November 4, available at https://www.theguardian.com/technology/2019/nov/04/microsoft-japan-four-day-work-week-productivity.

28. Ibid.

29. Kuta, Sarah, 2022, "The U.K. Is Launching the World's Largest Four-Day Workweek Experiment," Smithsonianmag.com, June 7, available at https://www.smithsonianmag.com/smart-news/the-uk-is-launching-the-worlds-largest-four-day-workweek-experiment-180980210/.

30. "Flexible Working: Striking a Balance," The Deloitte Millennial Survey, 2016, available at https://www2.deloitte.com/bd/en/pages/about-deloitte/articles/gx-striking-a-balance.html.

31. "3 Ways Gen Z Employees Are Transforming the Workforce," Metlife, 2019, available at https://www.metlife.com/stories/work-family/3-ways-gen-z-employees-are-transforming-the-workforce/.

32. Ibid.

33. Wikipedia, "Bleisure travel," available at https://en.wikipedia.org/wiki/Bleisure_travel.

34. Airbnb, 2022, "Airbnb 2022 Summer Release Highlights," Airbnb, May 22, available at https://news.airbnb.com/airbnb-2022-summer-release-highlights/.

35. Murry, Alan and Meyer, David, 2020, "Why Accenture Thinks the 'Henry Ford Moment of the Digital Era' Is Coming," Fortune, September 17, available at https://fortune.com/2020/09/17/accenture-julie-sweet-digital-transformation-ceo-daily/.

3 Grok the Empowered Mindset

In the spring of 2020, people all around the world were sent home to work remotely. Likely, you were one of those people. By the spring of 2022, nearly a million people in the United States and nearly 8 million around the world had died from Covid-19 infection.[1] In between, millions of workers navigated an existential crisis that left us deeply changed, although not all in the same way. We rode out the same storm, but in very different boats.

While the pandemic was experienced differently in one way or another by virtually everyone, one through line stands out. The relationship between individuals and the organizations for which they work has forever changed. We have reaffirmed our values. We have reordered our priorities. We have reassessed our work. And while we no doubt will debate where and when work takes place, it's clear that we are all rethinking where and how work fits into our lives. And while the Great Resignation grabbed the headlines, this Great Reset is the real game changer.

Employees across generations had a rare opportunity to pause and really think about the role of work in their lives. And why not? After sleep, we dedicate the most time in our lives to work, some 81,396 hours on average, according to the pollsters at Gallup.[2] Why wouldn't we want that time to be well spent?

For many workers, it's not. Gallup found that 60% of workers are "emotionally detached" and 19% are downright "miserable."

It's no wonder, then, that people began seeking a different relationship with work.

For large swaths of the workforce, that reassessment led to resignation. In 2021, over 47 million Americans quit the workforce. By the spring of 2022, more than 4 million people, on average, were voluntarily leaving their jobs each month.

Anthony Klotz, a professor of organizational behavior at University College London School of Management, spotted this trend line and was the first to use the term "Great Resignation" to describe this exodus.

It would be easy to assume that the pandemic was the cause of the Great Resignation, but Klotz is clear that it is not. For years prior to the outbreak, plenty of red flags suggested real challenges with employee engagement. "This is a drum that HR professionals have been hammering for a while. Humans have not been happy at work," Klotz told us.

Work fulfills many of our emotional needs, Klotz told us. The pandemic and remote work gave workers autonomy, yet it separated us from the collegiality and community of the physical workplace. "Being in a physical office, with the connections that it offers, fulfills the need for relatedness and belonging," he said. "I don't know how you keep both relatedness and autonomy but I think it is an important pursuit."

Klotz's observation might sound like an invitation to jump back to our pre-pandemic ways. As Covid-19 recedes to an endemic stage, businesses and their leaders can resume their normal programming. That, we think, would be a terrible mistake and – worse – a terribly lost opportunity.

The people who have been returning to work – whether in person, in a hybrid model, or remotely – are not the same as those you sent home in March 2020. No matter the age or stage of their careers, they have weathered a great workplace disruption with a mix of newfound agency, personal trauma, and self-preservation that has put everyone on new footing. And because everyone experienced the pandemic differently, there is no one-size-fits-all leadership style (if there ever was one).

Indeed, it is critical to remember that regardless of how *you* weathered the pandemic years, your employees' experiences were likely quite different from yours and from each other's. Now, you have the twin challenges of leading people with vastly different experiences and cultural knowledge and who may rarely, if ever, again assemble in a single physical space.

To many of the business leaders we talk to, that prospect is terrifying. Some now find themselves unmoored when the environment (office) and factors (driving productivity, long hours) that marked their success are not the operational levers they once were. After all, we've built careers on managing organizations, modeling business, and directing processes for optimal outcomes. Then along comes this great interruption and we're left leading actual, diverse, stressed, creative, messy, authentic *people*. People that won't respond well to dictates and demands. People you have to understand, empathize with, and persuade to motivate.

We understand that the people we work with are demographically and experientially diverse (Chapter 1) and that newfound autonomy has restructured their relationship to the work itself (Chapter 2). The third key to leading an empowered workforce is to really get to know how your workers think. So, let's break it down.

Rebalancing Work and Life

When Covid-19 moved work from office to home, so-called work/life balance disappeared into a long swirl of a day. Before the pandemic, life was what you had time for when your work was done. In the pandemic, the line between work and life blurred and work didn't always come first. You might have started your day with a virtual team meeting (work), then popped off the call to set your children up for a day of remote learning (life). Maybe you took a call while dashing to the grocery store (work and life) before returning home to corral the family for a walk in the park (life) where your kids played (life) while you checked email on your phone (work). Later, dinner (life), kids' bedtime (life), before sitting down to dive into a spreadsheet (work). There was no work/life balance; there was just getting through the day.

In time, we settled into routines and many of us found that we liked tucking work into life much more than before, when we stressed about having a life outside of work. This new balance was Revelation One for many of us. Work took on a new place in lives filled with family, caregiving, remote learning, and newfound hobbies (sourdough bread, anyone?).

This reordering of life over work has liberated workers to think very differently about where and how work happens (as we discussed in Chapter 2), and more importantly, the role of work in our lives.

We once built our lives around our jobs. We took a job in a city or town, invested in housing nearby, maybe found a secondary job for our spouse, made friends, joined churches and clubs and gyms, sent our kids to schools, discovered our favorite restaurants and entertainment spots, and organically, perhaps accidentally, formed our community. When remote and even hybrid work is less dependent upon place, or if we simply put life before work, we can flip that scenario to find a community in which we most want to live in a climate we prefer with people and activities we love, and *then* we fit our work into that life. That is, after all, one great benefit of remote work. We can be anywhere to do it. And while remote work does not work for all jobs and may not even work 100% of the time for jobs that can be done remotely, where work fits into our lives and how we prioritize work among a growing list of personal demands and interests have forever changed. According to research conducted by the distributed work platform company Upwork, currently 9.3% of working Americans – nearly 20 million people – are looking to relocate because the availability of remote work.[3]

A New Approach to Work

This rebalancing, though, is not just about reallocating time spent at work to time spent enjoying life. Our relationship to what we do and why we do it has also shifted.

In the 1960s, psychologist Frederick Herzberg wanted to understand what motivated people to work. He came to understand that satisfying basic requirements, such as a fair salary and safe working conditions, are not sufficient to motivate someone to work. He described two sets of factors: hygiene and motivation. In Herzberg's language *hygiene* simply means the factors that remove objections. Hygiene is the usually tangible things a company provides, like salary, a nice workspace, and perks, to keep an employee from being dissatisfied. Herzberg came to realize that failure to provide appropriate hygiene factors can lead to dissatisfaction and demotivation, and – more importantly – hygiene factors alone cannot be motivating. Instead, motivation comes from the often-intangible benefits of the job, like appreciation, promotion, and an inherent interest in the work. Hygiene is removing the pain; motivation is lighting the fire in your belly.

Herzberg's motivation-hygiene theory, sometimes called the two-factor theory, went even further to explain that satisfaction and dissatisfaction are not on a spectrum, but rather influenced by entirely different sets of factors.[4]

In other words, being paid does not, alone, lead to job satisfaction, whereas loving the work you do, even if you are not well compensated for it, is more likely to keep you motivated to do your job. (See "The Hierarchy of Work Engagement.") In the nonprofit world this reality is called the "sacrifice-privilege" bargain. Nonprofit workers sacrifice higher pay for the privilege of making a difference. While we don't believe this "bargain" is right or fair, it is an unfortunate reality. The same is often the case in caregiving and education-based careers. Let's be clear, though: this is oftentimes very critical work and these jobs ought to be well valued and workers paid a fair and livable wage, not exploited because of their passion and purpose. Rewards like salary, benefits, perks, and promotions are simply table stakes to engage someone with a job. Yet too often, discussion of job satisfaction begins and ends there. Enter the pandemic, with its stress and disruption, and those job basics are insufficient to motivate people to engage with their jobs.

Research done in 2012 and spanning 48 countries showed that job satisfaction depends on three core things: a sense of accomplishment, recognition for a job well done, and work-life balance.[5] This confirmed research conducted two years earlier that demonstrated the power of aligned values. The 2010 study looked at organizational surveys and public databases of nursing homes in the US Midwest and found that "value congruence can serve as a source of intrinsic motivation for employee effort and mitigate agency problems in the workplace."[6] That's a fancy way of saying that when workers feel valued and believe in what they are doing, they remain engaged on the job.

It's for this reason that we eschewed the stack of opinion columns that swore that at the first sign of a recession workers would return to their jobs like puppies with their tails between their legs. That, we think, is old think that misses – willfully or otherwise – the profound impact of the Great Reset. No recession will remove the workers' desire, or rather demand, for meaningful work. None of this should be new, but it took the painful experience of a pandemic to bring these truths into sharp focus.

Anthony Klotz would seem to agree. In an interview with CNBC reporter Michelle Fox, he said, "The pandemic brought the future of work into the present of work. Because these work arrangements give us more flexibility and control over our lives, and more autonomy and freedom in how we structure our lives, I don't think most people are willing to go back to a traditional work environment."[7]

The Hierarchy of Work Engagement

Eighty years ago, psychologist Abraham Maslow described "A Theory of Human Motivation" in the journal *Psychological Review*.[8] You may be familiar with this model that stacks – on top of our basic needs for physical survival and safety – our needs for love, belonging, and esteem, with self-actualization at the peak.

Work, it turns out, is not so dissimilar. In the 1960s, psychologist Frederick Herzberg recognized that basic requirements, such as a fair salary and safe working conditions, are necessary but not sufficient to motivate someone to work. These needs, then, are at the base of a Hierarchy of Engagement. To attract talent, the nonnegotiable foundation is fair and equitable compensation and a safe working environment. Herzberg uses the word "hygiene" to describe what we have long referred to as "perks."

To retain and engage talent, you must provide an environment that offers flexibility and prioritizes wellness, not as an employment benefit, but as a deeply embedded strategy to mitigate burnout in support of the organization. This is also hygiene, and essential to employee satisfaction, if not in and of itself motivating.

The key to the deep engagement that grows your organization is belonging, in the context of an authentic expression of workers' values and the agency to make an impact in the business and on the world. As we move up the hierarchy, these are the factors that begin to affect motivation and engagement.

At the peak of the Hierarchy of Engagement is mobility, providing a pathway for learning and advancement within your organization, and – perhaps ironically – beyond it. It's here, at the top of the pyramid where individuals can most fully express themselves (this is where you'll find your motivational fuel).

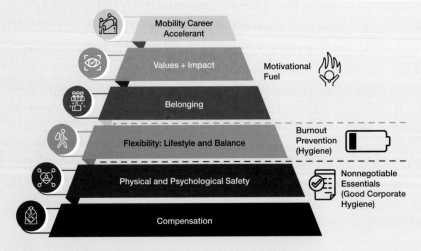

Figure 3.1 The Hierarchy of Work Engagement

Work That Is Worth It

Work, it seems, is now filtered through one basic question: Is it worth it? Workers in every kind of role are seeking work that satisfies both economic and emotional requirements in a careful calculus that measures purpose alongside pay and flexibility alongside status. Workers are seeking values alignment with their employment and their employer.

To be clear, this question is not one only for the privileged. Employees of every kind of work, from executive roles to custodial ones, will need to satisfy that question.

"Worth it" is an evaluation of the effort in exchange for the benefits (pay, status, security, etc.) of work. Surely, fair compensation is a critical consideration, and quite clearly wages have not kept pace with inflation over the last 50 years. (See "Origins of The Great Resentment.") In the era of industrial productivity, in fact, wage suppression was thought to be the primary lever of profitability. If that era had a mantra, it might have been "pay workers as little as you must," a sentiment stripped bare by one-time *Saturday Night Live* cast member and comedian Chris Rock, who took a jab at draconian pay policies. "You know what that means when someone pays you minimum wage?," Rock asks, "You know what your boss was trying to say? 'Hey if I could pay you less, I would, but it's against the law.'"[9]

But the question of a job's worth is greater than a paycheck. In a recent massive study, Microsoft found that folks use the term "worth it" to reconsider much of what we once – pre-pandemic – more easily tolerated. Fighting traffic to get to and from work, juggling work and caregiving responsibilities, earning little more than the cost of childcare, feeling abused and disrespected at work, accepting low pay. From the Microsoft report:

> In our study, 47% of respondents say they are more likely to put family and personal life over work than they were before the pandemic. In addition, 53% – particularly parents (55%) and women (56%) – say they're more likely to prioritize their health and wellbeing over work than before.[10]

Origins of the Great Resentment

Fueled by a newfound agency, the Great Resignation has seen millions of people walk away from jobs that were unfulfilling, mismanaged, or had misaligned values. It's also seen workers leave jobs that simply pay poorly. It's not an unreasonable economic decision.

In the United States, income inequality is nearly as profound a gap as it was at its peak in the 1920s. Low wages and high costs of living extract the greater price of social mobility. Harvard University economist Raj Chetty notes that people born in the 1940s had a 90% chance of doing better than their parents. Fast-forward 40 years; those born in the 1980s have seen that probability dropped to 50%.[13] Why is that?

For starters, minimum wage has been stuck at $7.25 since 2009 after getting a 71% bump over the 1992 minimum rate. Had it kept pace with productivity gains, workers would be making $23 an hour minimum in 2021.[14] But, it hasn't, even as inflation has ramped.

Developed by *The Economist*, the Big Mac Index serves as a proxy for inflation, pegging the cost of a McDonald's Big Mac foreign currencies to determine if they are over or undervalued against the US dollar[15]. The price of that ubiquitous sandwich has gone up over 147% in the last 30 years.

Worse, though, is the cost of higher education, inflating by 340% in the same time frame. When education, the pathway to social mobility, outpaces earnings, it's easy to see how workers grow resentful and decide that low-wage jobs just aren't worth it all.

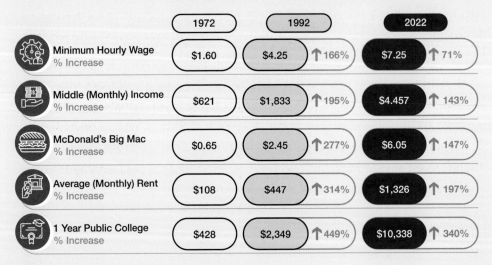

Figure 3.2 Origins of The Great Resentment

Data sources: US Department of Labor; McDonalds; Educationaldata.org; US Department of HUD; US Census.

Collectively, we have changed, and no one will willingly or easily trade their values for a paycheck. In fact, the paycheck isn't the greatest driver in job change. The report went on to say:

In 2020, 17% of people left their jobs, and we see that trend continuing – reaching 18% in 2021. The top five reasons employees quit were: personal well-being or mental health (24%), work-life balance (24%), risk of getting Covid-19 (21%), lack of confidence in senior management/leadership (21%), and lack of flexible work hours or location (21%). Somewhat surprisingly, "not receiving promotions or raises I deserved" landed in number seven on the list at 19%, further illustrating the shift in priorities.[11]

So how are we to make this calculus? In a 2015 essay, *New York Times* columnist David Brooks described two types of virtues: the résumé virtues and the eulogy virtues.[12] The résumé virtues are the skills that give people value in the workplace. Eulogy virtues are the attributes and stories people share about us after we die. Our résumé virtues are how we make a living; our eulogy virtues are how we make our lives.

Our résumé mindset wonders how things work. It is obsessed with external success. It seeks to acquire money, fame, attention, possessions. Our eulogy mindset contemplates why we are even here in the first place. It builds internal values and searches for love and opportunities to give back to others. These two virtues needn't be separate. In fact, we are at our best when we integrate our work with our inherent values. We are our best when we are both living and working our purpose.

This confluence of résumé and eulogy mindsets forms the heart of the new age of human-centric, or humanized, work. And it is the new organizing principle for companies and teams. Purpose acts as a magnet and filter. When organizations make their purpose clear they attract workers who are dedicated to those values. Workers who don't share those values self-select out of the employee pool, opting instead for workplaces that look, act, and believe more like they do.

Healing Our Whole Selves: Mental Health and Burnout Are Real

When our need for a balanced and purposeful relationship with work is too long neglected, the unfortunate result is burnout. And when burnout is ignored for too long, mental health issues take root.

By the beginning of 2022, Americans were reporting extraordinary levels of stress and burnout. Citing stressors that have become "persistent and indefinite," the American Psychological Association's 2022 Trends Report cites staggering figures: 79% of workers experienced work-related stress in the month prior to their Work and Well-being survey, 36% described cognitive weariness, 32% cited emotional exhaustion, and 44% said they experienced physical fatigue.[16]

Michael P. Leiter, an organizational psychologist and expert on burnout, believes we are experiencing an epidemic of burnout. "Whether burnout from life, in general, or specifically work burnout, or burnout from parenting, or burnout from anything else, it is very much in the culture at the moment," he told us. "People are getting overwhelmed, overtaxed or overextended in so many ways, and people aren't suffering in silence."

His observations are born out in Gallup's State of the Global Workplace: 2022 Report. Pollsters with the organization noted an "all-time high" in workplace stress in 2020, only to see that number climb even higher in 2021. "Those who agreed [that they experienced stress during a lot of the day before the poll] may not have been stressed about work, but they were certainly stressed at work."

While reported levels of worry, sadness, and anger fell in 2021, they remained above 2019 levels. And notably, 50% of working women in the United States and Canada reported high levels of stress, compared to the overall average of 44% worldwide.

At the same time that we are seeing higher than typical levels of stress, we're also experiencing a crushing amount of mental health issues. Mental Health America, a leading nonprofit mental health advocacy group, saw a 500% increase in people seeking support for mental health issues. In 2021 alone, over 5.4 million people took a mental health assessment and, across all demographics, 76% of these information seekers tested with moderate to severe symptoms of mental health conditions.[17]

Among those screening for mental health issues, the report goes on to say, 63% say that loneliness and isolation are among the top contributors to their mental health concerns. In the new world of hybrid and remote workplaces, this data is particularly troubling, not only because it affects the health and well-being of your employees, but because it has a very real impact on retention.

How to Spot Burnout

You probably know that feeling: near-total exhaustion that comes from a seemingly never-ending barrage of physical, mental, and emotional stress. That's burnout, and it is at an all-time high.

In the 2021 Work and Well-being Survey of the American Psychological Association, nearly 3 in 5 American workers reported feeling the effects of prolonged stress, including a lack of motivation (26%), diminished effort at work (19%), and physical fatigue (44%), a 38% increase from the survey two years earlier.[18]

The World Health Organization, calling it an "occupational phenomenon," says burnout is the result of "workplace stress that has not been successfully managed," characterized by lack of energy, performance deficits, and feelings of negativity or cynicism about the job.[19]

When pressure is unrelenting and workers have little agency to change the situation – or worse, they see no action from leadership to alleviate the pressure – exhaustion gives way to cynicism, Leiter told us. "The sign that burnout is a hanging threat," he said, "is when people start talking in a cynical way. It suggests they are losing that sense of confidence in the organization. That's when you know things are getting risky here."

There is a relatively easy fix for exhaustion: rest. Cynicism, on the other hand, is much harder to recover from. "You get suspicious when you are cynical. You lose trust in others, and in leadership. You need to catch exhaustion before it becomes cynical, and that means interacting with employees with authenticity. You have got to come from the heart."

(Continued)

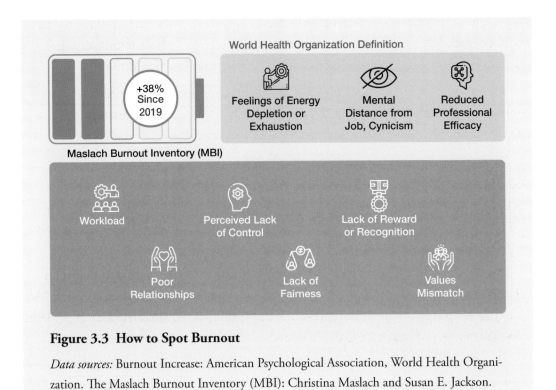

Figure 3.3 How to Spot Burnout

Data sources: Burnout Increase: American Psychological Association, World Health Organization. The Maslach Burnout Inventory (MBI): Christina Maslach and Susan E. Jackson.

Relationships Matter

Perhaps most important to our new attitudes toward work in an era of remote and hybrid teams, relationships matter even more. In an interview with *Fortune* magazine, Martine Ferland, CEO of benefits company Mercer, posits that employee loyalty is on the decline in part because remote work doesn't bind us in relationship to our companies and colleagues.[20]

That's simply a different way of saying that relationships matter, and it is our job as leaders to use our most human capability, empathy, to build the relationships that create the stickiness – the sense of belonging – that engenders engagement and builds organizational capacity.

That will be a big shift for some people, yet it can be simple, too. Instead of asking, "Where are you on that project?" lead with "How are you doing? What do you need? How can I support your success?"

"We're in this super big experiment, following a huge crisis that has changed the world of work forever," Ferland told *Fortune*'s Phil Wahba. "The question is whether this job jumping is elevated because of what we're currently going through."

Whatever is driving "job jumping" – a loosening of the employee/employer bond, a detachment from colleagues, a desire for greater flexibility, Ferland was clear on one thing: "We haven't cracked this hybrid work model yet."

In other words, because we aren't interacting in the physical space of work, we may not be building the sticky relationships that adhere us to our workplaces and colleagues. Echoing Herzberg's motivation-hygiene theory, Ferland said in *Fortune* that workers are becoming "more exacting" about compensation and perks while also increasingly comparing their employer's values to their own.

In a Mercer-sponsored survey of HR professionals, 70% predicted higher than normal turnover in their organizations, owing to the shift from perks to purpose. "A lot of our clients are focused on how to rebuild this culture of identity and of pride in being successful together as a team," Ferland told *Fortune*.

That data was reinforced by research firm Gartner, Inc., which predicted employee turnover will be up 20% over pre-pandemic levels and will likely stay elevated for some time.[21]

Humans Are Your Greatest Source of Value

All of these factors are messy, particularly for leaders who have spent their careers refining their business and process management skills at the expense of people skills. And it's made messier still by the disruption of a pandemic that did not cause work, cultural, and social norms to change, but did put those changes in sharp relief. The pandemic, then, is both a breaking point and an opportunity. It is a break from past work structures and an opportunity to refocus on the human capacity that drives value in work and in life. (See "History Rhymes: Our Opportunity Is Now.")

Making the effort to really understand how your workers are thinking now, to dive into what truly motivates people to engage deeply in their work and with their colleagues, is so worth it, not simply because it creates a more positive workplace, but because it is the single most important thing you can do to unlock value in your business.

History Rhymes: Our Opportunity Is Now

It has been said that history does not repeat itself, but it does rhyme. And it is really rhyming now. Consider the factors that shaped the 1920s and those that are transforming our current times.

A century apart, the world faced a deadly pandemic. In the 1920s, electrification made housework far less time-consuming, freeing women to consider more opportunities outside the home, including the push for the right to vote. Conversely, the shift to work from home in the 2020s proved taxing for women juggling full-time caregiving and full-time work. Many said "enough" and women left the workforce in larger numbers.

More than 100 years since Henry Ford and labor unions established a 40-hour work week, many studies now suggest less work may be more advantageous, and companies around the world are contemplating a reduction in hours for their employees.

The changing demographic composition of our society today from largely white and Christian to a plurality of races, ethnicities, and religions is challenging workplaces to become more inclusive, just as the rise in immigration and Jim Crow racism of 1920 demanded the march toward social justice.

What does all this mean and why does it matter? Centuries can be turning points, and we are surely standing on the precipice of one now. Workers are clearly saying what they do and don't want from career opportunities. Will we be wise enough to capitalize on this much disruption, uncertainty, and change to craft a future that is more inclusive and more engaging for more of us –thus unleashing more human potential? That is up to the one holding this book.

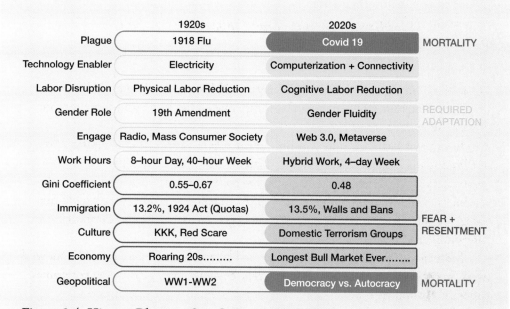

	1920s	2020s	
Plague	1918 Flu	Covid 19	MORTALITY
Technology Enabler	Electricity	Computerization + Connectivity	
Labor Disruption	Physical Labor Reduction	Cognitive Labor Reduction	
Gender Role	19th Amendment	Gender Fluidity	REQUIRED ADAPTATION
Engage	Radio, Mass Consumer Society	Web 3.0, Metaverse	
Work Hours	8–hour Day, 40–hour Week	Hybrid Work, 4–day Week	
Gini Coefficient	0.55–0.67	0.48	
Immigration	13.2%, 1924 Act (Quotas)	13.5%, Walls and Bans	FEAR + RESENTMENT
Culture	KKK, Red Scare	Domestic Terrorism Groups	
Economy	Roaring 20s.........	Longest Bull Market Ever........	
Geopolitical	WW1-WW2	Democracy vs. Autocracy	MORTALITY

Figure 3.4 History Rhymes: Our Opportunity Is Now

Data sources: Gini Coefficient, 1920: Berruyer, adapted from Doug Henwood; Census Bureau. Gini Coefficient, 2020: Statista.com. Immigration rates: Migration Policy Institute.

Changing the Goal

And let's be completely clear. In the past, businesses and their leadership had one goal: to drive and continuously increase productivity. Now, the goal must change. Your leadership must inspire human potential to create self-propelled talent that, by their productivity, create new value for your company. This is a concept we will talk about further in Part Three.

In Part Two, we'll show you how organizational structures can be shaped to better support your people and create that value. In Part Three, we'll help you refine your leadership style to get the most from those structural changes. But here's one clue before we leave this study of today's empowered workforce.

The single most effective and efficient tool in your leadership kit is your empathy, that ability to really see and understand the people you depend on.

Jamil Zaki, a psychology professor at Stanford University and author of *The War for Kindness,* shares this story to illustrate just how powerful empathy can be in your leadership.

I once asked a dentist friend of mine how important flossing really is. "Not that important," he replied. "You only need to floss the teeth you want to keep."

Leaders often ask me how important empathy really is during the Great Resignation.

"Not that important," I'm going to start telling them, "You only need to empathize with the people you want to keep."

We wrote this book to help you find your way to keeping more of your precious talent.

The Empathy Advantage

Notes

1 "Total Confirmed Deaths from COVID-19, by Source, World," Our World in Data, March 17, 2020, available at https://ourworldindata.org/covid-deaths.

2. Clifton, John, 2022, "The World's Workplace Is Broken – Here's How to Fix It," Gallup, June 14, available at https://www.gallup.com/workplace/393395/world-workplace-broken-fix.asp.

3. Ozimek, Adam, 2022, "The New Geography of Remote Work," Upwork, available at https://www.upwork.com/research/new-geography-of-remote-work.

4. Herzberg, Frederick, Mausner, Bernard, and Snyderman, Barbara B., 1959, *The Motivation to Work* (2nd ed.), Wiley.

5. Andreassi, Jeanine, Lawter, Leanna, et al., 2012, "Job Satisfaction Determinants: A Study Across 48 Nations." Proceedings of 2012 Annual Meeting of the Academy of International Business – US North East Chapter: Business Without Borders, Sacred Heart University, available at https://digitalcommons.sacredheart.edu/wcob_fac/220/.

6. Ren, Ting, 2010, "Value Congruence as a Source of Intrinsic Motivation," *Kyklos* 63(1): 109, February, available at https://ssrn.com/abstract=1536227.

7. Fox, Michelle, 2022, "Even When the 'Great Resignation' Wanes, the Workplace Changes It Spurred Won't, Says Psychologist Who Predicted the Trend," CNBC, July 12, available at https://www.cnbc.com/2022/07/12/great-resignation-workplace-changes-are-lasting-says-anthony-klotz.html.

8. Maslow, A. H., 1943, "A Theory of Human Motivation," *Psychological Review* 50, 4: 370–396, https://doi.org/10.1037/h0054346.

9. Rock, Chris, 2011, *Saturday Night Live*, April 27, available at https://www.youtube.com/watch?v=AtjTRTKHDjg.

10. Microsoft, 2022, "Great Expectations: Making Hybrid Work Work," Work Trend Index 2022, March 16, available at https://www.microsoft.com/en-us/worklab/work-trend-index/great-expectations-making-hybrid-work-work. Used with permission from Microsoft.

11. Ibid.

12. Brooks, David, 2015, "The Moral Bucket List," *New York Times*, April 11, available at https://www.nytimes.com/2015/04/12/opinion/sunday/david-brooks-the-moral-bucket-list.html.

13. Chetty, Raj, et.al., 2017, "The Fading American Dream: Trends in Absolute Income Mobility Since 1940," *Science*, April 24, available at https://www.science.org/doi/10.1126/science.aal4617.

14. Constant, Paul, 2022, "American Workers Would Make More Than $20 an Hour if Minimum Wage Kept Pace with Productivity, an Economist Says," *Business Insider*, April 7, available at https://www.businessinsider.com/minimum-wage-27-if-kept-pace-productivity-economist-opinion-2022-4.

15. "The Big Mac Index," *The Economist*, available at https://www.economist.com/big-mac-index.

16. Abramson, Ashley, 2022, "Burnout and Stress Are Everywhere," American Psychological Association 2022 Trends Report, January 1, available at https://www.apa.org/monitor/2022/01/special-burnout-stress.

17. "Mental Health and COVID-19 Two Years After the Pandemic," Mental Health Associates, April 2022, available at https://mhanational.org/mental-health-and-covid-19-two-years-after-pandemic.

18. Abramson, "Burnout and Stress Are Everywhere."

19. "Burn-out an 'Occupational Phenomenon': International Classification of Diseases," World Health Organization, May 28, 2019, available at https://www.who.int/news/item/28-05-2019-burn-out-an-occupational-phenomenon-international-classification-of-diseases.

20. Wahba, Phil, 2022, "Why Mercer's CEO Thinks Employee Loyalty Is in Decline—and What Managers Can Do About It," *Fortune*, June 10, available at https://fortune.com/2022/06/10/mercer-worker-loyalty-great-resignation/.

21. "Gartner Says U.S. Total Annual Employee Turnover Will Likely Jump by Nearly 20% from the Pre-pandemic Annual Average," Gartner, April 28, 2022, available at https://www.gartner.com/en/newsroom/04-28-2022-gartner-says-us-total-annual-employee-turnover-will-likely-jump-by-nearly-twenty-percent-from-the-prepandemic-annual-average.

Aqueduct Technologies: Really Great Ideas, Really Happy Employees

It's rare to find links to a company's Women's Collaborative or Buying Local initiatives on an information technology company's website. But, then, Aqueduct Technologies isn't your typical information technology company.

Founded in 2012 to provide its clients with networking, security, and cloud solutions, and infrastructure that supports collaboration and communication, this fast-growing company emerged from the pandemic with double-digit growth and a 40% increase in staff. The company's diverse technology expertise accounted for its revenue growth. Its culture gets the credit for its growing team.

Well before the so-called stay interview became popular, Aqueduct fostered a culture of "open transparent dialogue," founder and CEO Manak Ahluwalia told us. Developed by the Society of Human Resource Management as a retention tool, the stay interview is a catalog of questions intended to surface employee concerns before those issues drive the employee to quit. At Aqueduct, annual performance planning and regular manager reviews are supplemented by conversations between an employee and someone on the HR team.

Just as at most companies, managers at Aqueduct work with employees at the beginning of the year to set goals for performance and professional growth. And just as at most companies, those goals can be lost in the day-to-day efforts of doing the work. "We set these glorious goals at the beginning of the year, and then the very next day, we're asking about very tactical things: the project you're working on, what quantitative measurement do you have for the business, the next deal, the fire of the day. In the midst of those tactical questions, the dialogue gets lost," Ahluwalia said. The structured questions of the stay interview help the company take the pulse of employees throughout the year.

"We weren't worrying about employees leaving or needing to figure out what it would take for them to stay," Ahluwalia says, "but we found the questions led to greater dialogue and gives an employee the ability to advocate for themselves around what's really meaningful and important to them in their current job, how the organization can support them, and in many cases, what's personally important to them outside of their job and how the organization can help them fulfill their personal mission."

Ahluwalia is reluctant to call these conversations "stay interviews," however. The concept, he reminded us, was developed for organizations that were afraid of losing employees. "We look at it the opposite – like you're here, you're happy. How do we continue to nurture that? How do we get to continue to get you to stay without the concern or fear that you're going to leave? And then, obviously, if there is even a little bit of a red flag, we'd like to address them pretty quickly."

This candor, Ahluwalia said, has established trust among the team and fostered a willingness to be more open and to share information. And that, in turn, leads to a healthier organization, one that Ahluwalia describes as "an empathetic organization" that listens to the concerns and aspirations of employees. "An open, transparent dialogue within an organization tends to lead to really great ideas and really happy employees," he said.

Part II
Rethink Your Organization

In the early days of 2020, a group of friends were planning a once-in-a-lifetime expedition to Africa. They researched and planned for months. They studied local languages and customs, made travel arrangements, bought clothing and gear. A few of the friends had already begun to pack their bags. They were ready to go, until Covid had another idea. Fast forward two years. The Africa trip was called off, and a new adventure planned. They would hike the Canadian Rockies instead.

Both trips required specialty gear and appropriate clothing. They needed passports, guides, and permits for both trips. In either case, the travelers would benefit from a bit of local knowledge and physical preparedness. But as adventures go, the two trips could not be more different. Had they simply transferred the planning, luggage, and local knowledge from one trip to the other, our friends would surely have had a miserable time on the mountain trails in Canada.

You may be thinking to yourself: Of course, you plan for a safari differently from a mountain trek. It's obvious!

Yet in many cases, we'd bet, you're still going to work each day with a plan and approach that you adopted in your pre-pandemic career. And as often as not, that approach isn't working quite like it used to. Going forward, the trip is different. Why would you use the same maps and planning for this completely different adventure?

Applying the plans and approach of the past to this new future is unhelpful at best and, more likely, a liability.

As if finding new maps, models, plans, and approaches isn't hard enough, the future presents an even greater challenge; every day it becomes harder and harder to anticipate the disruptive changes that almost instantly make those maps, models, plans, and approaches obsolete. To succeed in this rapidly changing and uncertain future, you must learn to be comfortable with continuous change, a requirement that, for many, sounds like being asked to get comfortable having dental work without Novocain.

No doubt navigating to an unknown future is not without some pain. But you *can* structure your organization to have the flexibility and resilience to accommodate and adapt to change. In time, you will come to see these uncertainties as opportunities to learn and respond in ways that drive deeper worker engagement, build stronger customer ties, and create new business value.

In these next pages, we'll explore approaches to navigating this new world of work not just without our familiar maps, but in many cases without maps at all.

In the pre-pandemic world of work, we aligned organizational structures, metrics, and incentives to scale production and drive profits. The workforce, from highly-skilled management to minimum-wage line workers, were in many cases cogs in a machine that generated results based on long-held assumptions and prior performance metrics.

In the post-pandemic world in which the workforce has said "enough" to the drain and demands that favor corporate profits over worker well-being, workers aren't just an additive ingredient to a business model, they *are* the business. They are your most valuable resource as you forge a new path forward because they are on the front lines and best positioned to identify and respond efficiently to market dynamics.

As leaders, then, we need to reimagine most every aspect of the workplace and environment. Linear and hierarchical structures are too often slow to recognize and react to changing market dynamics. Can we push decision making to the edges and empower people closest to issues to act upon them? How might we align incentives and create a work environment where people are rewarded for achieving shared goals rather than compensated for grinding out the to-do list of a job description? How might we establish an organizational mindset that favors learning and experimentation for purposes beyond market validation and bias confirmation? Can we embrace "I don't know" as a critical corporate value that fuels discovery and opportunity mining?

The answers to all of these questions can be "yes!" if we embrace the idea that people working, learning, collaborating, and thriving together are the new fuel for business. People, when aligned behind a purpose bigger than the bottom line, can do amazing things.

To capitalize on your human workforce, your organization needs to flex to meet them where they are, rather than trying to jam people into rigid organizational structures. Indeed, we need to stop designing workplaces and begin designing "people places," a space and structure where employees come together to learn, collaborate, and get the needed resources in order to do the work, either in that place or at some remote location.

No matter where you fit in your company's leadership structure – C-Suite executive, line manager, shift supervisor, or frontline worker – you are a scout on a new frontier, drawing new maps for the future of your workplace.

So how do we do that? Read on.

Key Takeaways:

- Workers aren't just an additive ingredient to a business model; they *are* the business and they are your most valuable resource as you forge a new path forward.

- The maps and models we used to organize work pre-pandemic do not work effectively today. The power structure has permanently shifted from management to workers, and smart companies will build new systems that embrace that dynamic.

- New models will be built on agency and trust in a holistic and healthy environment that fosters learning, exploration, and collaboration.

- To activate the potential of your workforce, you must tap the intrinsic motivation that drives engagement. Purpose is every company's unique advantage and every employee's driving motivation.

4 Upgrade Your Operating Models

After many years of planning, Boston embarked on the Big Dig in 1991, a massive 16-year construction project that rerouted roadways around the city. Not long after the first shovels began moving dirt, Chris moved away from Boston after living there for more than a decade.

Each time she returned to Boston – flying into Logan Airport and renting a car, she'd shove the rental agency's map in the glove box, confident she knew her way around. Even though, over time, the rerouted streets look less and less familiar, she continued to drive confidently, certain that the next intersection would lead where she was hoping to go.

It took years of return trips to Boston before Chris finally admitted that she was lost, that her old map didn't work anymore.

Business leaders today are not so different. We have had a way of working, organizing, and leading that worked well enough when everything was familiar. These models and maps are comfortable; after all, they got us where we are today.

As Alfred Korzybski, the father of general semantics, aptly noted, "A map is not the territory it represents. But, if correct, it has a similar structure to the territory, which accounts for its usefulness."[1] Borrowing liberally, we would suggest that organizational structure is not the company it represents, but, if correct, powers a company toward its usefulness.

For much of the last century, the dominant organizational structures optimized for productivity, often at the expense of the people who filled rank-and-file positions. Still, those structures worked. Over the last 50 years, net productivity grew more than 60%, according to the Economic Policy Institute, a nonprofit, nonpartisan think tank. Never mind that the hourly pay of a typical worker grew less than 18% over that same period.[2]

Despite the inequity, we continue to cling to these maps because they are familiar and they have for a century guided our decision making. They are the structures that forged our career success. They bring comfort. And now, an increasingly worrisome false confidence. If the pandemic taught us anything, it has shown that our maps and models no longer work and layering them on top of a newly empowered workforce might just be dangerous.

Management guru and author Roger Martin tells us that when models don't deliver expected results, leaders tend to assume it's not the model, but its application that has gone wrong. Leaders, he says, "double down" on the model, much like Chris simply persisted in driving further through newly routed Boston streets, hoping to find her way again.

In a post-pandemic world of work, where old habits have been broken and new ones established, where workers have claimed their agency and become newly empowered, the old maps, no matter how fast you drive them, will not work. It's time, then, to throw them away.

What Are We Leaving Behind?

In 2019, the Business Roundtable, an organization composed of the CEOs of the largest and most influential American companies, took a bold step and rejected the shareholder capital doctrine, a 50-year-old principle that valued a corporation almost solely on its stock price. Instead, companies needed to embrace their *stakeholders*, the employees, customers, communities, and – yes – investors that in aggregate supported and benefited from the organization. To understand just how brave that declaration was, keep in mind that most if not all the executives participating in this panel were compensated and rewarded for their efforts to increase share price. Now, they were saying that by reorienting their self-interest with the interests of the broader community, the organization would be best aligned for success.

This change of alignment has, more than anything else, ushered in the Human Value Era, an approach to corporate productivity and purpose that puts the workforce at the center of organizational thinking and structure. (See "The Rise of the Human Value Era.")

The Rise of the Human Value Era

By asserting that the purpose of a company was nothing more than to create wealth for shareholders, Milton Friedman ushered in the Shareholder Value Era of business. In that model, workers were little more than a cost of business, a cost to be contained.

While no one wants to think of themselves as a line item on a balance sheet, a closer look at that ledger offers insight into that accounting. In 1975, fully 83% of the enterprise value of S&P 500 companies came from tangible assets such as real estate, manufacturing facilities, and equipment. Businesses then made things, and automation enabled businesses to make things more efficiently. The more automation, the fewer humans required, and the lower the cost of production.

Over the next several decades, though, our economy shifted. To keep the cost of making things cheap, American businesses moved manufacturing offshore, where the human components of the manufacturing process were substantially less expensive. In America, businesses focused on making ideas, rather than things, as we transitioned to a knowledge-based economy.

As human creativity, ingenuity, and service became the basis of value creation, intangible capital – ideas, patents, brand, customer loyalty – began to account for more and more of corporate value until, in the last decade, the balance flipped. By 2015, more than 84% of corporate value was attributed to human-created intangible value.

In 2020, the Securities and Exchange Commission (SEC) required public companies to document the value of their human resources on their financial disclosure documents. By 2020, 90% of the enterprise value was intangible – human ingenuity.

These trends have ushered in the Human Value Era, where the capacity and capabilities of our people are highly valued. The greatest investment companies and society can make is in human potential.

(Continued)

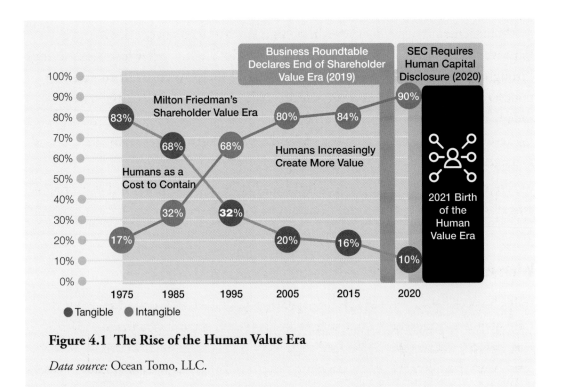

Figure 4.1 The Rise of the Human Value Era

Data source: Ocean Tomo, LLC.

Over his long career as the leader of Deloitte's Center for the Edge, John Hagel calculated the return on assets of public companies over more than 60 years. He discovered that the focus on shareholder value had come at the expense of actually creating value. Executives and corporate boards used financial tricks like stock buybacks and market manipulation to juice stock prices but failed to generate actual new value. According to Hagel's research, over the period from 1965 to 2015, return on assets fell by 75%.[3]

Still, we rely on the models of the last half of the last century largely because they are familiar. For many leaders, they were the models that shaped careers and delivered professional success. In hindsight, however, it becomes increasingly clear that these models – designed for industrial revolution–era business – become less and less workable in recent decades that have moved more toward knowledge and creative economies.

Management guru Roger Martin points out that while businesses have improved the cost of goods sold (COGS) through efficiency, they lost those savings through bloated sales, general, and administrative (SG&A) costs. In an excellent podcast interview with leadership consultant Mark C.Crowley, Martin calls today's modern offices "decision factories."[4] Declining productivity, he notes, is the result of the high cost of indecision and mismanagement of administrative and managerial overhead.

No doubt, this mismanagement is the result of calcified models and maps that no longer work. It's time to forge new ones.

What Are We Moving Toward?

In his book *A New Way to Think*, management guru Roger Martin writes about the mismatch between the nature of today's work and the way we organize around it. Companies structured and managed their workforce around what Martin calls "flat jobs," work that is more or less the same every day. It is a structure that makes sense if your goal is to optimize production, as you would in a factory or a call center or even a fast-food restaurant. As the economy shifted to creative and knowledge work, more and more people filled jobs that were anything but flat. Very little is the same from day to day, unlike traditional industrial jobs, yet businesses continued to organize around roles and job functions.

The better structure, Martin argues, is to organize around projects. "Projects arrive, ramp up, are handled, and disappear, often never to be seen again," he writes in a 2022 blog post.[5] "Because inherently project-based jobs are defined as if they are flat, they are highly inefficient."

Project work, almost by definition, ebbs and flows as one project concludes and another begins. That flow is challenging to staff. If you hire for peak demand, what do you do with staff when the project concludes? If you don't hire for peak demand, do you risk stressing your team to the point of burnout?

The solution, Martin writes, is to organize your people not around jobs but around projects, enabling people to come in and out of projects as needed, tapping skills when the demand requires them. It is an idea embraced by many consulting companies which organize employees' work in "tours of duty"

Lead Differently in Complexity

There was a time when the person who sat atop the corporate org chart was a know-it-all. Literally. Having come up through the ranks, leaders learned not just the job, but every aspect of the company, and they were expected to use that knowledge to direct efficient operations throughout the entire organization. The linear, if complicated, world of relative routine and predictable events and processes favored efficiency and rewarded unquestioned experts who led teams with a focus on driving productivity in the predictable.

Chances are, that's not the organization you are in today. Too many external and unpredictable forces – from emerging technologies to pandemics to geopolitical conflicts – create a complex operating environment beyond the scope and knowledge of any one individual. Add to that the rapidly emerging new knowledge across subject areas – from data analytics to cyber security to machine learning – and it quickly becomes clear that complete intelligence resides with the team rather than any one individual. In fact, if you have people reporting to you now, they most likely have skills and knowledge you don't have. That is as it should be and it requires leaders to shift their dependency from individual to collective intelligence.

We moved from a manufacturing-based to a knowledge-based economy by shifting output from a physical product to an idea. Yet too many assumptions remained the same. Jobs remained fixed, requirements static, and assumptions unchanged. That doesn't work anymore.

We know that technological change will happen, but we are not exactly certain when. We know climate change will have a profound impact on operations, but we do not know when or where. We know the economy retracts after periods of expansion, but we are challenged to predict when, by how much, or for how long.

As a result we have to create a greater buffer, build in a bit more redundancy, and dial up our agility and adaptability. That unquestioned expert making decisions in certainty is both a fool and a liability. We need a new type of leader and a new way of organizing work that harnesses the strengths and knowledge across and even outside the organization, as we make the profound shift from individual experts to a collaborative, collective intelligence.

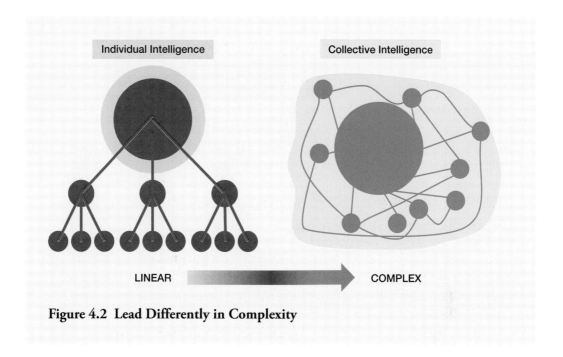

Figure 4.2 Lead Differently in Complexity

We liken this organizational principle to a cycling peloton.[6] Cyclists in a racing team have specialties, and depending on the leg of the race, the team organizes to optimize for the specific conditions of the course. If today's business is a patchwork of knowledge-based and creative projects, might it make sense to organize workers in a similar fashion, putting specialists on the case when they are needed, then reassigning them to another project where their skills can be put to better use again?

In the modern knowledge economy, work has shifted from linear and predictable to complex and variable. (See "Lead Differently in Complexity.") It's time, then, to organize differently to tap the full potential of your team.

More Frequent Disruptions

This shift from flat, jobs-based work to complex, project-based organizations is not just a nice idea; it's essential.

We are awash in disruption, whether by the forces of technology which drive rapid shifts in consumer adoption and behavior, the forces of nature which pummel us with the effects of climate change, or the forces of geopolitics that are pressuring alliances and altering governments in the United States and around the world.

By late 2022, Covid fatigue was a very real thing. People who had tired of distancing, mask-wearing, and isolation felt some measure of relief as the disease seemed on a path from its pandemic to its endemic stage. With vaccines widely available in the developed world – and rolling out, albeit slowly, globally, the always-mutating virus seemed to many that it was becoming more nuisance than life-threatening, something we could live with, if not eradicate. We were, largely, ready to move on after more than two years of collective chaos.

Yet, it's important to take a long, backward look if we are going to have a clearer view of our future. Covid-19 was often compared to the Spanish Flu pandemic of 1918, so you can hardly be faulted if you think we'll not see the likes of a global pandemic for another century. That, however, is not our history. In the space between the Spanish Flu and Covid-19, the world experienced two additional worldwide flu outbreaks (1957 and 1968), the Polio epidemic (1955), the HIV/AIDS epidemic (1980s), the Swine Flu pandemic (2009), and Ebola outbreak (2014), among other global health crisis. Note those dates: these outbreaks are happening more frequently and spreading more widely for a host of reasons.

"The same human activities that drive climate change and biodiversity loss also drive pandemic risk through their impacts on our environment. Changes in the way we use land; the expansion and intensification of agriculture; and unsustainable trade, production and consumption disrupt nature and increase contact between wildlife," Dr. Peter Daszak, President of EcoHealth Alliance, reported in an October 2020 investigation of the United Nations' Intergovernmental Science-Policy Platform on Biodiversity and Ecosystem Services (IPBES).[7]

The pandemic is the most recent and profound disruption we've faced in recent years, but interruptions to business as usual will be more frequent as we go forward. We can't plan for them, per se, but we can plan to adapt to them.

In Margaret Hefernan's latest book, *Uncharted: How to Navigate the Future*, she describes the pitfalls of the forecast-plan-execute model of running business. Citing research by the Good Judgment Project, Hefernan observes that most forecasters are only accurate within about 150 days.[8] The best, most attuned organizations are rarely accurate beyond about 400 days. Why, then, do we still toil over multiyear plans?

Listen Carefully: Change Is the Norm

We study and refer to "transformational change" and "change management" as if they are out of cycle events rather than the norm. Let us be clear, change is the norm now. Whether it is change in response to a disruption from climate change to a geopolitical event to an economic shock to a global health event like the pandemic, or change as part of a business model evolution in response to technology change or customer preferences, change is the norm.

Rather than resist change, we should embrace it. Research by Queens University in Ontario found that constant and consistent communication was highly correlated to successful transformational change.[9]

We tend to think of communication as telling and talking rather than listening and empathizing. But consider the old adage: we have two eyes and two ears, but only one mouth; that should guide your ratio of input (listening and seeing) to output (talking). Effective communication depends on both talking and listening. Listening is hearing what people say and watching what people express nonverbally. Listen to understand where your people are, what they want, and what they aspire to, care about, value, fear. Listening is the heart of empathy.

And it just may be the number one skill that establishes your leadership.

In survey after survey of people leaving their jobs in the Great Resignation, lack of empathetic leadership joined lack of career mobility, compensation, meaning and purpose, and collaboration as top reasons to leave.

We must, then, take a different path forward or, as Roger Martin will tell you, risk losing the talent you depend on to drive your business.

Forging a New Path to the Future of Work

If our old maps no longer work, the new territory ahead is complex and unpredictable, and our colleagues want a more meaningful and engaging work environment, how do we cut a path forward?

"The current way to organize knowledge workers/decision factories is just plain anachronistic and silly," Martin writes. "However, as with most norms of 'how business is done,' the shift will take a long time."[10]

It's not the maps and models that have to change; it's the organization. Because time is a nonrenewable resource, we need to find ways to accelerate the shift from "how business (was) done" to how business is done today.

So where do we start? To quote Peter Sheahan, Founder of Karrikins Group, "Organizations do not change; people do." In other words, this starts with you.

Understand the Relationship Between the Individual and Organization

In the past, as you climbed into leadership roles, you typically gained experience, learned skills, and developed institutional knowledge ahead of the people you would lead in an environment that was far more static than the one in which you work today. As a result, you could make decisions in certainty as you were the unquestioned expert. But if you are a leader today, you are managing people who know more – or, more aptly, know differently, than you do. Now, you need skills that are rarely acquired on the path to seniority – notably the ability to acknowledge not knowing.

Certainly, good leaders care about their direct reports, and it's reflected in the levels of social and emotional intelligence (EQ) generally reported in frontline leaders. As we gain seniority and become more insulated from the rank-and-file workers who are impacted by our decisions, we tend to shed a bit of our EQ. That might have been useful when people resources were viewed as an expense and a cost to be contained; it made the hard personnel decisions, well, less personal.

Today, though, people are not merely an expense on the balance sheet – or, they shouldn't be. They are your best asset, the living, breathing embodiment of your organization's capacity to create and serve your markets. And they are less prone to put up with impersonal management.

As Michael P. Leiter, author of *Banishing Burnout: Six Strategies for Improving Your Relationship with Work*, told us, the social dynamics that connect people are "a powerful part of work." Leiter refers to this social dynamic as "workplace civility" and it is at the heart of productive engagement. "If anybody is rude to you at work, just one little quip, just one failure to respond to your 'good morning' just throws you off a bit," he said, adding that his research data shows that a nod, a smile, or a simple acknowledgment ("it doesn't take very much," he said) makes a significant difference in employee engagement and burnout between employees who have a positive interaction with their supervisor and those who do not.

"What can you do to make the environment more pleasant and more engaging for each other?" Leiter asks. "More actively displaying consideration and that kind of human connection that moves people away from burnout."

Put more succinctly, your secret weapon to deep engagement and effective leadership is empathy, the ability to really see and share the feelings of others. It is undoubtedly the most important leadership skill in this new era of the empowered workforce.

Rethink Work and Learning

As the speed of change accelerates, linear, hierarchical structures – where decisions flow down and reporting bubbles up through complicated communications chains – simply do not offer the efficiency to respond quickly to changing market conditions and emerging opportunities.

The best way to move forward is to abandon command and control structures that were built for scalable efficiency and embrace experimentation and review systems that are designed for scalable learning. At the center of this design is the fundamental reconsideration of work. Work isn't a "job" with set requirements and specific tasks and duties. In that definition, any activity outside the scope of work is someone else's job, and there's tremendous waste in determining whose job it is to get something done.

Instead, think of work as a set of activities that require individual and collective effort in order to reach an outcome. In this definition, tasks aren't defined, outcomes are. The people doing the work have the latitude to do the work – the activities – required to reach the objective. That flexibility permits workers to be responsive to changing conditions, while staying fixed on the goal, rather than stuck in a job.

When we make that adjustment, we also need to rethink our bias towards skills hiring. Résumés – the cornerstone of hiring decisions – are typically a fair indication of what someone has done in the past. They may even document the skills that contributed to an applicant's past success. But résumés aren't crystal balls; they cannot accurately predict future performance, especially when the skills required to meet new challenges have yet to be defined. (See "The Skills Gap May Never Close.")

The Skills Gap May Never Close

Skills are a supply and demand game. Someone demonstrates a particular skill; the market values that skill and demands more. When demand outstrips supply, we call it a skills gap. Often, schools, businesses, and even economic development organizations attempt to meet demand – fill the gap – by providing training programs.

Unfortunately, the speed and complexity of knowledge formation today is just too fast for traditional education and training programs to catch up. IBM noted this challenge in its 2019 study which found that "in 2014, the median time it took to close a capability gap through training in the enterprise was three days. In 2018, the median was an astonishing 36 days. In just four years, the time to close a skills gap increased by more than a factor of 10."[11]

At that rate, especially given the pandemic-induced accelerated change, it's going to become impossible to catch up. So, let's look at skills differently.

There are three types of skills: competence, capability, and capacity. Competence is successfully repeating a task at an acceptable level or consistently finding the right answer to a given question. This is well-defined fundamental knowledge. Capability applies competence to a new challenge and deepens that knowledge through new applications. It is upskilling or advancing your knowledge in a focused area of growing expertise. Capacity is the ability to meet the moment. It is finding and framing new challenges or opportunities.

We tap capacity when we step out of our knowledge domain and enter the realm of exploration and discovery to formulate the new questions and frame new problems in order to find new answers and solutions.

Traditionally, we filled the skills gap by filling the space between what we do know and what we need to know with well-understood knowledge in order to build competence. That model doesn't work when we don't know what we will need to know. For that, we need the capacity to explore and learn. Competency and capability are the necessary foundation for many work functions, and so, too, is re-skilling and upskilling to maintain currency. The capacity for learning, however, is quickly becoming the most important part of work and the hallmark of the Human Value Era.

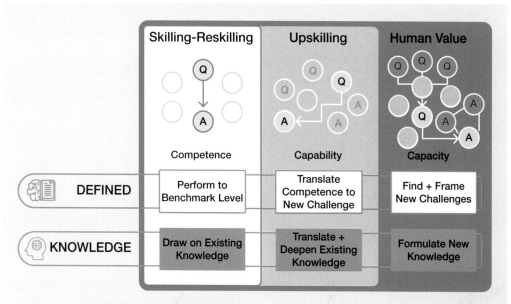

Figure 4.3 The Skills Gap May Never Close

The alternative to hiring for skills is to hire for learning. Seek out the curious mind, the person who has demonstrated an insatiable appetite for expanding their skillset. We'll talk about the importance of learning, curiosity, and culture more in Chapter 5, but for now think about how your organization can become more adaptive in a rapidly changing marketplace by organizing work around outcomes rather than job descriptions. Moreover, we need to view learning as an integral part of work, not simply a preparation for it. As we have often said: where we previously learned in order to work, we now work in order to learn continuously.

Recalibrate Your Metrics: Be Like Bhutan

Landlocked and tucked into the mountainous region of South Asia, tiny Bhutan turned heads when it proposed an alternative measure of geopolitical success – the idea of a Gross National Happiness (GNH) Index – at a United Nations forum in 1998. The index is every bit as rigorous as economic measures like gross domestic product (GDP). A survey of nearly 300 questions, with 9 domains and 33 indicators, is taken across the country's population to provide a holistic measure of the people and their economic, physical, and spiritual prosperity.

Decades on, Bhutan is economically and politically stable, real GDP has averaged 7.5% since the 1980s, poverty dropped from 36% to 12% between 2007 and 2017, and the country is carbon neutral.[12] That's a lot to be happy about.

And certainly a lot to consider.

Could it be that by shifting focus from work output to the workers themselves, businesses will find new energy to flourish and new paths to profitability?

The data suggests it can.

In his work following the global financial crisis in 2008, Thomas Wright, professor of management at Kansas State University, found strong links between happiness and financial performance in challenging economic times. "The benefits of a psychologically well workforce are quite consequential to employers. . . . Simply put, psychologically well employees are better performers. Since higher employee performance is inextricably tied to an organization's bottom line, employee well-being can play a key role in establishing a competitive advantage," Wright said in a news release from the university.[13]

Intuitively, it makes sense that happy, engaged people do good work, and Wright's research found statistically significant correlations between increased well-being and higher job performance. Workers with high levels of well-being, he said, tend to be better decision makers, have better interpersonal skills, and are more supportive of their coworkers. This is further evidenced by the marked performance difference of companies listed on the "Fortune 100 Best Places to Work". An analysis by FTSE Russell found that an equally-weighted index of the publicly-traded companies on the 100 Best list returned 11.66% annually from 1998 through the end of 2016 versus returns for the US all-cap Russell 3000 Index (6.72%) and the US large cap Russell 1000 Index (6.68%). Can creating favorable conditions for talent really be worth a 5% points premium over the market annually for nearly 20 years? Substantial evidence suggest so.

Conversely, Wright found that low levels of well-being – what we often and too casually refer to as burnout – correlate with lower performance and higher likelihood of job resignation.

"Burnout is a manifestation of chronic workplace stress." writes Paula Davis in *Beating Burnout at Work: Why Teams Hold the Secret to Well-being and Resilience*.[14] "Leaders may unintentionally make burnout worse by dismissing it or thinking it's the same thing as general stress," she adds. "Research shows burnout rates do decline during and immediately after vacation but return to prevacation levels within weeks."

Happiness, it turns out, is profitable. Burnout is expensive, layering in costs due to errors, lower efficacy, and turnover.

It's Time to Finally Address Burnout

For years now, chief human resource officers (CHROs) have been waving a red flag in the corpore C-suite. Their workers were disengaged, discontented, and unhappy. "It has been hard to get the CEOs' attention on these people issues, especially during a pandemic," UCL School of Management professor Anthony Klotz told us. "I think a lot of HR professionals have been trying to signal issues related to engagement for a decade or more. This is a drum that they've been hammering for a while—humans have not been happy at work."

People have a range of emotional needs, many of which are fulfilled by work. The pandemic and remote work gave people autonomy over many aspects of their work, and that met a very real need, according to Klotz. At the same time, people also have a need to belong and being present in a physical office offers connections that fulfill that need.

Klotz went on to describe the disconnect that many people have felt as they return to in-person work. "The disconnect in sentiments on return to work is based on the differences in how we feel when we are there," he said. "The office environment is empowering to many bosses. It is the place where they became successful. For many employees, it is not a place of empowerment. It could even be a place of distraction, vulnerability, or even misery. So, I think the differences in feeling about returning to the office may just be the differences in how that environment makes us feel."

Those differences are the focus of organizational psychologist Michael Leiter's long body of work. The social dynamics that connect people are a powerful part of work, he told us. "People come into the workplace with expectations, aspirations, preferences," he said. "They want some degree of control."

The organization itself also has expectations, aspirations, and preferences. It's the misalignment of these expectations between the organization and the people that creates stress, and unchecked, that stress can lead to burnout. "Burnout is treated as an individual problem when in reality it is an organizational challenge," Leiter said. "Burnout is a relationship problem where the relationship, and especially the expectations, between the individual and the organization are misaligned or misunderstood."

In his work with Christina Maslach, with whom Leiter wrote *The Burnout Challenge*, they identified six factors that contribute to burnout:

- The amount, intensity, and complexity of one's workload
- The control and autonomy they have on the job
- The intrinsic and extrinsic rewards
- The community and relationships that allows one to feel part of something special
- Fairness and justice as one perceives it
- Perhaps most importantly, the alignment of values

The idea that you may now be leading a workforce that is empowered and misaligned to the point of burnout is, in a word, terrifying to most leaders. After all, our MBA programs teach us to manage processes rather than people. When those processes are impacted by advancing technology and digital transformation, they are ever-changing around a core group of people who must continuously adapt. If it hadn't been clear before, it certainly is now: leaders don't lead organizations; they lead people.

Today, we are confronting a decidedly more fragile relationship between the people and the organizations in which they work and we need to double down on our focus on people. People as individuals, not as a monolith. Understanding your team is about empathizing with the individuals that comprise your team.

Benefits for Whose Benefit?

Love him or hate him, New England Patriot turned Tampa Bay Buccaneer Tom Brady is arguably the best quarterback in the history of the game. In 2017, the investor newsletter *The Street* estimated that the cost of Brady's diet was $16,000 per year, more than a quarter of the median household income of the fans who watch him play each week.[15] Add to that his well-reported routine that includes a personal trainer, near-daily massage and physical therapy, a personal chef, and a life coach and you quickly see why some estimate he spends as much as $1 million each year to maintain his fitness. The return on that investment? Seven Super Bowl wins and $475 million in on-field career earnings.

Make no mistake: Tom Brady is a business. A very fit, very disciplined, very profitable, very successful business. And he is the company's star employee. If personal training, nutrition, body work, and psychological support are "perks" of his job, his company is getting tremendous value by offering them.

Which makes us think: what if businesses, generally, began treating their employees with the care and concern that performance athletes receive? How would we invest differently in our people if "perks" drove performance outcomes that benefit the employee and the company? What if we stopped treating benefits as supplemental compensation and began to see them as an investment in the business?

In the Human Value Era, benefits like health-care, tuition reimbursement, and childcare combine to help your people better perform at work. By turning benefits on their head and thinking of them not as supplemental compensation but as an investment in your company's most precious asset, benefits become an investment in the business.

Almost every employee benefit is actually a benefit to the company. Even time off proves to be a benefit for the organization. A 2018 study by Project: Time Off, reported by the Society for Human Resource Management (SHRM), found that the employees of companies that encouraged workers to take time off were much happier than those who work in organizations where vacation time goes largely unused. In fact, the majority of managers say time off improves an employee's focus (78%) and reduces the risk of burnout (81%).[16] In its 2017 HR Mythbusters study of 125,000 employees, HR software provider Namely found that time off not only leads to greater happiness, but also higher performance. High-performing employees took, on average, 19 days of paid time off, compared to average performers' 14 vacation days.[17]

In other words, vacation time is as much a perk for the business as it is for the employee.

Flexibility Is Key to Empathetic Leadership

It's not just time off that matters, though.

Nearly all employees (94%) say that flexible work hours demonstrate an organization's empathy toward its people, according to Businesssolver's seventh annual *State of Workplace Empathy* report. Still, just 38% of employers offered flexible work.[18]

Clearly, workers want more flexibility and many more may be willing to rejoin the workforce if they were offered less "traditional" schedules.

Mercy, a top 25 health-care system in the United States, is making that flexibility work. Even as other health systems have struggled with nursing shortages, Mercy has been able to maintain its nursing staff by providing work shifts that better accommodate its workers. Once married to a 12-hour shift, three days per week model, the organization now uses a mix of traditional, fixed part-time, and "gig" scheduling to fill their nursing staff requirements, Mercy's EVP and Chief Administrative Officer Cynthia Bentzen-Mercer told us.

"We had a hypothesis that there is an untapped market of people that would love to keep their skills up to date if they could work in a schedule that met their needs," she said. Mercy developed a flex staffing model that included a traditional 3/12 schedule for workers who preferred that model, added a "part-time core" consisting of fewer hours across more days for workers who needed a consistent day-to-day schedule, and introduced an app-based gig model that allows nurses to pick up extra shifts as desired.

"It's a mindshift for leaders," Bentzen-Mercer told us, noting that doctors and nursing managers accustomed to the traditional scheduling have had to adjust and learn to see nurses in each of the staffing models as valuable team members on equal footing. Still, she says, "it is the complement of all these flex models that together ensure we don't have gaps and that we have continuity of care."

How We Lead Without Maps: Focus on Your People

We have covered a lot of ground in this chapter, from the challenges of a complex world, to the realities of the Human Value Era, why leaders as unquestioned experts are a liability, the likely phenomenon of more frequent if not constant disruptions, and the growing truth about burnout, and more. All of this points to a single truth: change is the norm.

The only way to successfully thrive in this much uncertainty is to focus on our people. The focus on value creation through scaled production of product and services was myopic, and blurred the importance of our most valuable asset: our people. To be successful in continuous change, we must focus on the development, engagement, well-being, and happiness of our people.

Notes

1. Korzybski, Alfred, 1995, *Science and Sanity: An Introduction to Non-Aristotelian Systems and General Semantics* (5th ed.), Institute of General Semantics, p. 58. (Originally published 1933.)

2. "The Productivity-Pay Gap," The Economic Policy Institute, August 2021, available at https://www.epi.org/productivity-pay-gap/.

3. Hagel III, John, 2020, "From Shareholder to Stakeholder Market Economies," John Hagel, September 7, available at https://www.johnhagel.com/from-shareholder-to-stakeholder-market-economies/.

4. "Roger Martin: It's Time for Leaders to Embrace a New Way of Thinking," Lead from the Heart Podcast, May 20, 2022, available at https://podcasts.apple.com/us/podcast/roger-martin-its-time-for-leaders-to-embrace-a-new/id1365633369?i=1000562851328.

5. Martin, Roger, 2022, "Organizational Strategy & Job Titles; When More IS Better," May 30, available at https://rogermartin.medium.com/organizational-strategy-job-titles-ba819ef95d99.

6. Shipley, Chris, 2010, "The Sumo Wrestler and the Peloton," TedX Austin, February 20, available at https://www.youtube.com/watch?v=LrTimHTdPV4.

7. "Reduce Risk to Avert 'Era of Pandemics,' Experts Warn in New Report," UN News, October 29, 2020, available at(https://news.un.org/en/story/2020/10/1076392.

8. Heffernan, Margaret, 2020, *Uncharted: How to Navigate the Future*, Simon & Schuster.

9. Beatty, Carol A., 2015, "Communicating During an Organizational Change," Queens University IRC, available at https://irc.queensu.ca/wp-content/uploads/articles/articles_communicating-during-an-organizational-change.pdf.

10. Martin, "Organizational Strategy & Job Titles."

11. LaPrade, Annette, Mertens, Janet, Moore, Tanya, Wright, Amy, 2019, "The Enterprise Guide to Closing the Skills Gap," IBM Institute for Business Value, available at https://www.ibm.com/thought-leadership/institute-business-value/report/closing-skills-gap.

12. "The World Bank in Bhutan," The World Bank, October 6, 2021, available at https://www.worldbank.org/en/country/bhutan/overview.

13. "K-State Researcher Says Happy Employees Are Critical for Organizational Success," Kansas State Media, February 3, 2009, available at https://www.k-state.edu/media/newsreleases/feb09/wellbeing20309.html.

14. Davis, Paula, 2021, *Beating Burnout at Work*, Wharton School Press. Kindle Edition, pp. 10–11.

15. Notte, Jason, 2017, "Tom Brady Can Afford This $16,000 Diet That You Probably Can't," The Street, September 26, available at https://www.thestreet.com/lifestyle/tom-brady-can-afford-a-16-000-diet-you-probably-can-t-14310464.

16. Frye, Lisa, 2018, "More People Are Taking Time Off and That's Good for Business," SHRM, June 1, available at https://www.shrm.org/resourcesandtools/hr-topics/employee-relations/pages/workers-taking-more-vacation-.aspx.

17. "Namely HR Data Report Reveals That High-Performers Take More Vacation Time," PRNewswire, June 20, 2017, available at https://www.prnewswire.com/news-releases/namely-hr-data-report-reveals-that-high-performers-take-more-vacation-time-300476454.html.

18. "2022 State of the Workplace Empathy," Businesssolver, Inc., 2022, available at https://www.businessolver.com/resources/state-of-workplace-empathy.

19. "Gartner HR Research Shows Organizations Are Eroding Employee Performance and Well-Being with Virtualized Office-Centric Design," Gartner, May 4, 2021, available at https://www.gartner.com/en/newsroom/press-releases/2021-05-03-gartner-hr-research-shows-organizations-are-eroding-employee-performance-and-well-being-with-virtualized-office-centric-design.

Mercy: Leadership Through Community

Many people who climbed the career ladder in the decades before the pandemic took as gospel the advice to show up and be seen. Arrive early. Stay late. Skip lunch. Spend long hours in the sightline of the boss. Often enough, those long hours paid off. We built the relationships that led to promotion, pay raises, and better opportunities. As we became leaders ourselves, we used the same relational measures to assess our teams.

Then, Covid-19 ushered in remote and hybrid work, and we could no longer see or be seen at work. How would we maintain and build relationships in the distant and virtual world when we have been so conditioned to equate presence with performance?

That's the question Cynthia Bentzen-Mercer has wrestled with since the early days of the pandemic, and the answer she and her organization landed on is quite remarkable.

As EVP, Chief Administrative Officer at Mercy, one of the top 25 health care systems in the United States, Mercer is responsible for creating the environment and culture in which the organization's more than 40,000 employees can thrive.

"Many senior leaders grew up in a culture that the more you were visible, the more you were seen, the longer you were there, the more promotable you were," Mercer told us. Now, she says, people need and demand more flexibility in their work, particularly women who tend to carry the greater weight of family caregiving.

Mercer points to a Gartner survey that found that a majority of managers (69%) feel they don't have visibility into their employees' workdays.[19] "How do you demonstrate your commitment and aspirations?" she asks. "There is a real concern that we are going to step backwards from a diversity, equity, and inclusion standpoint. The fear is that more women, Black, indigenous, and people of color who choose to work from home, because it is more fitting to their life, will not be seen in the hallways and may be overlooked for promotion and raises."

Mercy addressed this concern head-on, first by "giving it voice," Mercer said. "I don't know that we've figured it out, but we are talking about our need to think differently about how we measure impact and performance."

Then, leadership took the extraordinary step of reimagining their corporate workspace. Rather than creating traditional office spaces, Mercy wants to create spaces that are inviting to hybrid workers. The company is converting an entire floor into a corporate community meeting space that includes private meeting spaces, collaboration spaces, meeting rooms, and on-demand workspaces that have become typical to hybrid offices. Into this environment, Mercy will layer in a suite of "concierge services" – including meals, car washes, and dry-cleaning services – to make the office a "place that work and life can be in balance."

"We really think differently about the community," Mercer says. "We have made an investment in collaboration so that we don't lose the relational side of work and give people the opportunity to co-create, while also being visible."

Mercer sees the services as something more than a perk to entice people to come into the office. "They are a necessary construct to create an inclusive community," she says.

"Our culture grows and flourishes through a sense of community," Mercer adds, "We can pivot and embrace this hybrid work environment. People have a need to be with others and there is a creative process and a relational side of being in community that benefits the individual and benefits the organization."

5 Create the Conditions to Thrive

In two short years, everything we thought we understood about work changed.

Work was a job that you went to. In an office, a factory, a health care facility, a restaurant, shop, a shop floor. Work was a place where you had an office, a desk, a cubby, a locker. You cursed the commute that made you late and sometimes the boss that kept you late.

Work was a job with a set of tasks. Roles and responsibilities you performed for the reward of a paycheck and maybe, one day, a promotion. You stayed in your lane or you showed some initiative. Either way, it was the boss, the company, that had the leverage. You performed for their satisfaction.

Work was a job experienced with a set of coworkers. You pulled on the metaphorical oar together to move the company forward. Oftentimes, you competed with one another for bonuses, prized parking spaces, your picture in the "Employee of the Month" ensemble. You sat in meetings together and put in face time with company leaders and customers.

Then, in almost an instant, work became something different for so many workers. We worked at home, taking initiative to figure out how best to connect with coworkers and customers. We worked by ourselves or jumped on a Zoom call when we needed guidance from a manager or input from a colleague.

And perhaps without even knowing it, we crossed the threshold from the Shareholder Value Era that tied work to output and profit into the Human Value Era that married work with creative collaboration to build value for ourselves, our colleagues, and our companies. The Human Value Era forces us to rethink what a "job" is and create the conditions for a new measure of success. As we find new ways to organize work for a newly empowered workforce, our best path is one that creates the conditions that maximize individual and collective contribution, establishes an environment in which everyone can thrive, and builds the foundation for continuous learning. And let's be clear: many of the ideas we'll discuss were proposed long ago. Finally, their time has come.

Rethinking Jobs

In our previous book, *The Adaptation Advantage* (Wiley, 2020), we made the case that organizations ought to "fire the job description." Our thesis then and now is that fast-changing markets require adaptive organizations filled with people who can quickly learn new skills as the need arises. In these dynamic environments, past requirements may not be the best indicator of future needs.

Indeed, job descriptions are biased, often rigid boxes usually defined by the last person to hold that position. That prior occupant of the role, rather than the real needs of the organization, tends to set the standard for how *that job was performed in the past.*

By firing the job description, you stop searching for the candidate that ticks all the boxes that describe how things have always been done and instead hire the individual who demonstrates curiosity, flexibility, and an eagerness to take on new challenges *for the future*. In other words, it's time to end the practice of hiring people to fill jobs and begin the discipline of creating roles around outstanding people.

More than two decades ago, Timothy Butler and James Waldroop conceived the notion of "job sculpting," building definition and responsibilities around an employee's deeply embedded life interests, the "long-held, emotionally driven passions, intricately entwined with personality . . . [that] drives what kinds of activities make them happy. At work, that happiness often translates into commitment. It keeps people engaged, and it keeps them from quitting."[1]

Butler and Waldroop found that most people are driven by deeply embedded life interests. Mind you, these aren't hobbies or flights of fancy, they are deeply ingrained sensibilities that lead us to work we love. The researchers enumerated the "big eight" drivers:

1. Application of technology – the desire to understand how things work

2. Quantitative analysis – a passion for numbers as a system of understanding

3. Theory development and conceptual thinking – a focus on abstract ideas and big picture framing

4. Creative production – conceiving something new from whole cloth

5. Counseling and mentoring – a desire to teach and foster growth and development in others

6. Managing people and relationships – the satisfaction of leading people to achieve a goal

7. Enterprise control – a passion for "owning" decisions and leading projects and teams

8. Influence through language and ideas – the passion for ideas and influence shared through effective communications

The vast majority of people are driven by just one or two of these factors, and when they find work that taps that passion, they can become deeply committed to that work, Butler and Waldroop say. Search for someone who exhibits one or more of these drivers, then build a job around them.

We might assume that a CEO has a deep interest in having enterprise control, or that a CFO engages deeply with quantitative analysis. Certainly, a CEO, CFO, or any other person in your organization, has a job where they have to employ and build certain skill sets, but perhaps their underlying true embedded life interest drivers might be entirely different. In the Human Value Era, these same people might be able to better tap into their drivers to thrive and succeed in ways that weren't previously possible. Someone with a deep interest in enterprise control may have no interest in becoming a CEO, but may be the perfect candidate to lead the new corporate initiative to create a balanced hybrid work model, for example, or to create a corporate innovation lab. Someone with a deeply held interest in quantitative analysis might prove to be an exceptional data analyst, product pricing specialist, or inventory manager. Those who influence through language and ideas might just be your best frontline workers, interacting with customers at every level.

In the Human Value Era, everyone from C-suite leaders to hiring managers to shift captains must learn to tune in to the deeply embedded life interests of those around them. By shaping jobs to better align with interests, you not only engender happier and more engaged employees, but you can be more certain that you have the right people in the right jobs driving the success of the business.

Hire for Culture, Train for Specific Skills

But how do you suss out these deeply embedded life interests? Roger Hurni, founder and Chief Creative Officer of marketing agency Off Madison Ave in Tempe, Arizona, told us he uncovers some of the most important information about a candidate by asking more unconventional questions. Questions like "What is your guilty music pleasure?" or "When was a time when you went against the grain?" say more about a candidate's curiosity or entrepreneurial spirit than any resume can, Hurni told us. "I don't even care much about the specific answer," he said, "I am trying to figure out if they have a curiosity about the human condition."

Learning about a prospective hire's passion for scrapbooking, jazz music, acting, or anything else helps the Off Madison team understand what a prospect cares most about. It gives them a window into the candidate's creative process and potential contributions to the organization's culture. These avocations demonstrate a candidate's motivation and their self-propelled desire to explore a subject deeply. "We hire for cultural alignment, trust, and potential," Hurni said. "We train for skills."

The approach has served them well. Over the last 20 years, some 400 people have worked at the agency, and Hurni told us that he can "count on one hand the number of [hiring] mistakes."

And what about you? How do your deeply embedded life interests shape your work? Have you found the fit between your intrinsic passions and your work? That alignment is, after all, the very thing that will bring joy and meaning to your work. (See "Rethinking Work and Jobs.")

Rethinking Work and Jobs
Jobs Are Biased.

Job descriptions are often little more than a portrait of the last person to hold that position. They tend to be filled with irrelevant requirements and, often, requirements for outdated skills. That's because we tend to think of jobs as a set of relevant skills learned at a university or in a training program, and that worked when skills had a reasonable shelf life. That's rarely the case these days.

Consider your own career as a case in point. How much of your work is dependent on things you learned at school? We'd venture to bet – backed up by a 2022 study by the McKinsey Global Institute – that much of your value at work comes from experience, rather than explicit training. The McKinsey study found that when we begin our careers, 60% of our value comes from our skills and 40% from acquired experience. In the second decade of our careers, the ratio splits evenly, and by the time we cross into 30 or more years of work, the ratio flips; our value is composed of 60% experience and 40% skills.[2]

As the pace of change accelerates, we will see less of our value derived from predetermined skills and existing knowledge. Even today, from the time you identify a need in your workforce to the time you hire to fill that need, the need itself has shifted. A better approach is to seek talent with foundational skills and knowledge, yet screen for shared values and aspirations to find the new hires ready to learn together.

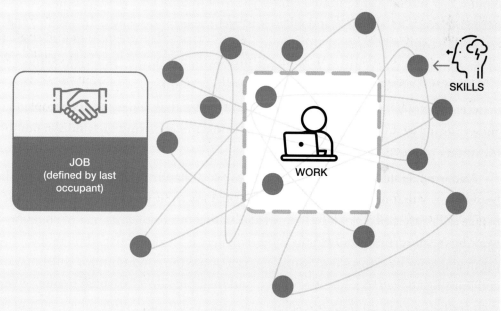

Figure 5.1 Rethinking Work and Jobs

Reporting for (Tour of) Duty

A decade ago, LinkedIn founder turned venture capitalist Reid Hoffman posited a different way of thinking about work, one he acknowledged wasn't necessarily new but that "hadn't taken hold."[3] Rather than the implicit contract between company and employee – namely, that your job was secure so long as both you and the company performed well – we needed a refresh to what he called "tours of duty." These tours, he suggests, are organized around a project or set of projects. They are opportunities to learn and apply new skills, collaborate with colleagues in the process of operationalizing an objective, and to build strong relationships to be carried from one tour to another.

There is a bit to unpack in this concept, so let's break it down.

First, in this model, the "job" is not a general set of tasks to be done in repetition across the lifetime of employment. The job, instead, is an outcome-focused collaboration among people of different and complementary skills who come together focused on a defined objective. Gone is the metaphoric "team" of coworkers sharing workspace while doing their respective and sometimes interdependent tasks, replaced by a literal team of colleagues committed to a result.

Second, this model replaces long-tenured roles – the concept of lifetime employment – with shorter engagements – the expectation that the project will require 2–3 years of concentrated effort. The tour of duty lasts as long as the team is needed to reach its objective and when it is over the team disbands. This is how most consulting companies operate today, and it's a model to pay attention to because in the future, we will organize work more like consulting firms. These companies are project based. Their relationship with the client is porous, with little distinction between talent in the firm and at the client. Together, they concentrate on learning and exploring new opportunities, while capturing and codifying their discoveries to fuel future products and services.

Understandably, many folks want to know what happens after the tour ends. The implication is that once the tour is over, so is the job. And that can be true for some people with specialized skills and knowledge who move from company to company working in short sprints on various projects. There is an alternative, though; by organizing your workforce into tours, you can create the conditions for collaboration and learning applied to a specific project, and then provide a "learning respite" where your people can top up skills or explore new areas of interest before taking on a new tour assignment. In some consulting firms, this time after a tour is called "time on the bench."

Where Work Gets Done

In the spring of 2020, we learned very quickly that a massive amount of work could be done from anywhere and without direct supervision. Workers at all levels adjusted to new routines, video conferencing, instant messaging, and digital tools. We didn't specifically need offices, just a digital device and a decent internet connection. Ironically, it took Covid-19 lockdown mandates to liberate workers from their offices.

Certainly, there are many jobs that require a place. Frontline workers from health care providers and caregivers to grocery store clerks and food services providers to delivery drivers and public safety officials, among many others, added to their work the burden of Covid prevention. But in a short few months we discovered that the default setting for work – an office – was more nice to have than need to have.

Yes, it was nice to huddle around a whiteboard with coworkers and sketch out new plans and designs. Sure, it was convenient to pop into someone's office to ask a question or get some advice. No doubt, putting in face time with corporate leaders made you and your work more visible to the higher-ups. But was it *absolutely necessary to work among others in an office*? We really don't know. Those who demand a return to the office, certain that workers must be together to build social capital or optimize innovation are doing so without empirical evidence. In truth, we need to be experimenting now to determine when, where, how, and why we come together in person.

Funny then, that as pandemic restrictions were lifted many bosses demanded a return to office. And not surprising that many workers simply refused. For leaders with a strong bias toward face-to-face work (after all, that's how they built their careers), the office creates space for creative collision, collaboration, and serendipity. For workers unburdened by a commute and the social pressures of in-person work, a return to office seems like an extraneous demand that makes them less – not more – productive.

Who's right?

Surely, some jobs, particularly those that require co-creation of a physical object, may benefit from more frequent in-person interactions, but there is little evidence that in-person work is nearly as beneficial to innovation, spontaneous collaboration, and creative engagement as we might imagine. In fact, the opposite is true.

Organizational behaviorists and Harvard colleagues Ethan Bernstein and Stephen Turban found that the trend toward open workspaces – work places with wide-open floor plans and fewer offices – did not lead to greater interaction among coworkers. In fact, "contrary to common belief, the volume of face-to-face interaction decreased significantly (approx. 70%)," they wrote. "Rather than prompting increasingly vibrant face-to-face collaboration, open architecture appeared to trigger a natural human response to socially withdraw from officemates and interact instead over email and IM."[4]

Writing for the *New York Times*, reporter Claire Cain Miller posited one reason why in-office face-to-face interactions don't work for everyone. "For many people, in-person office jobs were never a great fit," she writes.[5] We couldn't agree more. Many workers – women with caregiving responsibilities, people with disabilities, racial minorities, introverts, and social outsiders, among others – all experience some degree of emotional and physical overload from in-office work that burdens them *in addition to* the work itself. Quite frankly, return-to-office mandates may very well be at odds with your organization's diversity, equity, inclusion, and belonging (DEIB) initiatives, screening out those atypical workers who thrive outside the place-bound, 9-to-5 tempo of office work.

It seems, then, that this unexpected experiment with remote work that scattered colleagues near and far might – as digital technologies and our ability to use them improve and replicate many aspects of in-office work – actually encourage greater diversity and inclusion while improving productivity. No doubt businesses can and should make room for in-person work, but the best advice may well be to put more experimentation ahead of return-to-office mandates.

One such experiment, conducted by Stanford economist Nick Bloom in 2022, randomly assigned half the employees of a large technology company to work full time in the office, while the other half were given leeway to work from home (WFH) two days per week.

The results were striking. Attrition rates in the WFH group dropped by 35%, and self-reported satisfaction scores improved. The study also found that those in the WFH group shifted the hours they put into the job, working less on the days they were at home, but more on weekends and on the days they were in the office.

These workers also depended more on digital messaging and video communication tools, even when they were in the office. All while having no significant impact on performance or promotions.[6]

This is just one study, and we certainly need more of them to weigh the advantages and disadvantages of office-based in-person work on various populations, and on the types of tasked performed in these different environments. For example, if specific tasks or projects slightly favor in-person interactions, but exclude participation by some workers, the minor advantage may not be worth the major exclusion.

If office work is no longer the default, we can't simply assume that work from home or work from anywhere is the new defaults. We need more experimentation and an honest conversation about the trade-offs. We know that humans are social beings that run on connection. We know that human learning is often socially based. We know that mentoring and network growth are key to learning and career development. What we do not know yet is how to best construct where, when, and how we work. Evidenced by the rising rates of burnout, mental distress, and low employee engagement we discussed in prior chapters, we know that how we were working prior to the pandemic was not optimal. Yet we are still learning how best to manage geographically dispersed teams.

An executive in the automotive parts industry told us that he'd discovered a decade before the pandemic that he could not find the talent he needed in the region where his business operated. He decided to hire remote workers on a trial basis and experimented with when, why, and how frequently they needed to all meet in person. Over a decade, he discovered that meeting once a quarter for 3–5 days was optimal for his company. Many more companies, we suspect, will be working out these experiences for themselves.

Curating the Return to Office

As we move beyond fixed jobs and fixed workplaces, we will want to create purposeful environments for those times when it is essential that we come together face-to-face. After all, there's little value in simply relocating the same work from remote to office locations. Why go into an office if you're going to work at a desk by yourself or sit in the same type of meeting you could have on Zoom?

That question is at the heart of workers' resistance to corporate edicts to return to the office. And let's be clear: these are not recalcitrant workers who prefer to skip a commute and work in loungewear. They are challenging demands to return to the office, especially on set schedules, because few of these policies were crafted based on empirical evidence or any consultation with workers themselves. Return-to-office demands were a sudden loss of autonomy and, more importantly, trust. And, too often, executives have no good answer, except an instinct to return to the default office model that might have been more broken than we knew.

So much of office work is performative. The act of working becomes visible to others, even if the work itself remains largely unseen. When the pandemic sent office workers home, they substituted physical visibility with digital presence, developing a Pavlovian response to the chime of an incoming email or Slack notification. On a recent Friday afternoon, for example, a mutual friend slipped out to run a few errands. While standing in line awaiting a cashier, she looked at her smartphone, stepped out of line, and said without hesitation, "I need to respond to this message so they know I am still working." Never mind that she was 10 days from retirement and had already put in an eight-hour day.

Our obsession with evidencing our work through physical and digital presence is a hard habit to break, but break it we must. *Killing Time at Work 22*, a recent Qatalog and GitLab study of 2,000 knowledge workers in the United States and the United Kingdom, found workers are spending an average of 67 minutes a day sending superfluous emails and chats as evidence they are working: digital presenteeism is here.[7] If you think that is a waste of time, imagine the additional time tossed away reading and responding to 67 minutes' worth of unnecessary messages, all in service of the illusion of work.

Appearing on the *Ezra Klein Show* podcast, writers Anne Helen Peterson and Charlie Warzel talked with host Rogé Karma about the opportunity hybrid work presents if organizational leaders rethink this broken culture of work. Discussing their book *Out of Office: The Big Problem and Bigger Promise of Working From Home*, Peterson asserted that "really smart companies are reexamining . . . what excellence looks like and have decoupled it from any understanding of how many emails sent or how many meetings attended, and are looking more closely at what is the quality of the work."[8]

If hybrid work is to be successful, Warzel added, managers can't reflexively return to pre-pandemic leadership styles. Instead, he said, leaders should embrace the "massive opportunity" that is "building a different way to work."

How might that different way of working be expressed? Author and management consultant Roger Martin believes it comes from carefully orchestrating the office experience. "We're going to have to create reasons for employees to want to be in the office," he told Mark Crowley in a May 2022 podcast interview.[9]

He calls these reasons "curated events."

Sitting at your desk toiling away is "completely uncurated," Martin said. Leaders need to ask themselves what corporate needs require that people come together in real time in order to achieve a desired outcome, and then "put the investment into designing those experiences so that people wouldn't miss it."

That way, he said, when the event occurs, "It is exciting. It's generative. Something good comes out of that day."

Martin acknowledged that curation is a new skill for many managers, who will need to invest time into planning an agenda, setting expectations, assigning prework, articulating the goals and desired outcomes, perhaps even creating exercises and activities that engage participants. That may sound like a heavy lift, but it beats the alternative if you don't make the effort, he argued. "The alternative is that all those people resign."

It is not enough, then, to relocate work by demanding a return to office or a set hybrid schedule.

And we certainly can't fall back on old-style rewards and incentives to entice employees to return to the office. Employee-of-the-month programs and gold star reserved parking won't do it, and leaders can't fall back on the easy answers that are in their comfort zone. Instead, they need to find the motivators that their people care about. We have to really think about how we transform work by creating the conditions for well-aligned success.

Creating the Conditions to Thrive

If we are committed to the Human Value Era, we have to think about not just how we define work or even where that work takes place; we have to think about how we truly transform work so that the work itself can be transformative for those who do it.

But where to start?

Perhaps by looking at where we are and admitting honestly that the news isn't good. Life expectancy in the United States has decreased from 78.86 years in 2019 to 76.6 years in 2021, a loss of 2.26 years.[10] During the pandemic, rates of anxiety and depression globally grew more than 25%, and young people, people of color, and people in poverty were much more likely to report feelings of loneliness.[11]

Keeping Mental Health Top of Mind

We find ourselves mired in an epidemic of loneliness so concerning that the Surgeon General of the United States, Vivek Murthy, took to the pages of the *Harvard Business Review* in 2017 to argue that "reducing isolation at work" was good for business, reasoning that most people spend more time with colleagues at work than they do with families at home.[12]

In a 2022 Cigna study, 58% of Americans report being lonely, and while we might believe the younger "connected" generations are less lonely than older adults, the inverse is actually true. Seventy-nine percent of adults aged 18 to 24 report being lonely while only 41% of seniors aged 66 and older do.[13] Your young workforce is profoundly lonely; it is an epidemic that the Surgeon General suggests you might be best positioned to address. Our work/life balance has shifted in the years since Murthy wrote that article, but work still has a role to play in building community and belonging both inside organizations and across communities. And surely, what's good for the worker is good for business. It's time to ask: If the good mental health of your team is essential to the success of your team, are mental health benefits an employee benefit or your company's strategic advantage?

Embrace Diversity as Your Strategic Advantage

We cannot talk about reconceiving the workplace – in person or virtually – without establishing the foundation that is diversity, equity, inclusion, and belonging (DEIB). Too often, organizations get to the "D" and focus almost entirely on representational diversity – the stuff you can see, such as race, gender and gender identity, ethnicity and religion, and in some cases physical difference. There has been a sort of checkbox mentality, tallying people by outward classifications and declaring victory when the numbers found some balance.

Representational diversity is just the tip of the iceberg. The next frontier of DEIB is neurodiversity, recognizing that every person brings a different set of cognitive abilities, each with its own superpower. For example, in a paper by Helen Taylor and Martin David Vestergaard, "Developmental Dyslexia: Disorder or Specialization in Exploration?" the researchers posit that individuals with developmental dyslexia (DD) are "specialized in explorative cognitive search and . . . play an essential role in human adaptation."

Most literature on dyslexia focuses on the challenges and deficits, they point out, yet people with dyslexia often "have certain strengths – particularly in realms like discovery, invention, and creativity – that deficit-centered theories cannot explain."[14]

Thirty-five percent of entrepreneurs in the United States exhibit dyslexic traits, compared to a 15% occurrence of such traits in the US population as a whole, researcher Julie Logan found in a study conducted at the Cass Business School in London.[15]

Perhaps the most famously successful dyslexic is Sir Richard Branson, founder of the Virgin Group, which includes more than 400 companies. "Dyslexia," Sir Richard said in an interview with the *Times* of London, "is my superpower." His struggles with severe dyslexia caused him to surround himself with great people and delegate effectively. "I think that, by and large, dyslexics are more creative and good at seeing the bigger picture. We do think slightly differently to other people."[16]

Other types of neurodiversity include autism and Autism Spectrum Disorder (ASD), dyscalculia, epilepsy, hyperlexia, syspraxia, ADHD, obsessive-compulsive disorder (OCD), Tourette syndrome, and synesthesia, a perceptual phenomenon which links senses with unusual results. "Sounds may evoke colors, tastes may evoke shapes, or numbers may evoke spatial patterns – in all, over 40 unique pairings have been documented," writes Katherine Bryant for the *Neuroethics Blog*.[17] And in his 2014 paper, "Synesthesia on Our Mind," Lawrence E. Marks noted that "people with synesthesia do have enhanced creative abilities, creative cognition."[18]

Diversity across every axis is critical, to be sure. But if we are to intentionally build the conditions for a thriving, learning-centered, creative, and collaborative workforce, we need to embrace the entire acronym. Equity – creating a culture of fairness and level setting. Inclusion – seeking out and gathering in an array of perspectives. Belonging – building a community of trust in which your people can feel seen, respected, and valued. (See "Understanding DEI . . . and B."). True diversity is achieved by creating the conditions, building the culture, and embracing the value of equity, inclusion, and belonging.

Understanding DEI . . . and B

Let's make this point clearly: the most diverse companies outperform those that are less diverse. Full stop.

That's not our opinion; it's the finding of one of the United States' most conservative business media, the *Wall Street Journal*. "The 20 most diverse companies," the paper reported in 2019, "had an average annual stock return of 10% over five years, versus 4.2% for the 20 least-diverse companies."[19]

Diversity, Equity, Inclusion and Belonging (DEIB) has become so critical to business performance that in 2020, *Fortune* magazine and Refinitiv launched the Measure Up partnership to track the DEIB performance of the companies in the annual Fortune 500 ranking, prominently including Measure Up data alongside the financial data in the listing.[20]

Diversity is representation, making your organization look, feel, and act like the customers you serve. Equity is fairness, making policies that optimize the potential for each of your people as individuals. Inclusion is action, making decisions that reflect your commitments. Belonging is the feeling shared by every employee that they can be their full authentic selves at work. Without belonging, you lose the power of diversity.

DEIB is no longer a check-the-box concern for human resource leaders; it is an imperative for investors and the C-suite. Your company's commitment to DEIB underpins your ability to recruit top talent. In The Boardlist/Felicis Ventures survey of diverse executives (women and men of color), 84% say a company's commitment to DEIB is "incredibly important" when considering a position, and 41% rank diversity and representation in leadership as a top factor in deciding to take a job.

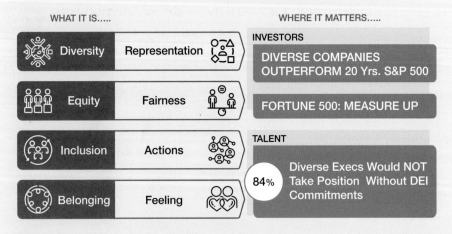

Figure 5.2 Understanding DEI . . . and B

Data sources: McKinsey: *Why Diversity Matters*; Fortune 500; Survey of 200 Diverse Executives Conducted by the Boardlist and Felicis Ventures.

Unleash the Power of Belonging

Diversity without belonging does not realize the potential of that diversity. Belonging is a powerful human emotion. It binds us to the communities we value and motivates us to work for and contribute to the shared objectives. In fact, in a Valuegraphics survey of 750,000 people that ranked personal values, belonging ranked above all other values for US respondents and ranked fourth worldwide. (See "The Importance of Belonging.")

"Simply feeling like you're part of a team of people working on a task makes people more motivated as they take on challenges" notes Stanford psychological scientists Priyanka B. Carr and Gregory M. Walton.[21] Across five experiments, Walton and Carr concluded that even subtle suggestions of being part of a team dramatically increased people's motivation and enjoyment in relation to difficult tasks. In each of the experiments participants first met each other in small groups of 3–5 people before heading to separate rooms – ostensibly as part of a study on solving puzzles. Although they were essentially working alone on the puzzles, those who were led to believe they were working as part of a larger group spent 48% more time working on the puzzles. In essence, the expectation of group collaboration led to greater perseverance and engagement and even higher levels of performance.

That perseverance and courageous exploration are at the heart of work collaborations, in which we work together as a team learning together. Belonging gives us permission to not know; it is the foundation for the psychological safety necessary to build a learning organization invested in Human Value.

The Importance of Belonging

Belonging. It's a basic human need, the desire to be accepted fully into a group or community.

"Psychological safety is built on a moral foundation of looking on our fellow creatures with respect and giving them permission to belong and contribute," writes Timothy R Clark, author of *The Four Phases of Psychological Safety*.[22] To achieve the first phase of psychological safety, we must move from exclusion to inclusion. Without that sense of belonging, we won't fully participate in an organization. We withdraw and self-censure.

We need to belong to be psychologically safe.

Belonging attracts and retains your people. "The primary reason people join and stay in a company or organization is . . . because they want to belong," writes Anthony Silard, associate professor of leadership and director of the Center for Sustainable Leadership at Luiss Business School in Rome. "The deepest intrinsic desire they wish to fulfill at work is to feel included, accepted, appreciated, and valued by a social group that, in their eyes, is worth belonging to."[23]

Belonging is the key to engagement. "Belonging is one of the values that drive people to do things around the world," says David Allison who has interviewed more than 750,000 people worldwide to develop a taxonomy of human values he calls Valuegraphics. Values, more than demographic data, motivate our actions, he contends. Belonging, it turns out, is a primary driver of behavior.

Belonging begets loyalty. Sid Lee, a global creative agency, developed the Brand Belonging Index™ to rank brands by their 40-point "belonging quotient." [24] Not surprisingly, the index's top brands are all companies that are purpose forward and have developed loyal communities by offering the exceptional customer and employee experiences that foster belonging. If brands like, Roblox, Patagonia, Disney, Nike, and Marvel resonate with you, it's likely that you feel an affinity, a sense of belonging, with them.

"Humans want to be with each other. It's one of the beautiful things we've discovered," Allison told us. "Belonging is the only consistent [value] across every target audience in every part of the world."

If it is not already, belonging needs to be the centerpiece of your employee experience.

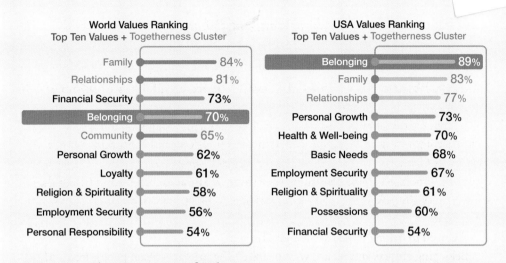

Figure 5.3 The Importance of Belonging

Data source: The Valuegraphics database is an accurate record of the core values of everyone on earth. It is a random, stratified, statistical representation of the population of 180 countries, collected from a half-million surveys conducted in 152 languages, measuring 436 values, needs, wants, and expectations with a +/– 3.5% margin of error and a 95% level of confidence.

Knitting a Psychological Safety Net

The term "psychological safety" was popularized by Dr. Amy Edmondson of Harvard Business School in her book *The Fearless Organization*. Psychological safety, she writes, is "a climate in which people are comfortable expressing and being themselves. More specifically, when people have psychological safety at work, they feel comfortable sharing concerns and mistakes without fear of embarrassment or retribution. They are confident that they can speak up and won't be humiliated, ignored, or blamed."[25]

As work, especially knowledge activities, becomes ever more the exploratory, messy, uncertain tasks of finding and framing new challenges (what some might call innovation), we need to make these explorations in an environment of trust, where failure can be celebrated as an opportunity to learn. But trust isn't bestowed with the wave of the hand and well-spoken assurances. It is carefully built, one step at a time.

In his book *The 4 Stages of Psychological Safety: Defining the Path to Inclusion and Innovation*, Timothy R. Clark describes the progression to psychological safety, each step building a foundation of trust for the next. He calls the first rung

Inclusion Safety, the feeling that you can be your authentic self at work. Just as belonging is essential to unleashing the potential in DEI, inclusion safety is essential to engagement. Workers who do not feel they can be their authentic selves will, as Clark describes it, "self-censor."[26] Once Inclusion Safety is established, the next step is Learner Safety, the ability to experiment, make mistakes, learn, and ultimately discover. The third step is Contributor Safety, the permission to contribute without waiting to be asked. Finally, at the top of the ladder, is Challenger Safety, the invitation to push back and even dissent without negative repercussions.

You might create an environment that offers safety to learn and contribute, but only when your organization climbs to the top of the ladder are you truly able to innovate, Clark argues, because innovation by definition means you challenge the status quo, offering new ideas, products, services, and methods that replace the current solutions.

While some old-school leaders might dismiss psychological safety as "woke," there are plenty of real-world examples that demonstrate the catastrophic results of a workplace without it. In 1986, for example, the (perhaps ironically named) space shuttle Challenger blew up 73 seconds after takeoff, killing the seven astronauts on board. The cause of the tragedy was not a big surprise. Colder than anticipated weather caused a rubber O-ring to turn brittle and fail to seal properly. NASA engineers knew O-ring failure was a possibility, but with the mission in doubt and a culture that did not invite objections, engineers kept quiet and allowed the liftoff to go on as scheduled.

Few situations are as tragic, but if we're honest with ourselves, most of us can all name a time or two when we or someone on the team knew a miss was probable yet failed to speak up for fear of reprisal. "Only when people feel free and able do they apply their creativity," Clark writes in his book. "Without challenger safety, there's little chance of that because threats, judgements, and other limiting beliefs block curiosity in ourselves and others."[27]

Creating the Conditions to Learn at Scale

The freedom to create is the freedom to learn, and it is learning that fuels your organization's future.

If Heather has a mantra, it is: Learning Is the New Pension. On a personal level, learning is how you create your future value every day. In an environment with a high degree of change and uncertainty, learning is as important as earning; it prepares you to advance in the organization or expand your options outside the organization. The investor and technology analyst and investor Esther Dyson put it best when she advised in a LinkedIn post, "Never take a job for which you are already qualified. Look for a job where the employer wants to invest in you. . . . That way, you will learn something, and the employer will end up with a knowledgeable, capable employee who understands the company's unique assets and challenges."[28]

Earlier, we shared that Off Madison Ave's Hurni hires for curiosity and teaches skills, but his practice is about more than skills fitting. Curiosity is his proxy for learning agility and aptitude. "I once hired a woman right out of college who had no experience, but when I asked her what she did for fun, she said she traded foreign currencies at night to make extra money. She was self-taught. I hired another guy after he told me about his passion for his rock band," he told us. "These are all signs of lifelong learners who are curious and self-motivated. When you have those qualities, you are seeking to understand the human condition and that is what makes you great in a creative agency."

Together, Dyson's and Hurni's ideas are powerful. As an employee and colleague, it's vital you seek a group with whom you can learn faster than you can on your own. As an employer and leader, search for talent that wants to join and learn with you to grow your capacity and theirs together. The more your team members are developing their own future potential, the more engaged they will be, and the more they will do every day to grow yours.

Social Capital Creates Collective Intelligence

No matter how our future work environment unfolds, we can always be more intentional about knowledge sharing and the creation of social capital. Whether in person or virtually, the social interactions of a shared workplace need to be intentionally constructed. Curated, as Roger Martin might say.

The National Bureau of Economic Research made that point in a study, published in early 2020, of people who sold cable television, internet, and phone services. In the experiment, sales people were randomly assigned to have lunch once a week with a coworker whom they had not previously met. Four months into the study, those salespeople who met for lunch had on average 24% higher revenue.[29] Why? Because when you meet somebody for lunch who has complementary knowledge, you end up giving and getting advice. You learn from each other.

By being intentional about designing these moments for cross-functional exchange, we build social capital and corporate collective intelligence.

Sun Microsystems cofounder Bill Joy captured this idea in a statement that has come to be known as "Joy's Law." "No matter who you are," he said, "most of the smartest people work for someone else." It's important, then, that we create moments for our teams to meet with "someone else" to expand their world view. As we begin to reimagine "where" work takes place, organizations have the opportunity to provide clever alternatives that satisfy the need to engage with someone else. Companies, for example, might sponsor employees' coworking space memberships where their people have the opportunity to expand their networks and knowledge. They might colocate with their best customers and closest partners to create a more porous border between your company and those who, by extension, participate in your business.

Organizing to Collaborate

We'll dive deep into culture and purpose in the next chapter, but we can't leave the discussion of organizational structure without mentioning the crucial role culture plays in how we organize work and structure the workplace.

In the old paradigm of work, which we are leaving behind, our work was organized into jobs. We owned our jobs, they were ours. Those jobs contained set tasks. We saw our peers as competitors. Competitors for the boss's attention. Competitors in the quality of work. Competitors for promotions and raises. When we move away from work organized like manufacturing production lines as if our knowledge work was as repeatable and skills-based as assembly work, we are left with collaborative explorations that rely on the knowledge and goodwill of those with whom we work. In this new mode, work is not a zero-sum game and our coworkers are not our competitors; they are our partners. They make us stronger. They make us smarter and stronger. They have our back. (See "Peers as Collaborators.")

In *The Adaptation Advantage*, we interviewed David Lewis and Alison Reynolds about their research that found that the combination of psychological safety and cognitive diversity lead to greater team learning and performance – especially around solving complex challenges. Their hypothesis is that cognitive diversity checks your blind spots. When you are open to your peers as collaborators, you have a better chance of identifying those knowledge gaps and increasing your performance.

Peers as Collaborators

When psychological safety is absent from the workplace and performance is measured in forced rankings – those performance measures that pit coworker against coworker, competition dominates the culture.

While some leaders think competition is the only way to bring out the best in people, evidence finds this is not always true. Competition works in sales when the targets are well aligned. When competition is ongoing and becomes personal, which it does in many organizations, it becomes a rivalry. Competition works when competitors have similar skills and knowledge. Given the pace of change and speed at which new skills and knowledge emerge, most organizations are filled with individuals with unique – rather than similar or redundant – skills and knowledge. Competition, then, must give way to collaboration, where the collective skills and knowledge of the team lay the foundation for organizational success.

In their paper "Whatever It Takes to Win: Rivalry Increases Unethical Behavior," researchers Gavin J. Kilduff, Adam D. Galinsky, Edoardo Gallo, and J. James Reade found rivalry among coworkers places a premium on self-worth and status, which in turn drives colleagues to "adopt a stronger performance approach orientation, which then increases unethical behavior."[30] In other words, highly competitive environments are at high risk for the bad behavior that can crush a company and its brand. Competition lowers trust, whereas collaboration requires constant alignment towards the collective goal.

At play in this dynamic are turf and trust. Turf wars rage in highly competitive environments, where trust is generally low. As a leader whose team is in competition with one another, you become the referee of their squabbles. Worse, you are the fuel for the competition. Progress comes in response to the stimuli-threat, punishment, reward - that you use to make incremental movement. Stop the stimuli and you stop the progress.

The alternative is to facilitate collaboration. Dialing down turf disputes, removing artificial stimuli, and building trust moves people from competition to collaboration. When workers see each other as collaborators, they are self propelled. You lead through motivation and necessary course correction rather than a often artificial stimuli-response mechanisms.

When your people collaborate, you remove the petty rivalries that prevent your team from reaching its full potential.

(Continued)

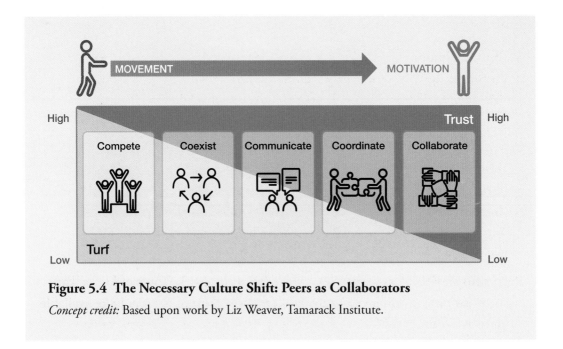

Figure 5.4 The Necessary Culture Shift: Peers as Collaborators

Concept credit: Based upon work by Liz Weaver, Tamarack Institute.

Finding Joy in Work

We have covered a lot of ground in this chapter, and you wouldn't be faulted for wondering right about now if this effort – to reimagine jobs and work, reorient your leadership toward learning and collaboration, and resolve to create an environment where every worker feels the agency to contribute and collaborate to their fullest – is worth it.

No doubt, it is work – a lot of work – to move into this new and strange territory.

It is also rewarding – incredibly rewarding. When your work is optimized for collaboration, aligned behind common objectives, and liberated from the constraints that dampen creativity, work can be a joy.

In the next chapter, we'll explore the secrets of uncorking that level of work satisfaction.

Notes

1. Butler, Timothy and Waldroop, James, 1999, "Job Sculpting: The Art of Retaining Your Best People," *Harvard Business Review*, September/October, available at https://hbr.org/1999/09/job-sculpting-the-art-of-retaining-your-best-people.

2. Anu Madgavkar, Schaninger, Bill, Smit, Sven, Woetzel, Jonathan, Samandari, Hamid, Carlin, Davis, Seong, Jeongmin, and Chockalingam, Kanmani, 2022, "Human Capital at Work: the Value of Experience," McKinsey Global Institute, available at https://www.mckinsey.com/capabilities/people-and-organizational-performance/our-insights/human-capital-at-work-the-value-of-experience.

3. Hoffman, Reid, Casnocha, Ben, and Yeh, Chris, 2013, "Tours of Duty: The New Employer-Employee Compact," *Harvard Business Review*, June, available at https://hbr.org/2013/06/tours-of-duty-the-new-employer-employee-compact.

4. Bernstein, Ethan and Turban, Stephen, 2018, "The Impact of the 'Open' Workspace on Human Collaboration," Philosophical Transactions of the Royal Society B, August 19, available at https://royalsocietypublishing.org/doi/10.1098/rstb.2017.0239.

5. Miller, Claire Cain, 2021, "Do Chance Meetings at the Office Boost Innovation? There's No Evidence of It," *New York Times*, June 23, available at https://www.nytimes.com/2021/06/23/upshot/remote-work-innovation-office.html.

6. Bloom, Nicholas, Han, Ruobing, and Liang, James, 2022, "How Hybrid Working From Home Works Out," National Bureau of Economic Research, July.

7. "Killing Time at Work '22," Qatalog and GitLab, 2022, available at https://assets.qatalog.com/language.work/Qatalog-Killing-Time-at-Work-22-Report.pdf.

8. "Transcript: Ezra Klein Interview with Anne Helen Petersen and Charlie Warzel," *New York Times*, August 16, 2022, available at https://www.nytimes.com/2022/08/16/podcasts/transcript-ezra-klein-interviews-anne-helen-petersen-charlie-warzel.html.

9. "Roger Martin: It's Time for Leaders to Embrace a New Way of Thinking," *Lead from the Heart Podcast*, May 20, 2022, available at https://markccrowley.com/roger-martin-its-time-for-leaders-to-embrace-a-new-way-of-thinking/.

10. Masters, Ryan K., Aron, Laudan Y., and Woolf, Steven H., 2022, "Changes in Life Expectancy Between 2019 and 2021: United States and Peer Countries," Medrxiv, April 7, available at https://www.medrxiv.org/content/10.1101/2022.04.05.22273393v1.

11. "The Loneliness Epidemic Persists: A Post-Pandemic Look at the State of Loneliness Among U.S. Adults," Cigna, 2022, available at https://newsroom.cigna.com/loneliness-epidemic-persists-post-pandemic-look.

12. Murthy, Vivek, 2017, "Work and the Loneliness Epidemic," *Harvard Business Review*, September 26, available at https://hbr.org/2017/09/work-and-the-loneliness-epidemic.

13. "The Loneliness Epidemic Persists."

14. Taylor, Helen and Vestergaard, Martin David, 2022, "Developmental Dyslexia: Disorder or Specialization in Exploration?" *Frontiers in Psychology*, 24 June 24, available at https://www.ncbi.nlm.nih.gov/pmc/articles/PMC9263984/.

15. Logan, Julie, 2009, "Dyslexic Entrepreneurs: The Incidence; Their Coping Strategies and Their Business Skills," Wiley InterScience, Wiley.

16. Sylvester, Rachel, 2022, "Interview: Richard Branson: Dyslexia Is My Superpower," *Times* (London), July 8, available at https://www.thetimes.co.uk/article/richard-branson-dyslexia-is-my-superpower-bh9m9zx58.

17. Bryant, Katherine, 2013, "Appreciating Neurodiversity: Learning from Synesthesia," *The Neuroethics Blog*, Emory Center for Ethics, April 23, available at http://www.theneuroethicsblog.com/2013/04/appreciating-neurodiversity-learning.html .

18. Marks, Lawrence E., 2014, "Synesthesia on Our Mind," May, available at https://www.researchgate.net/publication/314816855_Synesthesia_on_Our_Mind.

19. Holger, Dieter, 2019, "The Business Case for More Diversity," *Wall Street Journal*, October 26, available at https://www.wsj.com/articles/the-business-case-for-more-diversity-11572091200.

20. "Fortune and Refinitiv Launch Measure Up Partnership," 2020, available at https://fortunemediakit.com/fortune-and-refinitiv-launch-measure-up-partnership-encouraging-unprecedented-corporate-diversity-disclosure-and-accountability/.

21. Carr, P. B., and Walton, G. M., 2014, "Cues of Working Together Fuel Intrinsic Motivation," *Journal of Experimental Social Psychology*, 53, available at https://psycnet.apa.org/record/2014-16096-020.

22. Clark, Timothy R., 2020, *The 4 Stages of Psychological Safety*, Berrett-Koehler. Kindle edition, p. 124.

23. Silard, Anthony, 2022, "The Great Resignation Is a Crisis of Belonging. Here's the Real Way We Organize Ourselves at Work," *Fortune*, August, available at https://fortune.com/2022/08/25/great-resignation-belonging-work-leadership-anthony-silard/.

24. The Belong Index, 2022, available at https://belongeffect.sidlee.com/belong-index.

25. Edmondson, Amy C., 2019, *The Fearless Organization*, Wiley. Kindle edition, location 360.

26. Clark, *The 4 Stages of Psychological Safety*, p. 5.

27. Ibid.

28. Dyson, Esther, LinkedIn.com, available at https://www.linkedin.com/posts/estherdyson_careerkickstart-activity-6934900377574141952-hE_2/.

29. Sandvik, Jason, Saouma, Richard, Seegert, Nathan, and Stanton, Christopher T., 2020, "Workplace Knowledge Flows," National Bureau of Economic Research, January, available at https://www.nber.org/papers/w26660.

30. Kilduff, Gavin J., Galinsky, Adam D., Gallo, Edoardo, and Reade, J. James, 2015, "Whatever It Takes to Win: Rivalry Increases Unethical Behavior," Academy of Management, October 29, https://doi.org/10.5465/amj.2014.0545.

6 Enable Your Empowered Workforce

In his 1980 book *Fearfully and Wonderfully Made: A Surgeon Looks at the Human and Spiritual Body*, Dr. Paul Brand recounts attending a lecture by Margaret Mead. The anthropologist challenged her audience to identify the earliest signs of civilization, teasing the audience with possibilities – pottery, tools, cultivation. Then she answered her own question, holding aloft a fossilized femur. The bone showed a break that had healed. That healing, Mead asserted, was first evidence of a communal society.

In earlier fiercely competitive and predatory societies, a creature with such a significant injury would be left for dead. For the largest bone in the human body to have healed, Mead explained, someone must have cared for this person, tending the wound, feeding and protecting him for the four or more months it takes for this bone to heal. This act of kindness and caring, Mead might say, is the cornerstone of civil society, the belief that we are stronger together.

Fast-forward 15,000 years to the Industrial Age and it seems the workplace was too often reduced to a competitive and predatory environment. People were replaceable, if not disposable, parts of a production process, competing for resources (jobs, wages, benefits, the boss's attention, and other seeming advantages). Enter digital transformation and knowledge work, and *culture* and *collaboration* became the watchwords for highly effective teams. Yet, as one executive told us recently, the concept of culture seemed like a privilege reserved for select industries like financial services and high tech.

Perhaps so, if you view culture with a very narrow lens. We don't. Culture is the operating system of an organization. It is the code of conduct. The ethos, the purpose, and passion of an organization. The reductive view that culture is the place and style of work (nice offices, generous perks) fails the newly empowered workforce. It is a reflexive return to a pre-pandemic environment that stifles the collaboration and innovation most organizations, regardless of industry, hope to achieve.

Maybe, then, it's time to embrace the lesson of Margaret Mead's femur bone. Maybe it's time to heal ourselves at work?

Culture: The Operating Instructions for Your Organization

Over the near-decade of our collaboration, we have interviewed a wide range of successful leaders and nearly every conversation, at some point, comes back to the importance of culture. These leaders are mindful that culture is more than a wall-mounted list of virtues or a laundry list of amenities. Culture isn't about the work environment or benefits package and certainly isn't lip service to a set of ideals that are never fully realized.

Culture is a contract, sometimes written and often not, that directs how people within an organization choose to work together. Every organization has a culture. The best are intentional and well-articulated. High-functioning cultures are co-created, derived from the values and interests of leaders and employees and expressed in a shared understanding of the operating principles that drive success. They are celebrated and evidenced consistently in day-to-day decision making.

The worst cultures are accidental and unspoken. They are often the by-product of a leader's personality, and because they aren't well articulated, they shift. They lack consistency and clarity, are stressful, and often punishing. What works one day may not work the next. People assume context for decisions, but they can never be quite sure. They guess at what or how work is to be done. There is no clarity or consistency on what is expected, accepted, or tolerated. In other words, accidental cultures are almost always toxic.

Intentional culture is just the opposite. It may stem from an individual founder or leader, but it is documented and discussed. Organizational values are clear and these clear values underpin decision making. People know what is in – and out of – bounds. They know what is expected of them, usually without being told. Culture is just what you do.

Change happens on top of a strong culture, not to one. That consistency matters. Culture is the operating system. It's how everyone in the organization understands and has context for actions and decisions. Culture enables distributed decision making – because people understand the context and parameters for actions. You work and decide and act within the cultural framework. Culture – well-defined culture – allows a business to grow and scale because everyone knows what they are working for and how to work together.

Recognizing Toxic Culture

How can you tell if you're working in (or, worse, contributing to) a toxic culture? The signs are everywhere. Stress levels are high. Decision making is slow. People tend to feel underappreciated or believe they are treated unfairly. And the telltale sign? These organizations tend to experience high rates of employee turnover, as compared with other companies in their industry sector.

In a research paper published in *MIT Sloan Management Review,* Donald Sull, Charles Sull, and Ben Zweig analyzed LinkedIn profiles and more than 1.4 million Glassdoor reviews in search of the cause of the Great Resignation. They found that corporate culture, more than any other factor, is the most accurate predictor of employee attrition. A toxic culture, they write, "is 10.4 times more powerful than compensation in predicting a company's attrition rate compared with its industry."[1]

Using their "Natural Employee Understanding" technology to analyze employee comments, the researchers found "failure to promote diversity, equity, and inclusion; workers feeling disrespected; and unethical behavior" were the leading contributors to dysfunctional, toxic culture.

Building Mindful Culture

Work doesn't have to be that way, and in many, many organizations, vibrant cultures are built on a foundation of shared values and trust, and nurtured with mindful intention. In our work, we've found that this mindfulness toward culture is a leading indicator of a healthy, learning, and engaging workplace. We'll share two examples.

Nurturing Culture Through Dialogue

Culture is one of the most misunderstood and misused terms, bandied about by business leaders without much consideration.

Too often, leaders and employees focus on the artifacts of a culture – the perks of the job, the design of the workspace, the on-site services, and miss the culture itself. These things are a set of decisions that, in the best of circumstances, express the culture without being culture themselves.

This attention to the artifacts is often the result of a corporate culture crafted by leadership and dictated to the rank and file. When culture is a set of edicts – "This is who we are. This is what we believe. We seek people who are in lock step with us" – that is more cult than culture, a one-directional monologue from the C-suite to the line employee. A narrow culture with tight parameters used as a filter to screen for like-minded employees is a monolithic organization that is inherently at odds with diversity, equity, inclusion, and belonging (DEIB) initiatives.

A culture that values peers as collaborators rather than competitors creates a conversation. Shared values are a foundation to which employees can bring new perspectives. By contributing the things you believe, your aspirations for yourself and the organization and the individual and collective impact you hope to have in the world, you add to the culture rather than conform to it. Listening and evolving, then, are key attributes of a vibrant and enriching culture, one that senses, responds, and adapts to ultimately become the change you seek to be in the world.

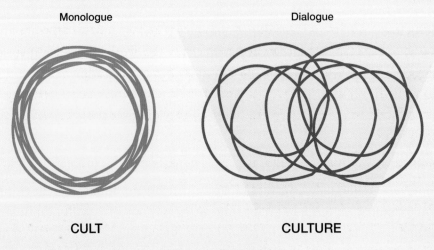

Figure 6.1 Nurturing Culture Through Dialogue

Concept credit: Based upon work by David Gray (Culture vs. Cult Circles).

One is a management and innovation consulting firm that focuses on funding and scaling high-potential start-up ventures. Over decades of work, they recognize the importance of nurturing their collaborative culture. They deeply value collective intelligence and affirm that commitment at the outset of every meeting. They embody the African proverb, "If you want to go fast, go alone. If you want to go far, go together." Their impressive track record shows they have cracked the code on how to go far together.

The second is an international social venture that enumerates its values and shares them anytime they bring someone new into the organization. They make mindfulness a practice of every meeting – in person or virtual – and they recognize that no one person, regardless of tenure or status in the company, has all the answers. Articulating that value with the simple notation "We > I," this organization embraces diversity and belonging as core tenets of their high-functioning culture.

To some, the idea of starting a meeting with a recommitment to values or a moment of mindful meditation may sound cultlike. In fact, it's quite the opposite. A cult is an unthinking devotion to a singular person or perspective. A living, breathing culture is a commitment to an inclusive conversation. A culture that values peers as collaborators is one that listens, senses, and responds, and adapts. (See "Nurturing Culture Through Dialogue.")

Living Your Values

It's one thing – one very important thing – to develop and articulate corporate values internally. It's quite another to live them in the marketplace. Yet doing so is increasingly tied to business success. By a large and growing margin (82%), consumers want to buy from brands that reflect their values and many (39%) say they will stop buying from even favorite brands if they discover those brands don't support their values.[2]

Few companies live their values as well as Patagonia, the adventure sportswear company. The company makes no bones about its progressive politics and its environmental advocacy. In fact, you're more likely to find an invitation to register to vote splashed across the top of the company's website than a come-on for one of their quality fleece pullovers. Click through on the Activism link and you'll find one of the company's core values: "We are in business to save the planet. We aim to use the resources we have – our voice, our business and our community – to do something about our climate crisis."

The company puts this belief into everything they do. They create products in the most environmentally responsible manner and when customers' gear or clothing wear out, they take it back in a program called Worn Wear, to repair, share, and recycle because, as the website shamelessly says, "The best thing we can do for the planet is cut down on consumption and get more use out of stuff we already own." Items in the Worn Wear shop are often less than half the price of new gear, which helps Patagonia and its customers work together to stay true to their values.

In 2018, the company earmarked the $10 million the company would save as a result of the Tax Cut and Jobs Act to support environmental causes. Writing on LinkedIn, then CEO Rose Marcario wrote, "Based on last year's irresponsible tax cut, Patagonia will owe less in taxes this year – $10 million less, in fact. Instead of putting the money back into our business, we're responding by putting $10 million back into the planet. We recognize that our planet is in peril."[3]

The next year, after seeing a post from an influential, though not values-aligned, Instagrammer who was showing off his branded Patagonia fleece vest, Patagonia changed its corporate sales programs to ensure that the companies it works with align to Patagonia's values.[4]

Most dramatically, in the fall of 2022, founder Yvon Chouinard transferred ownership of the company to a nonprofit organization to ensure that profits are channeled to fight climate change. To punctuate his point, Chouinard announced on their website and in press releases, "Earth is now our only shareholder."[5]

We belabor the point here to make a point. Patagonia is choosing values over profits and that choice is not impacting profits. The company continues to grow and does well by doing good. As a private company, Patagonia doesn't report its financials, but its annual B-Corp reports reveal a litany of positive, values-based impacts that could not be possible if the company didn't have the profits to support its impact.

Not every company can be a Patagonia, at least not at the start. But every company can decide to make its values the vanguard of its market presence. (See "Beliefs + Behaviors + Benefits = Culture.") Doing so, we're convinced, reaps tremendous benefits along multiple vectors.

Beliefs + Behaviors + Benefits = Culture

The word culture gets thrown around a lot in organizations. People say things like, "We have a great culture," and "He just didn't fit in our culture," and "I want to protect our culture." But ask those same people to describe their culture and the conversation gets a lot more quiet.

The sure sign of a thriving, productive culture is the ability for its members to be able to articulate what the organization really believes. It can be a simple statement that describes why the company was formed or what it hopes to achieve in the world.

Behaviors are expressions of the decisions we make in concert with our beliefs. The way we act and impact both inside and outside the company – how our products and production impact the world, how we treat employees and customers, how we distribute profits, all of that speaks volumes about what we really believe.

Benefits are the measure of the impact of our beliefs and behaviors. Very specifically, you might ask, who is advantaged by the business. In the Friedman Shareholder Value era, the list of beneficiaries started and ended with the owners of the company. In the Human Value Era, the list is much longer: owners and investors, certainly, but also workers, customers, suppliers, communities, and the environment.

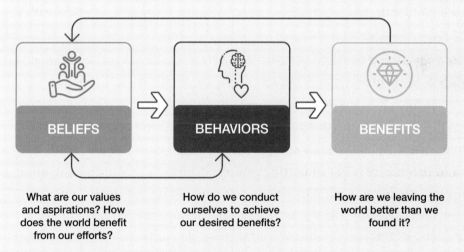

BELIEFS	BEHAVIORS	BENEFITS
What are our values and aspirations? How does the world benefit from our efforts?	How do we conduct ourselves to achieve our desired benefits?	How are we leaving the world better than we found it?

Figure 6.2 Beliefs + Behaviors + Benefits = Culture

Trust: The Cornerstone of Healthy Culture

Even the most elegantly framed culture is just an empty statement without trust. Culture is actuated by people, people who work in concert with shared values, mutual respect, and – most necessarily – implicit trust. Without trust, the potential of your culture cannot be realized.

But I *do* trust my people, you say, as you micromanage every task and deploy keyboard trackers and other surveillance software to monitor work-from-home hours and activities. That is not trust. Demanding that people return to the office only so that you can see them work is not trust. Team meetings centered on management monologues filled with directives and demands is not trust. Trust – or the lack of it – is expressed in every interaction, every mandate, every conversation. How you lead demonstrates your trust in your team. And whether your team can trust you.

Trust runs up and down the org chart. The simplest, and sometimes hardest, way to achieve that bi-directionality is to operate with transparency. You will make mistakes. Own them. Correct them. Owning and correcting errors is a sign you have listened, heard, and empathized with the concerns of your employees and your customers.

Another way to earn trust is to actively invite your employees into the decision-making process and – this is the important part – respecting and making room for their concerns and contributions. Throughout 2022, companies everywhere are debating (and oftentimes mandating) return-to-office (RTO) policies, and many corporate leaders have been stunned by employee resistance to these directives, perhaps none more publicly than Apple. An employee group calling itself Apple Together launched a petition that gathered more than 1,000 signatures in a matter of days after Apple CEO Tim Cook issued a return to office mandate for the entire company. "This uniform mandate from senior leadership does not consider the unique demands of each job role nor the diversity of individuals," the petition website asserted.[6]

Compare that approach with that of Cockroach Labs, Inc., a database software developer. As the Covid-19 virus seemed to ebb in the spring of 2022, the company engaged their staff as they created a workable RTO program and together they devised three options: fully in-office (main lab), hybrid (mixing labs), or fully remote (nodes). Employees can choose the options that best fit their unique personal and professional needs. Financial incentives are equalized by offering in-office "main lab" people dedicated workspaces and meal plans while giving hybrid "mixing labs" and remote "nodes" workers budgets to outfit their home offices. And every employee, regardless of where they work, has learning, development, and advancement opportunities because, after all, these programs that develop human capital are in the best interest of the company.

"We are in completely uncharted waters," Cockroach Labs' Chief People Officer Lindsay Grenawalt observed in an interview with *Fast Company* magazine. "But not knowing is exciting. It means we can define the future. We can find out what works, give our employees options so they feel in control of the experience, and design this new world together."[7]

Prioritizing employee preference, well-being, and experience does more than shore up company culture. It has real-world financial impacts. For the first time in its more than two-decade history, the 2021 Edelman Trust Barometer found that business leaders now believe their employees – more than customers, investors, or any other stakeholders – contribute most to their company's success. Even more interesting, we think, 90% of customers said brands must be good to their employees, prioritizing worker well-being and financial security over corporate profits, or risk losing brand loyalty.[8]

That finding correlates with the work of Tiffani Bova, author of *Growth IQ*. Her research shows that companies in the top quartile of employee experiences had both higher revenue and profitability.[9] It makes sense. Companies that create positive experiences and trusted relationships with their employees have higher levels of retention and engagement, which in turn means that a more experienced staff is better equipped to handle customer needs. Meeting customer needs, by extension, drives higher revenue and profitability.

Finding Purpose at Work

Hand in hand, culture and purpose are the super fuel of your organization and the key to unlocking scale. Purpose, though, is not one singular thing. It is faceted and nuanced. (See "The Three Faces of Purpose."). Purpose can be inwardly directed, as in a goal, or outwardly projected, as a deed undertaken for others. But, when people throughout the organization share common values and are aligned by purpose, they have an aspirational and shared understanding and solid frame in which to do their work.

In a late 2021 survey, Gartner found that 52% of workers questioned the purpose of their efforts on the job.[10] Sit with that for a moment. More than half of all people who show up for work are wondering if their work fulfills something bigger in their lives and in the world.

The Three Faces of Purpose

Purpose. A simple word with a complex set of meanings, each of which has some impact on how you lead. We looked at the many ways purpose is expressed and found three basic applications.

Intentional Purpose is internalized, often individualized, purpose. It is an inward idea, directed outwardly. When something is not an accident, it is done "on purpose." Our actions are directed toward an outcome. We do things with purpose – with intent – hundreds of times a day. Inventions can be ordinary – for example, I intend to do the grocery shopping after work. They can become a habit, like morning coffee. They can be motivating: I intend to see this through. In business, intention tends to be the everyday goals and objectives of the organization: sales targets, product plans, marketing initiatives, that sort of thing.

Intention is a practical kind of purpose. It is *doing to*. It is me-to-you or us-to-them. It is self-directed toward a goal or achievement, and when you achieve your goal, it's often quite satisfying. In that way, Intentional Purpose can be very transactional.

Extrinsic Purpose runs in the opposite direction. It is a desire to deliver something that others want or need. Think of phrases like "purpose built." You know exactly what the customer wants because you have – at best – co-created the product or service with them. Extrinsic purpose is *doing for*. It is you-to-me or them-to-us. In business, Extrinsic Purpose can be opportunistic. You see a problem, a need, a desire and you rush to meet it with exactly what the customer wants.

The third type of purpose – and the one that really drives your unique competitive advantage – is Aspirational Purpose. It is, what some might say, a calling or a passion. Aspirational Purpose is an ideal that is bigger than any one person, any one product, or any one quarterly result. It's the reason you open the doors – real or virtual – of your business each day. It is your reason for being. It sustains you when things get really hard. And it is the reason for celebrating when things go right.

Aspirational Purpose is *doing with*. It is a collective "we" that asks what does the world need from us and how can we achieve it together. Aspirational Purpose serves the greater good. The goal is so audacious and worthwhile that it becomes its own source of energy.

Collectively, these three faces of purpose provide the motivation that turns your organization into a self-guided operation, taking that lead or a back seat depending on the situation, but always present together to achieve better outcomes.

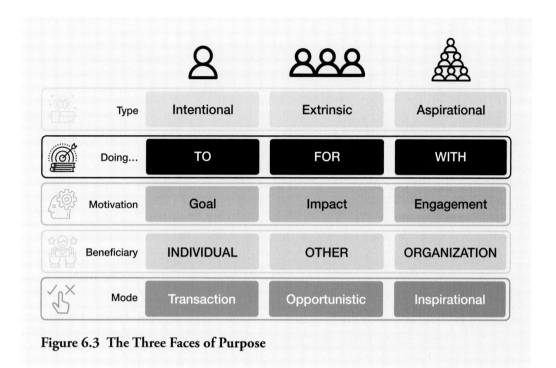

	Type	Intentional	Extrinsic	Aspirational
	Doing...	TO	FOR	WITH
	Motivation	Goal	Impact	Engagement
	Beneficiary	INDIVIDUAL	OTHER	ORGANIZATION
	Mode	Transaction	Opportunistic	Inspirational

Figure 6.3 The Three Faces of Purpose

And this: Gen Z – the age cohort that will soon represent a third of the US workforce – would rather work for a company that gives them a sense of purpose than one that gives them a bigger paycheck.[11]

People are more motivated and more engaged when they feel a sense of shared purpose. That shared purpose makes people feel valued and appreciated. It makes them feel seen, respected, validated, and empowered. Because purpose is bigger than any one person, command-and-control management becomes virtually unnecessary because everyone operates by a set of common assumptions. Decision making becomes more distributed because the criteria of choice are well defined by organizational objectives. Hierarchical reporting structures flatten into more efficient information and decision flows because the guidelines of culture and purpose are both instructive and directive.

Consider what happened at one Fortune 500 technology company, known for its strong culture and well-articulated values. An obviously upset customer reached a customer service agent who, following protocols, quickly resolved the customer's issue. Before ending the call, though, the agent asked an atypical question: "Ma'am, are you okay?" The customer sighed and apologized. She was not her usual calm and happy self, she explained, because her beloved dog had died that morning. The agent made his condolences and finished the call.

Then, he did something extraordinary.

He looked up the customer's address, called a local florist, used his personal credit card, and sent a bouquet of flowers along with the company's expression of sympathy. A few days later, social media was abuzz with this act of kindness. It was an authentic customer endorsement that no company can buy. Why did the support agent send flowers? Because the primary tenet of the company is to delight the customer, and this customer needed a lift.

Some companies could find a lot wrong with this agent's actions. He went off script in the support call. He didn't pick up the next call immediately. He wasn't authorized to send flowers on behalf of the company. That's not what happened here. Instead, the company created discretionary spending accounts for customer-facing employees so that they wouldn't have out-of-pocket expenses when faced with an extraordinary opportunity to delight the customer. As importantly, the company didn't put a lot of rules and reporting around the use of this account. Instead, it trusted that the shared culture, values, and purpose was enough to guide employee decision making.

It's a story worth telling because it illustrates our key point: culture and purpose are the foundation for the trust and autonomy that empower workers to engage as a team working in league to a greater end.

Purpose: Your Most Enduring Competitive Advantage

If our advice to embrace trust and autonomy have not been a clarion call for you, allow us to make this one additional point. Workplace trust and worker autonomy are not an act of faith. They are an alignment of purpose. When we know that we are working toward a shared purpose, trust is easy and autonomy is respect.

This is no doubt why return-to-office mandates are meeting so much resistance. Without clear and obvious purpose, the requirement to be present in the office – made worse by mandating scheduled appearances – sends a clear message to your team: I don't fully trust you, and I don't fully respect you.

Instead, use purpose to fuel your organization.

Consider all the ways that can happen.

It is your best recruiting tool.

It is your best retention tool.

It is your best sales tool.

It is your best brand tool.

In the Human Value Era, people have greater agency and more alternatives. To compete for talent, your organization needs an advantage. That advantage is your Aspirational Purpose. (See "Three Faces of Purpose") Material compensation can be matched and topped. Another company is always willing to give your best worker more pay, a more flexible schedule, a tonier title. Purpose, though, is the *ultimate reason* for the work. (See "The Great Reset Opportunity: Why We Work.")

That's why Aspirational Purpose is your unique competitive advantage. Your Aspirational Purpose is a signifier. It does the heavy lifting of attracting workers, customers, and stakeholders. By wearing your purpose on your sleeve, you are sending signals to your tribe. You are making a declaration about where you uniquely stand in the world. You are also sending a clear message to those who do not share your purpose: this organization is not for you.

And never has that been more important than now, in today's market.

Purpose plays a role in doing the work, too. When things get tough – and these last few years have demonstrated just how tough things can get – purpose keeps your people and your customers coming back. Purpose is the work that must be done. It demands your time and attention. It is what you want to do, not what you have to do. It makes hard, messy work, even unpleasant work, doable.

It is the clarifying context that frames every decision. Most of all, it is a magnet. It attracts like-minded, equally passionate people to your organization.

Purpose also enables your organization to adapt, because it centers the business on a motivation that is bigger than any one product, service, or business plan. We saw this writ large during the pandemic. The companies that survived – and even thrived – in those initial challenging months and beyond, those that adapted to new realities more easily, were the companies, organizations, or teams that had living, authentic, well-understood cultures, and even more importantly, these companies had a clear purpose.

The Great Reset Opportunity: Why We Work

In a call to offer Chris her first professional job after college, the recruiter rattled off details of the offer, including "many, many benefits." The recruiter wasn't able to enumerate any of those benefits, but assured her that this was a job awash with perks. The perks, it seemed, were the selling point.

Many years later, too many employers lean on salary, title, and perks to sell the job, never mind that most potential employees have moved well beyond those incentives. Compensation is just one of many levers, and employers would do well to work them all, in combination, to find the mix that is truly motivating for each employee.

Compensation. Yes, of course, pay your people well and fairly, particularly in the competitive market of empowered workers.

Physical and Psychological Safety. Workplace safety, long the province of OSHA and HR, took on even greater importance in the face of a pandemic. Now, simple interactions with coworkers and customers pose real risk, and employers need to honor the concerns and provide a range of options for workers to feel physically safe at work. As importantly, you need to let your people know that it is okay to mitigate personal risk, just one (major) step toward providing the psychological safety workers need so that they feel able to contribute fully. As work explores new frontiers of creative productivity, your teams also need the assurance that experimentation, learning, and sometimes failure are valued in the process of innovation. Failure is an option and an opportunity to learn, rather than a permit to punish.

Values and Impact. In an existential crisis – and face it, for many the pandemic was exactly that – it is reasonable to question the role of work. With Gen Z and Millennials at the vanguard, many workers retrenched in their values, deciding to work only with companies that allowed them to be their authentic and vulnerable selves. As an employer, you will attract the very best people by expressing your values, celebrating your impact in the world, and making clear the alignment of your corporate purpose with their identity and self-expression.

Flexibility: Lifestyle + Balance. We are facing a burnout crisis in the United States. Of those switching jobs in 2021, 89% cited burnout and lack of flexibility and support as reasons to leave a job.[12] LinkedIn has seen a 343% increase in mentions of flexibility in job postings since 2019.[13] In this milieu, employers simply must provide flexibility to workers who are no longer willing to sacrifice life for work.

Career Accelerant. Learning is becoming as important as earning. Learning is the accelerant to advancement and opportunity, and employees at every level see education as the path to more fulfilling work. In fact, Pew Research found, after compensation workers cited "no opportunities for advancement" as the second driver for leaving a job.[14] Ask yourself: What are you doing to build learning into every job?

Figure 6.4 The Great Reset Opportunity: Why We Work

Consider one of the most hard-hit industries in 2020, the restaurant business. The fine dining establishments that realized they were in the food business – not the "serve people in our dining room" business – adapted menus for takeout and kept their supply chains in business by becoming retail grocers and butchers. Some offered clever, purposeful marketing offers, becoming philanthropists by offering buy one/give one meals that fed both customers and essential workers at hospitals and care facilities. And in a very specific act of business need meeting community need, restaurants in the Cape Cod outpost of Provincetown, Massachusetts, began offering grocery delivery to assist the immunocompromised folks in a community with a high percentage of people with HIV/AIDS.

When the pandemic shuttered a number of high-end restaurants in San Francisco, the brigade of chefs started Zoom-based cooking classes, sending ingredients by courier to enrolled students. Their purpose – to introduce people to extraordinary food – was bigger than a restaurant venue. And so a thriving business bridged these chefs until they could get back to their restaurant kitchens.

Our bet: none of these restaurant entrepreneurs intended to go into food delivery, grocery, or digital learning businesses. But the alternative – closing their businesses for good – was a far more scary outcome. So they braved the steep and rapid learning curve, took a bet that the finances of the business model would break even, and trusted that loyal customers would form the core clientele for their classes, takeout services, grocery delivery, and other business experiments. Their passion for food and a deep desire to retain and support their people and their customers provided the incentive to find new ways to do what they love amid extreme limitations.

It's the same for you, regardless of the challenges you face. Clear-sighted purpose is the foundation of effective culture and the key to successful business adaptation. It is, in fact, the unique expression of why your company exists – and sets you apart. It can set you above.

The Trouble with Purpose

Now, here's the trouble with purpose: it keeps you true. You cannot claim one thing and do another. If your purpose, for example, is to reduce landfill waste, you can't fill the company refrigerator with water in plastic bottles and ship your products in layers of bubble wrap. Those behaviors do not square with your purpose.

If your purpose is to make people secure in a connected, digital world, you probably can't open a revenue stream selling customer data. It isn't aligned.

If your purpose is to turn customers on to healthy organic foods, you shouldn't fill the break room vending machine with processed snacks. It isn't aligned.

We can think of many examples, but the point is this: you have to look for alignment in every part of your business. In the products and services you sell, in the way you market them, and in the way you compensate and treat your employees and partners.

And this is important: you have to create an environment where it is safe for someone to tell you when you're out of alignment. In fact, not just safe, but celebrated. When everyone looks out for misalignment, everyone is working to the same purpose.

Make your purpose evident in everything you do, everything you say, everything you sell, everyone you hire. Make your purpose a beacon so that your tribe can find you. Other companies can build similar things. They can provide better pay and perks. They can buy more advertising. But they can't *out-purpose* you once you have established your one, true, immutable purpose.

That advantage will always fall to you.

Notes

1. Sull, Donald, Sull, Charles, and Zweig, Ben, 2022, "Toxic Culture Is Driving the Great Resignation," MIT Sloan Management Review, January 11, available at https://sloanreview.mit.edu/article/toxic-culture-is-driving-the-great-resignation/.

2. Bounfantino, Giusy, 2022, "New Research Shows Consumers More Interested in Brands' Values than Ever," Consumer Goods Technology, April 24, available at https://consumergoods.com/new-research-shows-consumers-more-interested-brands-values-ever.

3. Marcario, Rose, 2018, "Our Urgent Gift to the Planet," Linkedin .com, November 28, available at https://www.linkedin.com/pulse/our-urgent-gift-planet-rose-marcario/.

4. DeFrancesco, Dan, 2019, "The 'Midtown Uniform' Is Now in Peril as Patagonia Isn't Accepting New Finance Clients for Its Ubiquitous Fleece Vests," Business Insider, April 2, available at https://www.businessinsider .com/the-midtown-uniform-is-now-in-peril-as-patagonia-isnt-accepting-new-finance-clients-for-its-ubiquitous-fleece-vests-2019-4.

5. Chouinard, Yves, 2022, "Earth Is Now Our Only Shareholder," Patagonia website, https://www.patagonia.com/ownership/.

6. "Tell Apple: We Demand Location Flexible Work," Apple Together, available at https://act.appletogether.org/flexible-work-arrangements.

7. Grenawalt, Lindsay, 2022, "What Flexibility Really Looks Like in the Future of Work," *Fast Company*, April 22, available at https://www.fastcompany .com/90741975/what-flexibility-really-looks-like-in-the-future-of-work.

8. Roach, Cydney, 2021, "Employees Now Considered Most Important Stakeholders in Long-Term Success" Edelman Trust Barometer, available at https://www.edelman.com/trust/2021-trust-barometer/spring-update/ employees-now-considered.

9. Gautier, Kate, Bova, Tiffani, Chen, Kexin, and Munasinghe, Lalith, 2022, "Research: How Employee Experience Impacts Your Bottom Line," *Harvard Business Review*, March 22, available at https://hbr.org/2022/03/ research-how-employee-experience-impacts-your-bottom-line.

10. Wiles, Jackie, 2022, "Employees Seek Personal Value and Purpose at Work: Be Prepared to Deliver," Gartner, January 12, available at https:// www.gartner.com/en/articles/employees-seek-personal-value-and-purpose- at-work-be-prepared-to-deliver.

11. "2022 Great Resignation: The State of Internal Mobility and Employee Retention Report," Lever, 2022, available at https://www.lever.co/ research/2022-internal-mobility-and-employee-retention-report.

12. "From the Great Resignation to the Great Reskilling: Insight on What's Next for the 'Great Resigners,'" Cengage Group, January 2022, available at https:// cengage.widen.net/s/78hrkqgfj7/cg-great-resigners-research-report-final.

13. "2022 Global Talent Trends: The Reinvention of Company Culture," LinkedIn Talent Solutions, 2022, available at https://business.linkedin.com/ content/dam/me/business/en-us/talent-solutions-lodestone/body/pdf/global_ talent_trends_2022.pdf.

14. Parker, Kim, and Menasce Horowitz, Julia, 2022, "Majority of Workers Who Quit a Job in 2021 Cite Low Pay, No Opportunities for Advancement, Feeling Disrespected," Pew Research, March, available at https://www .pewresearch.org/ft_22-03-09_resignation-featured-image/.

15. Braham, Jeanne and Peterson, Pam, 1999, *Starry, Starry Night: Provincetown's Response to the AIDS Crisis,* Brookline Books.

16. "Massachusetts HIV/AIDS Epidemiologic Profile Statewide Report," Massachusetts Department of Public Health, Bureau of Infectious Disease and Laboratory Sciences, February 2022, available at https://www.mass.gov/doc/ statewide-report-data-as-of-112022/download.

The Canteen: Becoming a Place of Purpose and Belonging

Follow Route 6 down Cape Cod, and you will eventually come to Provincetown, Massachusetts, or "P-town" as the locals and regular vacationers are more apt to call it. Just off the shores of Provincetown, the Pilgrims signed the first governing document of the New World, the Mayflower Compact. Fishermen maintain an active commercial harbor there, regularly hauling in more than three million pounds of lobster, sea scallops and mussels, among other fish each year. Yet P-town is perhaps best known as a vibrant artist community and a gay enclave, a safe harbor, a place of belonging and self-expression.

In the 80s, this community came together like few others when the HIV/AIDS crisis gripped this hamlet of about 3,500 full-time residents. In their 1994 book *Starry, Starry Night: Provincetown's Response to the AIDS Crisis,* writer Jeanne Braham and psychologist Pam Peterson describe the "extraordinary . . . communal response" to the AIDS crisis in Provincetown and the "astonishing degree of trust"[15] that tie residents together in a landscape that is idyllic in summer and outright treacherous in winter.

Against that backdrop, more than 30 years later, the community of Provincetown came together again as Covid-19 spread across the country. In a community where more than 16% of the population is living with AIDS[16] and the median age is 56, the pandemic presented a specific risk to immunocompromised and older residents. And it is here where we see the confluence of purpose, adaptation, and belonging.

Rob Anderson and his partner Loic Rossignon are the owners of the Canteen, a restaurant neatly tucked among the shops on Commercial Street in Provincetown. Since it opened in 2011, the Canteen has grown from a casual New England eatery to the center of community life, employing 50 people, hosting a winter carnival, catering holiday meals, and remaining open year-round in a highly seasonal tourist town. It's no surprise, then, that what began as a personal response to COVID-19 turned into something much larger for these two restaurateurs.

"When the pandemic first started, I was afraid to go to the grocery store, so instead of going, I thought I would order things from the restaurant purveyors, who would be coming here anyway," Rob told us. The owners kept the restaurant open but changed its service to "keep things safe." Soon he realized that his staff had the same need as he and Loic. "Since I was ordering food for myself, I might as well order food for our staff, since they were afraid of going to the store too. And, if I could help them limit their exposure to the outside world, it would be good for them, for the business, and for us personally."

It didn't take long before Rob widened the circle further, inviting people throughout the community to order what they needed, too. "I realized that if a lot of people were getting their groceries this way, we might even be able to help keep infections down in our community."

Pretty quickly, the Canteen evolved into a 24-hour grocery ordering and delivery service, then morphed once again into community activism. Because P-town depends on the kind of businesses that were hit hardest by Covid-19 – tourism and restaurants, primarily – many residents had lost their jobs and were struggling to make ends meet. Moreover, P-town struggled with the same supply chain issues that hit communities across the country; simply getting food and supplies to town was a challenge. "We started offering free groceries to people who were financially unable to afford them. Our intention was to just pay for those groceries ourselves – one or two people a day. But then people started offering to donate money to us to help us expand the program. We received thousands of dollars in donations, which allowed us to really give anyone who identified themselves as being in need anything they needed."

By adapting their business to meet the moment, Rob and Loic put the power of purpose and belonging in sharp relief. They became not just a transactional business but a relational place of community and belonging. "It became a win-win-win-win-win for everyone really. It kept Loic and me busy. It kept people safe at home. It helped a lot of people who were struggling, either health wise or financially or both. It even helped people who had the means to help people find an outlet to do that," Rob said.

Most importantly, "It helped to create a lot of connections and joy between people. It was fun and joyful during a dark time."

Part III

Rethinking Your Leadership

"**I**'m CEO, bitch . . ."[1]

The storied tagline on Mark Zuckerberg's early business cards, made famous in the 2010 docudrama *The Social Network* and confirmed by the designer who created the card, speaks volumes about the young founder and the culture of leadership he created. "It's no secret that Mark looked up to Steve Jobs," Andrew Bosworth wrote in response to a question about the tagline on the query site Quora. Zuckerberg ran meetings "in that classic 'aggressive' Steve Jobs-style. It was during one of those meetings where I remember him first uttering the phrase, 'I'm CEO, bitch . . .'"

Boswell recalls Zuckerberg's business cards as "an excellent representation of the company culture at the time. Their [eventual] replacement reflected the changes a young Facebook needed to go through in order to be where it is today."

Whether grounded in insecurity or arrogance or something in between, young Zuckerberg's story echoes across generations of leaders who presume that to lead is to be the unquestioned boss, the one with all the answers, and all the authority. It's a tall order to be the one in charge, and many leaders, feeling they aren't up for the challenge, overcompensate with a business card, a booming voice, an intemperate management style. That "impression management," first described in 1959 by Erving Goffman in his book *The Presentation of Self in Everyday Life*, is the conscious or subconscious behavioral adjustments in order to present oneself as powerful, positive, and in control.

Human insecurity comes as a result of our rapid ascension up the food chain, Yuval Noah Harari posits in *Sapiens: A Brief History of Humankind*. Most top predators found their spot in the pecking order over millions of years. Humans jumped from middle to top in just about 100,000 years. "Most top predators of the planet are majestic creatures," Harari writes. "Millions of years of dominion have filled them with self-confidence. Sapiens by contrast is more like a banana republic dictator. Having so recently been one of the underdogs of the savannah, we are full of fears and anxieties over our position."[2]

Surely there is a metaphor here for how quickly many leaders climbed their career ladders, scurrying from rung to rung, never fully confident that their expertise had developed fully for the moment. Just. Like. Everyone. Else.

Speaking to the leadership team at a large media company, Heather reassured the audience that most leaders find themselves in this same spot. They are leading people with more and different experiences and expertise. After the talk, one executive took her aside. "You are speaking about me," the executive said. "They just did a massive reorganization and now everyone reporting to me has skills and knowledge I do not have. They are the experts. I have never felt this unsure and unsettled."

Chances are, you've felt the same way. Or you will.

At the very least, you are in good company. But the news is even better. As uncomfortable as it may be, and as counterintuitive as it may seem, this is *exactly where you need to be* to lead the newly empowered workforce.

Modern leadership requires a reckoning with our discomfort. It demands courage to not know and the vulnerability to admit your gaps to your team. Leadership now leverages a whole new skill set that we are just beginning to understand.

In *The Adaptation Advantage,* we noted marketing guru Seth Godin's belief that "managers manage processes and leaders lead change." To that maxim we add this: "It is all change now, and that requires a shift from management to drive productivity to leadership to inspire human potential."[3]

Now, we push that notion even further and perhaps make it less daunting. After all, few of us feel capable of delivering the rousing Knute Rockne locker room pep talk that inspires championship performances season after season. Most of us, however, do have the compassion and patience and temperament – and above all else, the *empathy* – to find that thing that helps our people find their intrinsic motivations and strong desire to work effectively, individually and collaboratively.

That's the new work of an organizational leader. Part coach, part mentor, part safety monitor, part interpreter, part career counselor, and maybe even part therapist, all to identify what makes individual workers tick so that you can provide the motivational fuel and connect their work to organizational needs. You are a catalyst now, and you work for your people, so that they will work for your organization.

If you are apprehensive about this new role, you are not alone. In the next few chapters, we will explore what it means to make the leap from unquestioned leader, devising game plans and shouting orders from the sidelines, to the collaborative coach, identifying the unique contributions of each team member and aligning them to the ambitions of the organization.

It should come as a relief that the new leader of the empowered workforce is not an all-knowing, authoritarian, directives-barking, stress-eating boss. That's an exhausting role that takes from you more than it returns. The new leader is a coach, a catalyst, an empath, an actual human being helping other human beings do their best work for a common goal.

In these next chapters, let's breathe deeply together and discover what it takes to achieve the satisfaction that accrued to the enabling leader.

Key Takeaways:

- The role of leader has shifted from all-knowing, authoritative director to curious coach and enabling mentor of a multitalented team.

- Work has changed from tasks executed in isolation and reliant on individual contributions to collaborative navigation and discovery that leverages collective intelligence.

- You have within you the capacity to be the empathic leader inspiring your team to achieve more than you collectively thought possible. It's time to tap that capacity.

- To thrive, we must embrace the Human Value Era.

Notes

1. Veloso, Bryan, 2010, "What's the story behind Mark Zuckerberg's fabled 'I'm CEO. . .bitch!' business card? Is that a true story? Does anyone have a copy of that card?" Quora, June 16, available at https://www.quora.com/Whats-the-story-behind-Mark-Zuckerberg%E2%80%99s-fabled-Im-CEO-bitch-business-card-Is-that-a-true-story-Does-anyone-have-a-copy-of-that-card.

2. Harari, Yuval Noah, 2015, *Sapiens: A Brief History of Humankind*, Harper Perennial; eBook location: 229 of 7353.

3. McGowan, Heather E. and Shipley, Chris, 2020, *The Adaptation Advantage: Let Go, Learn Fast, and Thrive in the Future of Work*, Wiley, p. 219.

7 Pilot Your Expedition Team

On May 24, 2010, Alison Levine reached the summit of Mt. Everest. That touch at the top of the world completed her Adventure Grand Slam, conquering the highest peaks on every continent and reaching both the North and South Poles.

As Levine tells it in her must-see Ted Talk,[1] reaching the summit was not nearly as important as "the journey and how you will use its lessons to be better and stronger." The author, leadership consultant, and inspiration knows of what she speaks. Her 2010 summit wasn't her first attempt.

Nearly a decade before, Levine captained the first American Women's Expedition, a quest that turned back by bad weather just a few hundred feet from the summit. "You have to be able to make tough decisions when the conditions around you are far from perfect," Levine told her audience at TedX Midwest in 2011. (Levine recounts the story of this expedition in *On the Edge*, published in 2014.)

Conditions were far from perfect when she set out for the top of Everest a second time on May 24, 2010. She describes ominous weather, snow and wind with "absolutely horrible" visibility. With sheer drop-offs on either side of the trail and fellow climbers turning back, Levine pressed forward. "Sometimes," she said, "you don't have to have total clarity to just put one foot in front of the other."

That is quite possibly the most important insight for leaders embracing the new challenges of the Human Value Era. You may not always have a clear line of sight to your objectives, but you can still move forward, taking your team on an expedition of learning, collaboration, discovery, and value creation in this new world of work.

What Is an Expedition?

An expedition is a journey into the unknown. In your work, it may be the white space exploration for a new product, service, or business model. It might be a collaboration to secure a new customer or launch a unique marketing campaign. It could be the daily journey of serving and supporting customers.

To run a successful expedition, it is essential that you put the right people in the right roles at the right times. Some people excel at problem finding, some at problem solving, others at scaling the novel idea while reducing risk. (See "Understand Your Expedition Team."). Knowing how to field your people properly is the most critical part of your job as expedition leader. But, if you have established psychological safety and your team members view each other as collaborators rather than competitors, your work is well underway.

Almost by definition, an expedition traverses uncertainty to find opportunity. For all practical terms, the Covid-19 pandemic thrust us all into a collective expedition. Those rapid shifts in norms caused us to rethink work, shopping, education, childcare, retail, and more. Some of it was temporary, some of it is permanent, and some of it will linger until we, collectively, decide how to proceed.

So, frankly, this expedition idea shouldn't be all that new to you.

What to Leave at Base Camp

As you head out on your first expedition, leading your newly empowered workforce, consider what you need to bring and what you might be better off leaving behind. Drop some of the things that may weigh you down. Relinquishing these ideas, self-perceptions, and behaviors that no longer serve you well will lead to a more successful expedition.

Relinquish the Primacy of Your Expertise. Maybe you become a leader because you were a star. The best salesperson, the rock star engineer, the creative genius designer, the fastest on the line, or the wiz with numbers. It felt great to be a star, didn't it? Dragging that glory from the past to the present is as appropriate as wearing your high school letter jacket to a work function or carrying an old trophy into a business meeting. Let it go, and with it your ideas about yourself as an all-knowing leader, a role that is simply impossible to fill. You are leading people now who have

Understand Your Expedition Team

Most businesses function on a cycle of exploration, creation, and exploitation. They explore the market in search of a need, respond to that need by creating a product or service to meet market demand, then produce that product or service, exploiting the proven business model until it is disrupted or replaced by better solution.

Each of these phases of business require a different mindset, aptly described by researcher and strategist Simon Wardley as Pioneers, Settlers, and Town Planners.

The Pioneers venture into unknown and uncharted areas to discover unmet needs and opportunity. They are comfortable in ambiguity and uncertainty. They are comfortable that failure is an essential part of learning, discovery, and innovation. Do you have at least one pioneer in your team?

Settlers take a problem that has been framed and structured from the Pioneer and build out insights into a viable reality. They are problem solvers and creators. No doubt you have a few settlers in your group; most organizations can't operate without them.

The Town Planners focus on scale and risk reduction. They enter the cycle to improve the product, reduce cost and risk, and maximize profits. Town Planners are efficiency experts, a vital role on most teams.

The best teams have all three types on their expedition team, working in collaboration through a product life cycle that begins in discovery and ultimately returns to discover when, in the waning life of a product, the Town Planner sends the Pioneer to discover a new need or opportunity.

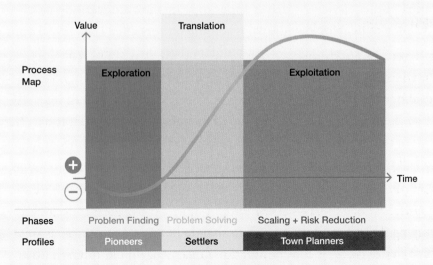

Figure 7.1 Compose Your Expedition Team

Concept credit: Based upon work by Simon Wardley (Pioneers, Settlers, Town Planners).

skills, knowledge, experience, and perspective that you likely don't have. Your job isn't to outshine your people; it's to guide them to bring back answers and approaches you might not have discovered on your own. So, drop the old models and embrace the journey.

Give Up Command and Control. For too long, the boss drove productivity with a carrot and stick. The boss gave an order and enticed performance by rewarding good work or punishing those who fell short. To lead a successful expedition and create a culture of learning, you need to move beyond command-and-control leadership. Your job is to bring out the best in each of your people, freeing them to apply their unique talents to the task. You needn't be the inspirational mentor for every person on your team, but increasingly, leadership will be measured less on what you did as a leader and more on the leadership pipeline you left behind. That only happens when you loosen your hold and enable your workers to contribute as uniquely and best as they are able.

Abandon the "No News Is Good News" Mantra. Too often, workers in fear of reprisal fail to share important information or sugarcoat bad news, lest they raise the ire of the boss. Strong leaders, however, know that their challengers are their secret weapon. And as author of *The Four Phases of Psychological Safety* Timothy R. Clark admonishes, you cannot cross the innovation threshold until your people are free – *and encouraged* – to dissent. As we learned in Chapter 5 from Alison Reynolds and David Lewis, cognitive diversity – and a safe environment in which to express varied points of views – drives superior teams toward learning and innovation. Embrace the people who make you uncomfortable. They reveal your blind spots. These challengers remove the blinders that limit your view of the future landscape.

Leave Meetings Behind. If leadership expert Roger Martin is right in his observation that the knowledge economy turned manufacturing facilities into decision factories, then the meeting is the knowledge era's production line. Why is your calendar full of meetings? Why do people start meetings by noting when they need to stop for their next meeting? Why do we spend so much time in meetings? When do we have time to actually do our work?

Microsoft researchers found the answer in a study of remote meetings, discovering that multitasking is common in those meetings with as much as 30% of meeting time spent doing email.[2] Why are so many people checking email during meetings? Either we have evolved to a perpetual state of partial attention or many of the people in those meetings don't need to be there.

So how do you cut down on meetings? Allan Chochinov, Chair of the MFA Products of Design program at Savannah College of Art and Design, has one simple answer: stop calling them meetings. In a 2018 blog post, Chochinov posits that when you change the word "meeting" to "review" participants' expectations change dramatically.[3] You might just show up for a meeting, he suggests, but you wouldn't dream of going into a review unprepared. He goes on to say that he rigged autocorrect on his computer and phone so that the word "meeting" would change to "review," eventually breaking the habit of scheduling "meetings" altogether. Imagine that rather than scheduling meetings, you hold a "briefing" to start a project or a "review" to assess the progress of a project. You might even schedule a "postmortem" to evaluate the challenges and successes of a project once it is completed.

In the summer of 2019, Microsoft Japan achieved a 40% increase in productivity by implementing an experimental four-day work week.[4] How did they decrease work time by 20% and increase productivity by 40%? The secret was time management training and, most importantly, putting their teams on a meeting diet. Meetings were cut from 60 to 30 minutes and attendance was capped at five people.

You can do it. No more "meetings."

Continued Uncertainty Means Continual Expeditions

Business takes place today against a backdrop of constant geopolitical, social, and economic disruption and uncertainty. Consider that in a span of fewer than 10 years, the United Kingdom left the European Union, the United States careened toward increasingly divisive politics, trade tensions between China and the United States intensified, Covid-19 brought the world to a halt, and Russia invaded Ukraine. Any of these things on their own would have had repercussions for global business. Coming as they did one on top of the other, they severed supply chains, drove inflation, and left consumer confidence shaken. Add labor shortages that show no signs of abating and mounting climate catastrophes, and it becomes clear that the outlook ahead is continual uncertainty.

Navigating Rising Global Uncertainty

Charted by counting the frequency with which "uncertain" or a similar word was used in the Economist Intelligence Unit's global reports, the Economic Policy Uncertainty Index was created by a group of scholars to measure economic confidence around the world. The trend line is a who's who of geopolitical disruption, the kind that makes it difficult to lead a team with a high degree of certainty.

How is a leader to navigate these rough waters?

One of those scholars, Stanford economist Nicholas Bloom, suggests a three-step approach:

1. Pay close attention to geopolitical and economic trend lines. Your business doesn't exist in a vacuum. Make it someone's job, if not your own, to track and understand the global issues that may affect – or worse, disrupt – your business.

2. Stay flexible and keep your options open. Uncertainty demands it. Don't get locked into long-term agreements, rent rather than buy, and round out your team with contract workers. "Pay more to avoid long-term commitments as these make it hard to be nimble in the face of major shocks," Bloom advises.

3. Have a contingency plan and be ready to make quick decisions if you have to activate it. These plans, Bloom says, are like insurance; you hope you never need to implement them, but if you do, you're glad you have them.

Following these steps, putting one foot in front of the other, will push your expedition forward.

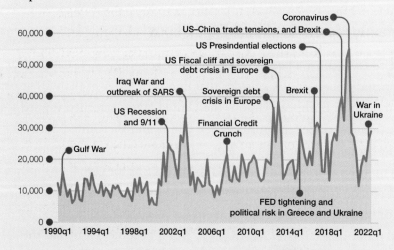

Figure 7.2 Navigating Rising Global Uncertainty

Source: Courtesy of Economic Policy Uncertainty (http://www.policyuncertainty.com).

Likewise, social and political unease seeped from the headlines into workplaces, until it was no longer an option for business leaders to hedge on issues from Black Lives Matter to Roe v. Wade to changing gender norms. Just ask Disney CEO Bob Chapek. When Florida Governor Ron DeSantis signed the controversial Parental Rights in Education Act, known colloquially as the "Don't Say Gay" bill, Chapek kept quiet on the issue. One of Florida's premier businesses and an anchor to the state's tourism industry, Disney had long been a champion of the LGBTQ+ community. Chapek's silence was met with outrage by employees and customers. And when he finally chose to speak, he faced backlash from the governor and his conservative allies.

Simple to say and much harder to do, leaders will have to navigate this confluence of change with candor to be clear with their employees, customers, and community just where they stand. That in and of itself is a continuous expedition.

Prepare to Cut a Different Path

For all the planning, map-making, and preparations, expeditions always encounter the unexpected. It's just the nature of the complex and continuously changing environment in which we operate. And the more complex the scheme, the more necessary it is to adapt to accommodate the unexpected. An entire field of study looks at Complex Adaptive Systems, the networks of independent parts that interact in ways that are often difficult to predict. As an expedition leader, you needn't become an expert in these theories, but you will do well to heed the message of mountaineer Alison Levine: In an environment that is always changing and evolving, a plan is outdated as soon as it is finished. And make no mistake, your environment now, and for the foreseeable future, will be continually evolving. The key to getting through these unexpected disruptions, she says, is being able to take action based on the situation. "Focus on execution rather than sticking to some plan," she advises.

Let's then consider the delivery of the first coronavirus vaccines in the United States in the winter of 2021 to illustrate the importance of adaptability in a complex operation. The Pfizer-BioNtech Covid-19 vaccine required ultra-cold (between −90°C and −60°C (−130°F and −76°F)) containers for transport, deep refrigeration for short-term storage, and had only a 12-hour window of viability after it was thawed. That's one layer of complexity.

Early doses were reserved for frontline health care workers and people at highest risk for Covid-19 mortality, creating a hierarchy of eligibility. Distributing vaccines based on risk profile layered more complexity. And social and political considerations – unprecedented demand, vaccine hesitancy, and political jockeying for allocations – added yet one more complex layer.

So how successful was the system developed to meet these complex requirements? Heather began tracking that answer as vaccines rolled out. Using Becker Hospital Review's tracking system,[5] she was able to compare the number of doses allocated, administered, and the overall percentage administered in each state with a set of assumptions about vaccine receptivity based on population, quality of health systems, and social and political factors that are typically an indicator of positive health outcomes.

She guessed that Democrats might be more likely to take the shot than their Republican counterparts who were more prone to be exposed to vaccine hesitancy and conspiracy theories circulating in right-wing media. (Incidentally, that assumption was confirmed by the Kaiser Family Foundation, noting that unvaccinated adults were three times more likely to lean Republican[6] and almost twice as many Democrats (62%) than Republicans (32%) reported receiving a booster shot.[7]).

She further assumed that states with high population density and highly ranked health care systems would be advantaged because people would be in closer proximity to, and thus more likely to access, vaccination centers and the well-established health infrastructure. Because higher education attainment is highly correlated with better health care outcomes, she also assumed that states whose populations had a high percentage of post-secondary degrees might have an edge.

Turns out, these assumptions did not bear out in the early days and months of vaccine distribution. Massachusetts is the fifth most densely populated state in the Union according to 2020 census data, ranked #2 by *US News and World Report* for access to health care, ranked #2 for educational attainment by *The Global Partnership for Education*, and went for Biden by more than 33 points. Surely, Massachusetts would get more shots in arms than other, more sparsely populated and conservative states.

So where did Massachusetts land? According to the Becker Hospital Review's tracking system for vaccine distribution, Massachusetts was 48 of 50 states with a utilization rate of just over 48%. North Dakota – with one of the lowest population densities, solidly red Republican, near the bottom rankings of health care access, and far lower educational attainment – landed at number two with almost 76% of doses utilized. How could that be? How could these assumptions be so far off?

Like many large established companies, Massachusetts relied on rigid protocols and procedures that slowed them down. They weren't scrappy and couldn't adapt. States that have far fewer resources and are used to pulling in volunteers to make do tapped those networks to support vaccine distribution rather than relying on bureaucratic processes.

A case in point: Kittitas County in Washington state.

Kittitas County is a small, rural, under-resourced community accustomed to fighting the forest fires that frequently strike the region. Fires are fickle and can turn in a minute, experience that has taught this community to react and adapt to the changing situation. Oddly enough, that firefighting experience served the county well when it came time to give shots. Charged with vaccine distribution in the county, Deputy Fire Chief Richard Elliot led a team of essential workers and volunteers that took the same adaptive approach to vaccine distribution. Their objective: do not waste a dose. If the vaccine was unused at the end of the day, they went down their list to the next eligible group, official guidelines be damned.

"Everybody communicating, everybody willing to be flexible and play whatever role's necessary . . . gives us the framework to do it," Elliott told CNN. "You're not supposed to tell people how to do your job. You're supposed to tell them what the objectives are, give them the resources, give them the time frame, and then stay out of their business."[8] That mindset delivered more than twice the vaccine doses than the average across the state.

Over time and having worked out a new processes for vaccine distribution, Wisconsin, Massachusetts, and Connecticut emerged as the top three states for vaccine distribution, more aligned with Heather's initial assumptions, but it took these states considerable adaptation and rethinking to move to scrappy adaptation.

Whereas Massachusetts relied on bureaucracy and existing infrastructure, Kittitas County focused on the goal of zero lost doses. The team, a mix of skilled and unskilled volunteers, was given guardrails and the autonomy to act as they saw fit within those parameters. As you will learn, your expedition may never get off base camp if you operate as you have in the past. Giving your people the goal, the guardrails, and the autonomy to operate will serve you best in your expedition.

Imagine if those guardrails and goals had been in place at United Airlines in the spring of 2017. Faced with an overbooked Flight 3411 from Chicago to Louisville and the need to get four employees to another airport, the airline identified four passengers based on an algorithmic calculation of ticket price and airline status, and asked them to give up their seats. Three left the plane and one refused. The rest of the story was captured on now-infamous video as Dr. David Dao Duy Anh was forcefully dragged off the plane.

Technically, the algorithm was right in selecting Dr. Anh and the United crew acted by the book, following rules and forcing a confrontation rather than adapting to a changing and difficult situation. Given the latitude to override the algorithm, the crew might have explored other options to find other passengers willing to give up their seats, or make alternative arrangements for the four employees, or, really, any other solution than physically beating up your customer.

But the damage was done. A Morning Consult survey of nearly 2,000 air travelers found that more than 40% would choose a more expensive and longer flight to avoid flying United.[9]

Work is increasingly a journey into the unknown with higher and higher rates of uncertainty. Increasingly, organizations navigating complexity and uncertainty will need to give leaders the flexibility to creatively solve challenges. To change direction as they explore new frontiers.

Care for Your Expedition Team

As you embark on your expedition, you have the critical task of caring for your team, ensuring that all are fit and ready for the journey. It is a substantial responsibility.

Recall Frederick Herzberg's theory of motivation. (See "The Hierarchy of Engagement," Chapter 3.) Simply put, Herzberg identifies two human drivers: the basic biological need to avoid pain, what he calls "hygiene," and the psychological need to achieve and grow, what he calls "motivation." These drivers act independently and are equally important. One removes dissatisfaction, the other provides satisfaction. You might, for example, eliminate factors of dissatisfaction by offering more and better perks, but if you have not also stoked intrinsic drivers of personal growth, you will have failed to engage and motivate your team. A great salary and a nice office won't compensate for lack of recognition, advancement, or even interest in the work itself.

To that understanding, let's add another dimension, what psychologist Guy Winch calls emotional hygiene. Much like brushing our teeth and bathing attend to our physical hygiene, Winch writes in *Psychology Today*, emotional hygiene is "being mindful of our psychological health and adopting brief daily habits to monitor and address psychological wounds when we sustain them."[10]

Before you discount emotional hygiene as some touchy-feely nonsense challenging your stoic leadership, take a minute to think about the power of emotion.

Research shows that an emotional response travels a millisecond faster than a cognitive one.[11] That is, feelings move faster than thoughts. And feelings drive our biology, a point clearly made in Mark C. Crowley's fascinating book *Lead from the Heart*. "We now know it's our emotions that drive our biochemistry – not the other way around," says Rollin McCraty, HeartMath Institute's director of research, in an interview with Crawley. "Feelings and emotions, therefore, determine our level of engagement in life, what motivates us, and what we truly care about."[12]

Managing to others' emotions is a heavy lift, indeed. As a leader in a stressful and increasingly uncertain world, you are caring for team members who come with a range of emotional and mental states. How can you wrap your arms around that? Remember the pre-flight safety admonition to "put your oxygen mask on first before helping others"? That's how.

Winch advises us to look inward, offering these five tips: (1) pay attention to emotional pain, (2) stop emotional bleeding, (3) protect your self-esteem, (4) battle negative feelings, and (5) become informed about the impact of emotional wounds. By tending to your emotional well-being, you are best able to support your team. And with the current level of emotional distress from the aftershocks of the pandemic, the loneliness epidemic, and the skyrocketing rates of mental illness, our ability to better read, understand, and process our own emotions is paramount. Understanding the cartography of your own emotional landscape makes you a better expedition leader. (See "Focus on the Fundamentals.")

Focus on the Fundamentals

Time. It's your most precious resource. Time is finite. Too often, we act like money is finite and time is infinite, but it's the other way around. You can make more money; you cannot make more time. Mindfully manage your time. Do you need to be doing that work right now? Or is your time better spent at dinner with family or to surprise your daughter at her soccer game? Embrace the adage, "Live every day as if it is the last and sooner or later you will be right."

Trust. It's your most important asset. Every product or service a customer buys or rents is a souvenir from the trust they have in you. People come to work with you or become friends with you because they trust you. People follow you as a leader because they trust you. Virtually every commercial activity is a transaction of trust. So, with every interaction think: "Am I building or burning trust right now?" You are almost always doing one or the other.

Capacity. It's your investment into yourself, your people, and your organization to increase your capacity to meet the moment. Your intellectual capacity, your curiosity capacity, your passion capacity, your wellness capacity. Capacity is your ability to be effective, well, and balanced. Capacity, in this sense, is not your ability to do more or everything, but to meet the moment and know what things deserve your time and trust.

Focus on these three things – time, trust, and capacity – and you will be well equipped to lead nearly any expedition.

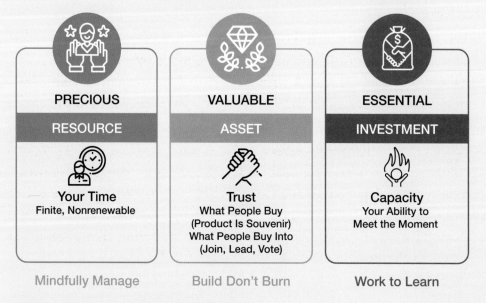

Figure 7.3 Focus on the Fundamentals

Create Enthusiasm Around the Expedition

Expeditions are about exploring the unknown, finding opportunity, and continually managing change. Navigating uncertainty and managing change will be the majority of what you do. And let's be honest: these deep dives into the unknown can be frightening for many of the people around you. New experiences – expeditions – can trigger fear and panic, which in turns trigger our freeze, flight, or flight responses. How do you move your people on from these unproductive states? By building trust, and that requires empathy. In her 2018 TED talk "How to Build (and Rebuild) Trust," Frances Frei shared her experience working to turn around the culture at Uber. It was, she said, a journey of redemption, rooted in rebuilding trust.[13]

Trust, she said, is founded on three components: Authenticity, Logic, and Empathy. "If you sense that I am being authentic, you are much more likely to trust me. If you sense that I have real rigor in my logic, you are far more likely to trust me. And if you believe that my empathy is directed toward you, you are far more likely to trust me. When all three of these things are working, we have great trust, but . . . if any one of these three wobbles, trust is threatened."

The most "wobble," Frei tells us, is empathy. "People just don't believe that we are just in it for them." she says. But without empathy, "everything is harder."

The solution, she concludes, is to "look at the people right in front of us, listen to them, deeply immerse ourselves in their perspectives, then we have a chance at having a sturdy leg of empathy."

When you ask someone to jump into the unknown, you are asking them to be uncomfortable and potentially insecure. You must tap into *their* emotions to truly understand their motivations and hesitance in order to coax them from a negative emotion to an emotion of action and autonomy, guiding them with authenticity and shared vulnerability.

Fellow optimist, CEO, and speaker Cassandra Worthy believes negative emotions are signals of our greatest opportunities for growth and has architected a three-step process she calls "Change Enthusiasm Growth Cycle": (1) embracing emotions as signals, (2) explore the opportunity, and (3) consciously choose to evolve. Worthy notes, "Emotions exist to serve. The question is, how do we allow them to serve us in the most productive way?"[14]

Worthy believes it is possible to transform fear into hope and anxiety into anticipation. Better yet, the cycle is self-reinforcing as we build resilience and perspective with every turn. Or – in the parlance of an expedition leader: The more expeditions we embark on, the more equipped we are to explore the unknown. We need to lean into our emotions and see them as our guides for transformation and growth, rather than leaving them outside the office door or off the Zoom call, always remembering, as Mark C. Crowley told us, that the heart sends more signals to the brain than the brain sends to the heart. Our emotions are often the driver of our behaviors. Understanding how to comprehend them in ourselves and others, and learning to redirect emotions from negative and paralyzing to positive and action oriented are essential for any leader today.

Yes, You Are a Career Coach Now

If you had to write your own eulogy today, what would you say? Would you focus on your role as leader? Would you talk about the budgets you managed, the products you launched, a surging stock price, or your latest acquisition? Or would you talk about the people you inspired, the teams you built, the things that they accomplished together?

The latter, we'd guess, is the most fulfilling part of your leadership. Yet too often coaching and mentorship is seen as a side gig of leaders who instead ought to stay focused on the big decisions and negotiations and policies by which the company runs.

Not long ago, Heather was having dinner with a friend who has spent her entire career in one industry and the majority of that with one company. Now a senior leader, the friend was lamenting the number of people in her organization who, in her view, focused more on where they want to go than in the job they are in. "Come on," she harrumphed, "I am not a career coach." A lightbulb went off for Heather who responded, "If you're not, you should be."

The greatest impact a leader can have is not on the product or the stock price, but on the people, especially the pipeline of talent you develop. An organization is only as sustainable as the people it attracts and engages. Your best work is to inspire your team to thrive and grow in the work in front of them today and help them realize where their careers may take them. That, perhaps more than any other aspect of your work, brings sustainable value to your organization and sustained engagement to your people. As Frances Frei and Anne Morriss succinctly write in their book *Unleashed: The Unapologetic Leader's Guide to Empowering Everyone Around You*, "Your job as a leader is to create the conditions for the people around you to become increasingly effective, to help them fully realize their own capacity and power. And not only when you're in the trenches with them, but also when you're not around, and even (this is the cleanest test) after you've permanently moved on from the team."[15]

In a world moving this quickly, what you learn is as important as what you earn. Leaders must work to increase everyone's capacity. In 2021, as the first wave of the Great Resignation washed over business, Pew Research found that the top two reasons people left their jobs were insufficient compensation and lack of opportunities for growth, both tied with a net score of 63%.[16]

When we speak of purpose, as we have repeatedly in this book, we have attempted to be clear that there is not one singular purpose. We all have personal purpose. Our organizations have collective purpose. We can have a purpose in the job we are in today, and the careers we are building. When our individual purpose connects to purpose in our work and aligns with organizational purpose, incredible potential for value creation is unlocked. When you fill the role as expedition leader who coaches your team, you are helping them align their purpose with the organizational purpose – and that makes magic happen.

Take That First Step

Your transformation from commander to expedition leader may not seem clear. You may not know how or where to place your footing. That is OK; we don't know either (we will get into the power of saying "I don't know" in the next chapter). But as the proverb goes, "The journey of a thousand miles begins with a single step."

Go ahead.

Notes

1. "Lessons from the Ledge: Alison Levine at TEDxMidwest," available at https://www.youtube.com/watch?v=6hUybmqUVmM.

2. Hancheng Cao, Lee, Chia-Jung, Iqbal Shamsi, Czerwinski, Mary, Wong, Priscilla, Rintel, Sean, Hecht, Brent, Teevan, Jaime, and Yang, Longqi, 2021, "Large Scale Analysis of Multitasking Behavior During Remote Meetings," CHI Conference on Human Factors in Computing Systems (CHI '21), May 8–13, available at https://hci.stanford.edu/publications/2021/cao_remote/CHI2021-RemoteMeetingMultitask.pdf.

3. Chochinov, Allan, 2018, "Change Everything You Hate About Meetings with This ONE SINGLE WORD," *Products of Design* blog, September 25, available at https://productsofdesign.sva.edu/blog/nomeeting.

4. Gatlin-Keener, Courtney and Lunsford, Ryan, 2019, "Four-day Workweek: The Microsoft Japan Experience," available at https://www.aabri.com/VC2020Manuscripts/VC20032.pdf.

5. Bean, Mackenzie, 2021, "States Ranked by Percentage of COVID-19 Vaccines Administered," Becker Hospital Review, November 30, available at https://www.beckershospitalreview.com/public-health/states-ranked-by-percentage-of-covid-19-vaccines-administered.html.

6. "Unvaccinated Adults Are Now More Than Three Times as Likely to Lean Republican than Democratic," Kaiser Family Foundation Newsroom, November 2021, available at https://www.kff.org/coronavirus-covid-19/press-release/unvaccinated-adults-are-now-more-than-three-times-as-likely-to-lean-republican-than-democratic/.

7. "KFF COVID-19 Vaccine Monitor: January 2022," Kaiser Family Foundation Polling, January 2022, available at https://www.kff.org/coronavirus-covid-19/poll-finding/kff-covid-19-vaccine-monitor-january-2022/.

8. Zdanowicz, Christina, 2021, "A Rural County in Washington State Hasn't Wasted a Single Covid-19 Vaccine Dose. Here's Its Secret," *CNN*, January 25, available at https://www.cnn.com/2021/01/25/health/kittitas-county-washington-covid-19-vaccine-trnd/index.html.

9. Nichols, Laura, 2017, "Poll: People Won't Fly United If Another Airline Has an Identical Flight," Morning Consult, April 16, available at

https://morningconsult.com/2017/04/16/poll-people-wont-fly-united-another-airline-identical-flight/.

10. Winch, Guy, 2014, "5 Ways to Improve Your Emotional Health," *Psychology Today*, December, available at https://www.psychologytoday.com/us/blog/the-squeaky-wheel/201412/5-ways-improve-your-emotional-health.

11. Sterrett, Emily A., 2014, *The Science Behind Emotional Intelligence*, HRD Press, available at https://www.hrdpress.com/site/html/includes/items/SBEI.html.

12. Crowley, Mark C., 2022, *Lead from the Heart,* Hay House Business, p. 16.

13. Frei, Frances X., 2018, "How to Build (and Rebuild) Trust," TED Talk, available at https://ed.ted.com/lessons/how-to-build-and-rebuild-trust-frances-frei.

14. Worthy, Cassandra, 2021, *Change Enthusiasm*, Hay House Business, p. 8.

15. Frei, Frances X. and Morriss, Anne, 2020, *Unleashed: The Unapologetic Leader's Guide to Empowering Everyone Around You,* Harvard Business Review Press. Kindle Edition, Location 117 of 3251.

16. Parker, Kim and Menasce Horowitz, Julianna, 2022, "Majority of Workers Who Quit a Job in 2021 Cite Low Pay, No Opportunities for Advancement, Feeling Disrespected," Pew Research, March, available at https://www.pewresearch.org/ft_22-03-09_resignation-featured-image/.

8 Embrace Your Superpowers

"I. Don't. Know."

Say it. Again. Get comfortable with those words. Because there is so much that you don't know. So much that others know that you do not. And that's just fine. Even if it is uncomfortable.

In the face of unprecedented uncertainty, ambiguity, change, and rapid formulation of new skills and knowledge, no leader can know it all. To acknowledge that you do not know, to be vulnerable to that truth, is a profound act of courage.

New York Times best-selling author of *Daring Greatly* and other works, Brené Brown writes and speaks about the power of vulnerability as the "birthplace" of those characteristics that make for a great leader. Vulnerability, she writes, "is the source of hope, empathy, accountability, and authenticity."[1]

It is a recurring theme in Brown's work, and one she touched on again in a 2021 talk at Learn Serve Lead 2021. "Vulnerability is not weakness," she said. "It's the ability to show up and be seen. It's the ability to be brave when you cannot control the outcome."[2] The ability to show up, to acknowledge that you don't know, to be brave in the face of uncertainty, these are the cornerstones of empathic leadership in the Human Value Era. And it is, sometimes painfully, quite the inverse of long-held expectations of leadership.

The Power of Vulnerability and Not Knowing

For so very long, and especially since the advent of knowledge work, we've come to expect our leaders to be experts, rarely questioning their knowledge and perspectives. After all, they worked their way up the career ladder by building expertise. It was simply assumed that anyone on a rung above had learned more, experienced more, and knew more than you.

That idea began to unravel amid rapid digital transformation and exponential advances in technology. The formulation of new knowledge accelerated and began to outpace our ability to consume that knowledge and maintain our expertise. What's a person to do when they're expected to be the all-knowing leader in a world where it is impossible to keep up? For many, the answer was "fake it."

The clinical term is impression management, endeavoring to control how we are perceived by others, and it is too often the crutch of those in leadership positions. Impression management is rooted in insecurity, shame, and the fear that others will not respect our leadership, especially if they know how much we simply did not know.

The antidote to impression management and the liabilities it creates for you and the organization you lead is to establish psychological safety. We've talked about this important concept throughout this book, and it is important enough to bear repeating: Psychological safety enables your team to show up as their authentic selves without self-censoring and with the security to learn, contribute, fail, and challenge. If your team doesn't feel it can challenge assumptions or offer a dissenting opinion, they do not have psychological safety and – more importantly – you do not have a team that will have your back when new information enters the scene.

How do you lay the foundation for psychological safety? In a word, vulnerability. Your vulnerability. When you open yourself to reveal your full, imperfect, authentic self you invite your people to be their true selves with you. You create a true connection and build the foundation of belonging.

There's one more advantage to taking the vulnerable step to acknowledge you do not know: It lifts a tremendous burden from your psyche and allows you to focus on what you and your team collectively know, identify gaps, and learn together. Not knowing is a huge relief, *and* it is the path to innovation and creative collaboration. Not knowing is the first step in learning or building something new.

It takes courage to recognize you don't know, and it is well worth the risk. Doing so imparts agency to your team, freeing them to contribute more fully and giving them a greater stake in the outcome of decisions. That, as an empathic leader, is your highest objective. And it is the key to unlock all the other superpowers of your leadership.

The Power of Awareness

Much of what you do as a leader is make decisions with imperfect information and guide humans in social interaction. Leadership has shifted from managing processes in a certain and stable environment to guiding your team in ambiguity and uncertainty. Your work, then, is essentially to make decisions and manage both your emotions and help others to manage theirs. Doing that well requires a high degree of both self-awareness and social awareness. It requires emotional intelligence.

According to Travis Bradberry, author of *Emotional Intelligence*, emotional intelligence is measured in the balance of how we see the world (self-awareness and social awareness) and how we act in the world (self-management and relationship management).

No doubt, if you are human, you've found yourself on the wrong side of an in-the-moment emotional reaction. Anger or frustration floods in, and all effective communication is washed away. Self-awareness is that self-check, taking a moment or more to understand what you are feeling and why, and harnessing those emotions more productively before responding. Surely, you know that it's best to hold your tongue or wait to respond to an email or text in the heat of emotion. But self-awareness plays into every level of decision making.

Consider the study "Extraneous Factors in Judicial Decisions," a peer-reviewed survey of over 1,000 rulings by eight judges. The researchers found time of day, more than any other factor, contributed to the likelihood of a favorable parole ruling. And not by a small margin. Jonathan Levav, associate professor of business at Columbia

University and one of the authors of the study, noted that an inmate is as much as six times more likely to be paroled if the case is heard early in the day than if the case is among the last before a lunch break or the day's adjournment. "The likelihood of a 'favorable' ruling peaked at the beginning of the day, steadily declining over time from a probability of about 65% to nearly zero, before spiking back up to about 65% after a break for a meal or snack."[3]

If judges who are trained to make life-altering decisions based on law and reason can be influenced by hunger and fatigue, what does that say for the rest of us? In the days of steady and reliable processes, a late lunch or a poor night's sleep might not have mattered so much. But most leaders today need to make decisions with imperfect information and often with some urgency, not unlike those judges. Judges grant parole, or not, by weighing a series of unknowns. Will this person reoffend? Does this person have the will, perseverance, and support systems to lead a new and different life? Has this person overcome addiction or mental health struggles that drove their criminal behavior? Judges make their best assessment, and apparently do it best on a good night's sleep and a full belly.

So many of the decisions we make today – from hiring for the ability to adapt and learn to designing business models against a changing competitive landscape – are not unlike the decisions of these judges. We are often navigating the unknown, working with incomplete information, to place a bet on the future. That kind of decision making requires the emotional intelligence to sit in your own feelings, the empathy to feel what others do, and the situational awareness to see a picture bigger than the immediate moment. Being aware gives you the power to get closer to a "right decision."

The Power of Candor

In his powerful essay, "The beautiful clarity of true candor," *Axios* founder and CEO Jim VandeHei write that candor is a "time-saving, culture-strengthening, clarifying gift." [4] And so it is. Nothing cuts to the core like direct, honest communication, carefully and clearly delivered. It leaves nowhere to hide. It leaves nothing to guess. In that way, candor is extraordinarily efficient. It saves your people from speculating about where they stand or what you expect. It saves you from waiting, usually in vain hope, for someone to figure out what you lack the courage or compassion to tell them directly.

Candor is easy when the going is good. There's little risk in giving direction and acknowledging good and hard work. Candor is tougher when the honest truth is less pleasant. But that's when it matters most. Years ago, when Chris was part of an executive team navigating a difficult restructuring, the day arrived when certain employees would be told they were losing their jobs. In that moment, her boss offered a bit of wisdom that has served her well throughout her career. Don't be nice, be kind, he advised. Sugarcoating the news might seem nice, but it was unkind. Be direct. Be clear. Be careful in your words. Candor, then, is the ultimate act of kindness that your people deserve.

There is a subtle and important difference between truth and candor. We have heard leaders say that they will always tell the truth, and they do. On their terms and in their own time. No doubt there are times when leaders must hold their counsel, waiting for the culmination of factors before communicating with their teams. But withholding necessary truth ("I didn't lie; I just didn't say anything.") flies in the face of a culture of trust and candor. Candor doesn't wait. It doesn't allow unease to fester. It won't permit a veering off course.

But let's be clear: candor cuts two ways. Your direct and honest communications will drive your team to perform to clear expectations, perhaps even to exceed them. And you must also invite your people to be honest with you, and without fear of reprisal. Candor does not allow the unquestioned expert leader. Rather, bilateral candor is an act of trust, of respect, and ultimately of compassion.

In a constantly shifting world, commit to candor. (See "The Four Essential Leadership Shifts.")

The Four Leadership Shifts

Can we be candid? Everything you likely learned about leadership is changing. Let's take a closer look.

- *Mindset.* This is the big shift, and it's a tough one. You are no longer managing people; you are enabling their success. The organizational psychologists at SAP SuccessFactors sifted through academic journals and business publications to better understand the evolving role of people managers and concluded that the managers have moved from overseeing work and evaluating performance to become "performance coaches that invite feedback, cultivate psychological safety, and provide individualized interpersonal support," the psychologists wrote. It is the role of the manager "to make their team successful, foster meaningful and engaging team member experiences, and empower them for future career opportunities that may lie beyond the team."[5] Put another way, your people no longer work for you; you work for them.

- *Culture.* When your people all worked for you and you were the all-knowing and unquestioned boss, your people vied for your attention, direction, push, and praise. In that sense they operated as competitors, an idea reinforced by management policies like forced rankings that pitted people against each other in a *Hunger Games*–style death match to land as number one. Now and especially as we strive for employee engagement and collaborative explorations, we need teams to operate with collective intelligence because no one person has all the knowledge required to be successful. Your people are collaborators, not competitors. When your team members perceive each other as collaborators they free you to become a mentoring coach rather than flag-throwing referee.

- *Approach.* You will not be successful getting your people to learn and adapt at the speed, scale, and scope required by the extraordinary rates of change by threatening punishment or dangling rewards. This extrinsic approach just won't work. Instead, shift to helping your people identify their own intrinsic motivation. Give up fixed job descriptions and overly structured org charts, and embrace job sculpting rooted in people's values, curiosity, and interests. That way, they are intrinsically motivated and become self-propelled to work, learn, and adapt.

- *Behavior.* In the not-so-distant past, leaders were expected to take command, make decisions in certainty, and drive productivity – often by instilling fear. (Keep in mind that, too often, fear brings out the worst in people. Why was it ever thought to be an effective means to drive productivity?) Now, leaders must slip into the role of coach and motivator-in-chief. Your role now is to guide effective behaviors, balance wellness, avoid team burnout, and inspire your people to do their best work. Your job is to create the optimal conditions for your team to thrive.

Who wouldn't want to work under these conditions?

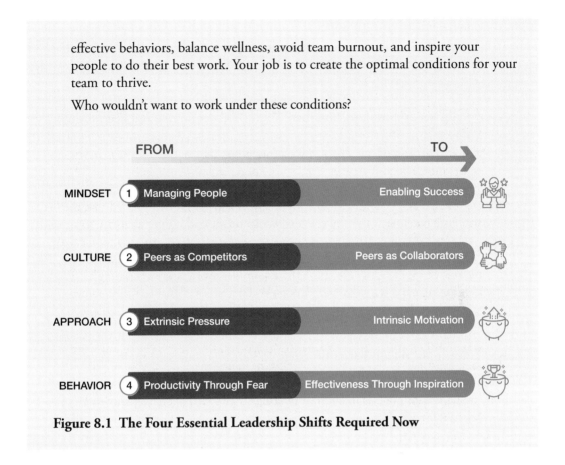

FROM ———————————————————————→ **TO**

MINDSET	① Managing People	Enabling Success
CULTURE	② Peers as Competitors	Peers as Collaborators
APPROACH	③ Extrinsic Pressure	Intrinsic Motivation
BEHAVIOR	④ Productivity Through Fear	Effectiveness Through Inspiration

Figure 8.1 The Four Essential Leadership Shifts Required Now

The Power of Listening

The essential partner of candor is listening. Deep listening. Like candor, listening is an act of vulnerability. As a leader, you need to be open to really hear the ideas and concerns of the people who work with you. More importantly, you need to commit to following up on what you hear. That's not to say that you have to adopt every far-fetched idea or placate every grievance. You do, however, need to respond. "Thanks for sharing" isn't enough.

In fact, that sort of half-hearted listening does more harm than good. Survey after survey finds pockets of employees who are deeply dissatisfied and disengaged with their work because management doesn't listen and respond to employee input, even input that management directly solicits. And we're talking here about more than the annual employee satisfaction surveys which, from our experience, drive more self-congratulations among the management team than actual change for the rank and file.

So, listen carefully. Then, reiterate that you heard, acknowledge what you can and cannot do, clearly set expectations, and then work to deliver on that implied promise. To listen deeply, you need to create opportunities – both formal and informal – for your team to have a voice. One company we work with makes feedback an essential part of *every* company initiative, using a simple "I like/I wish" format. Participants are invited to talk about what worked well and about what they "wish" would be different in the future. Those "wishes" are taken seriously by the leadership team, and visible changes occur with haste. (In one meeting, someone wished for a particular brand of soda. When we gathered for the next meeting, that soda was in the cooler to the delight of the participant. It's a simple example, but it demonstrates the power of listening and being heard.)

To be clear, we're not suggesting you implement everything your people suggest (and sometimes even demand) you do. President Barack Obama famously asked his advisors for input on all matter of issues. When everyone said their piece, he reportedly thanked everyone for their insights and information, then explained the decision he made based on what he had heard.

Listening has remarkable benefits for employee morale. Who doesn't want to be asked for their ideas? Listening deepens employee engagement. Who doesn't want to work for someone that invites their regular feedback and contribution? Listening is vital to innovation. Do you really know where all your best ideas will come from?

If you really want clear and transparent feedback, and you should, make listening to your people a top priority. Manak Ahluwalia, CEO of Aqueduct Technologies, sits with we discussed in Chapter 6. Cockroach Labs deeply engaged its workforce before setting its return to office policy. Each employee at least once a year to *specifically* listen and learn about emerging problems, needs, and desires so he can proactively address them. (See "Aqueduct Technologies: Really Great Ideas, Really Happy Employees," Chapter 3.) Be like Manak.

As businesses adapt for a post-pandemic workplace, listening to employees – and acting on their feedback – is more important than ever. Employers everywhere, for example, are asking employees where and how they prefer to work. The best organization uses this input to create flexible strategies that meet the reasonable desires of their employees. Consider the example set by Cockroach Labs, a data security company for cloud applications. Among the company's key tenets is to "build a space for our employees that inspired innovation while still encouraging employees to find their unique balance of personal and professional commitments."[6]

By engaging with and deeply listening to employees, Cockroach Labs (they chose the name to signify resilience and survival) navigated to a policy solution that worked for company and workers alike. With this approach, it's not hard to see why Cockroach Labs is repeatedly rated a top place to work by Crains, Inc. and NextGen 100.

If only all companies worked like Cockroach. Too many organizations tried to impose arbitrary back-to-office mandates that seemed to pay little mind to what employees were saying they wanted and needed. These edicts were met with quick and decisive backlash. It wasn't unusual to see employees resign rather than comply. That fierce feedback had many CEOs walking back their mandates, having discovered the newfound power and agency of their employees.

And quite frankly, those return-to-work mandates fly in the face of everything we learned during the heat of the pandemic. You trusted your employees in the pandemic work-from-home necessity; why not trust them now? People *did* work from home, most of them quite successfully. To be clear, we do not know yet where, when, and how various tasks are best completed. Those experiments should begin now, absent of bias and unqualified assumptions. Why would you now ignore their wish to continue flexible work in favor of a cookie-cutter, return-to-office policy that doesn't clearly satisfy a differentiated reason for the work that must be done in person? That type of performative listening is a sure recipe for employee turnover.

Active listening is one facet of leading in trust, and trust is the superpower that motivates and engages your team. Together, listening, candor, and trust rebalance your role and relationship from omnipotent boss to empowering coach. So much so that you might just start to believe that *you work for your employees*. And that just might be a very good thing. (See, "Mindset Shift: You Work for Talent.")

Mindset Shift: You Work for Talent

You were the boss. Now, you are the coach.

Workers manage themselves on the continuums of engagement to disengagement and directed to self-directed. When people worked for you and you managed people, your team looked to you to provide the direction for their work. In that world of "movement," your people reacted to the stimuli you provided – threats, promises, punishments, or rewards. Your team's progress depended upon your push or pull. Their progress was a limited reaction to the direction and stimuli you provided. You stop the stimuli, they stop.

When you inspire your people to be self-directed or self-motivated, they provide their own motivational fuel, and that lessens the pressure on you to make progress. Optimally, you want to lead your team to a state that is both self-directed and self-motivated. There, they become "self-propelled."

Self-propelled workers have the agency to harness collective intelligence to make progress with and without you. You offer coaching and course correction. You block and tackle. You provide resources. You counsel, frame, and focus from within your broader understanding of your organization's goals and objectives. You are like a coach of professional athletes. You will never play their positions better than they can, and they cannot knit together the team toward the goal the way you can.

This is a big shift: You now work for your people, not the other way around. And for some leaders, who like the *idea* of being the boss perhaps more than they actually like *being the boss,* that's going to take some adjustment to their ego. It's a major adaptation, but one worth doing to arrive at a more effective team.

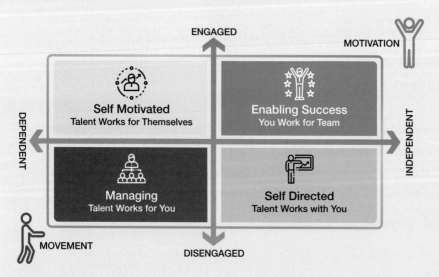

Figure 8.2 The Mindset Shift: You Work for the Team

The Power of Being Human

For too long, we prized leaders who could "make hard decisions," and too often, we validated ruthless, anti-worker behavior for the sake of the bottom line. Now, we're seeing cracks in that image. BusinessSolvers' *The State of Employee Empathy* report found a 3–4% decrease in empathy from 2021 to 2022, and cites that decline as a contributing factor in the Great Resignation.[7] The trust granted and earned in employees during the crisis began to fade when the virus ebbed. Now, the report says, we are renegotiating the social contract between worker and employee. In that negotiation, we are free to be more human as leaders and managers and to develop relational rather than transactional relationships with our work force. (See "Behavioral Shift: Change in Leadership Profile.")

In a *Chicago Tribune* op-ed titled "Airline Meltdowns Are the Canary in the Coal Mine," Matt Sigelman and Ken Mehlman address this issue. These two leaders of the labor market analytics firm Lightcast posit that the tightening labor market demands a shift in leadership style.

Since the 1960s, they write, a transactional approach to labor dominated corporate hiring and firing practices. That approach "works" when the workforce is plentiful and people can be quickly trained. Now, as the labor market has tightened, the time has come for a new way of thinking, they say. "That means considering the workforce as a relationship, not just a transaction – one that is less disposable and more enduring through ups and downs."[8] Leaders must, they add, invest in our workforce.

This changed relationship between individuals and organizations means you can drop the charade of the tough-minded boss and embrace your empathic self.

You can be fully human, and that may just be the greatest superpower of all.

Behavioral Shift: Change in Leadership Profile

The archetype of "leader" is changing, and for the better, we believe.

Selection Criteria. Leaders used to be plucked from the ranks of up-and-comers because they were the "best" – the best technical expert, the best engineer, the best finance wiz, the best designer or marketer or that person who just crushed in sales year after year. Business valued outstanding individual expertise without any qualification of management or leadership skills. Now, more than ever, we need to put people leadership first, selecting leaders from those who demonstrate the best human skills like empathy, collaboration, connection, and communication. We need as leaders those with the unique ability to coach the best performances out of people. Those who can foster the best connections among team members. Those who can kindle that special connection among members of the team so that they perform to their collective best.

Focus. Let's face it, we are moving from managers who home in on process oriented tasks to those who focus on people-centric activities. Treating humans as depersonalized units of productivity never made sense. And now, as technology picks up the dull and routine tasks and delivers increasing productivity, leaders can shift away from being process managers and instead focus on inspiring the human potential of their most valuable assets – their people.

Valued Traits. Too many leaders of the past sat in the role of the unquestioned expert. Work got done as the leader wanted because "the boss said so." Now, with rapidly shifting and emerging skills and knowledge, you will never see the full landscape without the help of your people sharing valuable insights and connecting the dots that you can draw into a full and rich picture. In fact, that unquestioned expert making decisions in certainty is a full-blown liability. You need a humble, curious learner who is comfortable making decisions with imperfect information and increasing ambiguity. You need a leader with the ability to say those very hard words, "I do not know."

Motivate With. Now that the days of the productivity-driving, boss-in-charge leader are over, we need leadership that can inspire and care for the workforce. "Lead with love," says management consultant and author Mark C. Crowley, "and your people will follow."

This is a markedly different leadership profile, one that sets a new mold for management training and its leadership pipeline. And it may be a profile that is uncomfortable for many existing leaders to assume. You will be asking the existing leaders in your organization to abandon the leadership style that got them where they are today. They can adapt, no doubt, but it will be a leadership challenge *for you* to embrace with time and patience and empathy

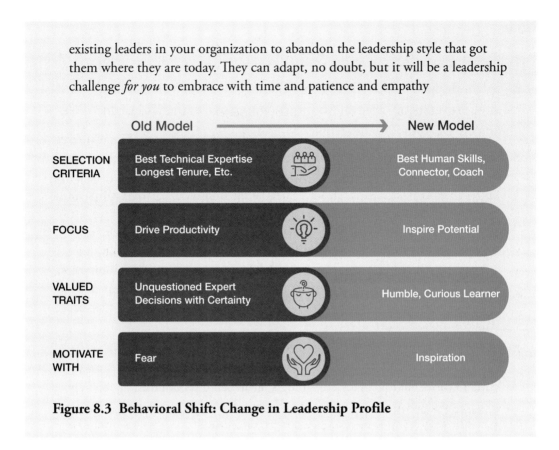

Figure 8.3 Behavioral Shift: Change in Leadership Profile

Become the Resilient Leader

In another parlance, these super powers are what human resource managers and business consultants might call "soft skills." Unlike accounting or engineering or supply chain management, so-called soft skills are not taught, the thinking goes, they are intuited. You are a nice person or you're not, and if you are, well that's an added bonus on top of your technical skills and knowledge.

By now, though, it should be clear that the shelf life of technical skills and experiential knowledge is growing shorter and shorter. But those soft skills – what we called "human skills" in *The Adaptation Advantage* – are here forever. They are the currency of leadership in the Human Value Era. And the good news is that you *can* learn to be more self-aware. You *can* practice radical candor. You *can* develop your skills as an empathetic listener. You *can* build a culture of inclusion, belonging, and – yes – even love.

These human skills are the foundation of a resilient leader, exactly the kind of leader you want to be.

Notes

1. Brown, Brené, 2012, *Daring Greatly,* Penguin. Kindle Edition, p 34.

2. Balch, Bridget, 2021, "There Is No Courage Without Vulnerability," AAMC .org, November 9, available at https://www.aamc.org/news-insights/there-no-courage-without-vulnerability.

3. Danziger, Shai, Levav, Jonathan, and Avnaim-Pesso, Liora, 2011, "Extraneous Factors in Judicial Decisions," Proceedings of National Academy of Science, April, available at https://www.pnas.org/doi/10.1073/pnas.1018033108.

4. VandeHei, Jim, 2022, "The Beautiful Clarity of True Candor," *Axios*, June 30, available at https://www.axios.com/2022/07/01/candor-leadership-management-hard-conversations-at-work.

5. Acosta, Joshua, 2022, "Transforming People Management," SAP SuccessFactors Growth & Insights.

6. Grenawalt, Lindsay, 2022, "Cockroach Labs Named #1 Large Company on Crain's 2022 Best Places to Work," *Cockroach* blog, September 29, available at https://www.cockroachlabs.com/blog/crains-best-places-2022/.

7. BusinessSolver, 2022, "BusinessSolver 7th Annual Report: 2022 State of Workplace Empathy," available at https://www.businessolver.com/resources/state-of-workplace-empathy.

8. Sigelman, Matt and Mehlman, Ken, 2022, "Airline Meltdowns Are the Canary in the Coal Mine," *Chicago Tribune*, August 31, available at https://www.chicagotribune.com/opinion/commentary/ct-opinion-airline-meltdowns-travel-labor-shortage-20220831-3griatp6i5f45b6l363cl7a3ra-story.html.

sparks & honey: Building a Practice of Gratitude

In the wee hours of April 20, 2018, Iola Killian received an email from her mother's boss.

"We are incredibly lucky to have Annalie as part of the sparks & honey family," wrote Terry Young, founder and CEO of the culture intelligence company, "and we know that Annalie is very fortunate to have your love and support in her life."

This was just one of dozens of messages that went out that night to the company's 65 employees and their invited guests, spouses and partners, children, siblings, best friends, and family members who would enjoy lunch the following day at the sparks & honey offices turned five-star caliber restaurant for the afternoon. A half dozen years into the consultancy's business, it was time to show some gratitude.

Across the afternoon, Young addressed each employee directly, letting each one know their value to the company and, in the process, reframed the office as a place of celebration.

"We didn't know how it was going to work," he told us, "but it was kind of mind-blowing that everyone in the room spoke. They told stories and jokes and we just kept going."

"Sometimes we are not always vulnerable leaders because we don't know what's going on in someone's life outside work," Young continued. "That day was really emotional. As a leader, there are times that we get ourselves into those situations and it can feel pretty, pretty uncomfortable. But it's really powerful in that you build a much stronger bond with your employees by being willing to go there."

The Gratitude Lunch was the kind of leadership move that signaled to employees that they were bigger than the organization and that the organization was better because of it. The event, says Annalie Killian, "changed the working relationship not only between myself and my daughter, but also my daughter and sparks & honey as the entity that competes for my attention. It gave her a better understanding of the work that we do and also the community that we are a member of. It really helped to cultivate this sense of this is not just a job. It's a community."

"Every organization talks about how your work is your family," added Kristin Cohen, the firm's Chief Marketing Officer, "and oftentimes that feels like a little bit of BS. When you actually bring your family or your closest loved one into the actual community, there's empathy to what you have going outside of the organization as well."

The notion that employees have interests and work outside their day jobs is challenging for a lot of companies. Indeed, many people would never want their employer to know they had a side hustle. Not so at sparks & honey. "It's very much encouraged as part of our learning culture," Killian told us. "We have formalized a strategic priority about becoming a learning company."

In fact, the company has a "Curiosity Budget" that employees can tap to learn about "whatever takes their interest," Killian said. "If you have a hobby or passion, pursue it and then share that with the rest of the company." On the day we spoke, the company had just approved a request from an employee who wanted to take piano lessons.

"We have to create meaning and purpose for our work," Young said. "We are cultural observers. Everything we do to learn and be curious benefits our work."

9 Emerge the Empathic Leader

On March 11, 2020, after more than 118,000 cases and 4,291 deaths in 114 countries, the World Health Organization declared Covid-19 a pandemic. Within weeks, if not days, the world came to a halt. Offices emptied and businesses closed as people went home to wait. And wait.

Despite assurances from government agencies that we needed just "15 days to flatten the curve," it soon became clear that this pandemic was about to change everything.

Our first book together, *The Adaptation Advantage,* dropped in the midst of this upheaval – an upheaval that put us to the adaptation test. Plans for in-person book events were scrapped for virtual interviews that invariably turned to the question on everyone's mind: "When will we get back to normal?" From the earliest days of the pandemic through to today, we have the same answer: "You won't be going *back*, ever." In fact, on March 23, 2022, Heather wrote an article in *Forbes* based on our conversations predicting that not only was the pandemic accelerating our transition into a future of work, but it might be the greatest catalyst for business transformation.

The premise of that first book pivoted on the singular idea that change is inevitable, constant, and quick. The pandemic-induced lockdowns put that in sharp relief. Change in the circumstances around you requires change in understanding, change in methods, change in process, change of mind, change in self-perception. And, we get it, change is hard, and the magnitude of change brought on by Covid-19 seems nearly impossible.

Now, as we write the final chapter of this current book in the fall of 2022, the World Health Organization cautiously said the end of the pandemic "is in sight." The US president, with an eye no doubt to the November election, was more definitive. "The pandemic is over," he told *60 Minutes* reporter Scott Pelley. These declarations are welcome relief after nearly three years of "business as unusual," and the impulse to return to the before-times mode of operation and leadership is understandable.

But here's the thing: you can't. You won't be going back, *ever*.

Because everything *has* changed. Everything about the who and how and where of work is different; if you've read this book from the beginning, that should be evident.

So, just when you thought you might get some relief, we're here to say two things: there is no respite from change, and you are already doing a great job navigating it.

In fact, even change has changed. In 1947, psychiatrist Kurt Lewin described three phases of change. A successful change requires an "unfreezing" of the current state, effectively letting go of the past. Next, you must move on to a new and different state. Then, finally, you "freeze" in a new state. "Since any level is determined by a force field," he wrote way back when, "permanency implies that the new force field is made relatively secure against change"[1] His "unfreeze, change, refreeze" model delivers a sense of hope that change is a one-time thing to endure in order to arrive at a new and consistent state of statis. Neither is true today.

Think of it: these pandemic years have been a long expedition, thrashing through the underbrush of unknowing, hoping to arrive at something familiar, at the very least some "new normal" that feels as solid as life and work before the pandemic. Instead, you have arrived at the Now Normal, a moment in time that will be comfortable and familiar for only a moment in time, until rampaging change can no longer be ignored.

The good news, though, is that every muscle you built and every instinct you honed thrashing through the jungle of the unknown these last three years is *exactly* what you need to move forward as an effective leader now. More change is certainly ahead. It may be economic uncertainty, geopolitical conflict, social unrest, another pandemic, rapid technological change, or something that we cannot even imagine today.

The Pandemic Was a Quiet Teacher

No matter what your leadership style was at the start of 2020, the pandemic challenged it and enabled you to grow as you shepherded your team through upheaval and uncertainty to find a new way to work together. Pause for a moment to think about that experience and all that you have learned.

The necessity of work from home environments demanded that your people be given the agency to determine how best to deliver their work. Quickly, you learned that – given clear guidance, the right tools, a little coaching, and a bit of flexibility – you could trust your people to get their work done independently. That should come as a huge relief to leaders who felt the need to manage the minutiae of daily work. Now, you are liberated to focus on the higher-order challenges and emerging opportunities, *and* you are discovering a breadth of new capabilities among your team.

Even if your workers were willing to give up their newfound agency, why would you want them to? Why would you want to go back to a leadership style that made you more taskmaster than talent agent? In the currently emerging Human Value Era, great leaders no longer rule with an iron fist. Instead, their best work is tapping the potential of the people around them, enabling and encouraging them to do their best work rather than the work you think is best. An unbridled team will inevitably find the most efficient, creative, cost-effective, and quality solution to the challenge at hand because in most cases they are closest to it and understand it best. (See "The Cumulative Shifts Between Individuals and Organizations.")

Surely, we have been clear on that point. Simply put, your team – certainly collectively and often on an individual basis – knows more than you do. It's time to flip the script and invert your relationship with your team. You now work for *them* supporting them to do their best work. Their success is your success.

The Cumulative Shifts Between Individuals and Organizations

The Great Reset is a convergence of trends some decades in the making that culminate in a changed relationship between individuals and organizations. Let's break down the five "Great Rs" that collectively give us the empowered workforce:

- **The Great Resignation**, posited first by Professor Anthony Klotz in a May 2021 interview in *Businessweek*, was originally thought to be a short-term post phenomenon triggered in the pandemic when the nation's quit rate hit a 20-year high. In reality, churn has been building since 2009, and Gartner predicts churn will increase 20% over pre-pandemic levels[2].

- **The Great Retirement** has been long in coming as the Baby Boomer generation moves into retirement. Although we knew this was coming, we were still caught flat-footed as the pandemic created the conditions for droves of Boomers to leave the workforce sooner than even they may have expected. Economists believe the resulting labor shortages will continue for at least a decade.

- **The Great Reshuffle** is occurring as people have reskilled and switched industries during the pandemic. Of those who changed jobs in 2021, more than half changed careers entirely, according to Pew Research.[3] While this reshuffle has left many industries scrambling for workers, the positive news here is that many of these reskilled workers are now working in fields of greater interest to them.

- **The Great Refusal** took hold as people turned down bad jobs with low pay. The Reddit thread r/antiwork is a showcase of workplace travesties that are leading workers to walk away from bad jobs, and today's federal minimum wage certainly falls well short of an incentive to make dehumanizing work worth it. Until 1968, the minimum wage kept pace with inflation and rose with productivity. If the minimum wage had continued that trajectory, it would be over $21 an hour today, according to the Center for Economic and Policy Research. But it hasn't. The minimum wage hasn't budged in a decade. Humans are assets to develop, not costs to contain, and some sectors of our economy are seeing higher than average labor shortages as workers reject these underpaying jobs. And here's another incentive to better engage your workers: customers experience your brand through interaction with your frontline workers. Engaged workers are better brand ambassadors.

- **The Great Relocation**, fueled by the shift to remote work, is allowing workers to pick where they want to live first to build community around place rather than work. It is the shift from work-life balance to life-work balance. The pandemic period of 2020–2022 saw the initial wave of relocations, as many people left large cities for more space to social distance. Now as the location and flexibility of jobs has become clearer and people prioritize work and life differently, more than 19 million adults are now looking to relocate due to availability of remote work, according to findings from Upwork.[4]

Collectively, these shifts are **The Great Reset**, with an empowered workforce that has tasted autonomy and flexibility. We are no longer centered on where we work, but rather where work fits in our lives, and there is no putting this genie back in the bottle. We have created new habits and new requirements.

Tapping into these new habits may well be the key to keeping an engaged workforce. Gallup's employee engagement numbers have not moved more than 10 points over 20 years. In the United States, engagement sits at 32% and it rests at 21% globally.[5] More worrisome, Gallup finds that global unhappiness is the highest ever recorded; 33% of people report being pretty much miserable.[6] Baseball batting averages are better than this. Let's hope that an empowered workforce that puts work in the proper place in their lives is the key to better engagement and greater happiness.

GREAT RESIGNATION + Talent Is Mobile, Get Used to It

GREAT RETIREMENT + The Boomer Retirement = Labor Shortages

GREAT RESHUFFLE + Reskilling: People Working to Their Potential

GREAT REFUSAL + Humans Are Assets to Develop Not Costs to Contain

GREAT RELOCATION + Remote Work + Life-Work Balance Recasts Settlement Patterns

GREAT RESET: THE EMPOWERED WORKFORCE = Not Just Where We Work, But Where Work Fits in Our Lives.

Figure 9.1 The Cumulative Shifts Between Individuals and Organizations

We're also going to guess that you learned a lot about the people that work with you. About their work skills and professional capabilities, certainly, but even more importantly about who they are as complete and complex human beings. Work from home suddenly gave us a digital window into our colleagues' lives. Blurred backgrounds and digital backdrops aside, we showed up for work more authentically than ever before, dressed for comfort, laptops propped up in home offices, on dining room tables, in spare bedrooms, or any corner of any place that might provide enough quiet to get through a Zoom meeting uninterrupted. With cameras on, we got to see our coworkers' home decor: their kitchens, their bookcases, their artwork, and maybe even an extensive and impressive sneaker collection. We met their dogs and cats and kids and partners, dipping into the digital frame just long enough for us to share the disruption and sometimes disorder that is the work from home life that we were all experiencing together, if apart.

It has become common to begin a virtual business meeting with a preamble about where you are and who's at home and what interruption may occur. We've all been there. We all understand. And in that understanding we found the seeds of empathy.

Understanding Empathy

The call to empathetic leadership gets louder by the day. Leading business journals fill their pages with articles extolling the virtues of empathetic leadership, but what does that mean, exactly?

We know that the days of leaders as unquestioned experts driving productivity with reward and fear are over and that the best leaders for our current era are competent, caring, humble, and curious learners who can say, "I do not know" and who can model vulnerability, demonstrate empathy, and coach and champion everyone to achieve their highest potential.

It is instructive, then, to take a deeper dive to fully understand empathy.

Perhaps first, we should dispatch the notion that empathetic leaders are simply nice. Surely kindness has a role to play in empathetic leadership, but nice is a different matter. Nice allows you to skirt hard conversations so as not to upset someone. Nice can be empty platitudes, hollow compliments, and forced smiles. Too often, nice dodges the hard conversations and leaves people to act from their assumptions. Nice – when not coupled with candor – is not, in fact, nice at all. Kindness, on the other hand, is honest, providing the feedback that enables someone to act from knowledge and assurance. Or, as author and professor Brené Brown is wont to say: "Clear is kind, unclear is unkind."

Empathy, though, is more than that. At its most basic level, empathy shifts the focus from you to the other to see a situation from another person's perspective and understand the unique experiences, thoughts, and emotions that create context for that person's ideas and actions. Empathy allows you to move beyond simple facts to get to the true drivers of behavior. Empathy allows you to tap into the concerns and passions of your team, finding the unique levers to engage and motivate them.

Empathy is no magic looking glass, to be sure. It is a layered social and psychological ability to connect uniquely with another person. Psychologist Daniel Golman has written extensively about empathy in his two best-selling books, *Emotional Intelligence* and *Social Intelligence*. He describes three types of empathy: Cognitive, Emotional, and Compassionate.

As the label implies, cognitive empathy is a basic knowledge of how another person feels and how they might be thinking. It's recognizing, perhaps, that a coworker is stressed because they are facing a big deadline, their partner is out of town, and their toddler just spiked a fever.

A layer deeper, emotional empathy shares the feelings of another. You relate through your own lived experience. You feel what they feel. You deeply understand the anxiety of the new staffer on their first day of work because you had that same anxiety when you started out.

Most deeply, compassionate empathy moves from understanding through feeling and to action. You balance cognition with emotion to find the space to offer support and act in concert and cooperation with your colleague.

More than anything, though, empathy creates the context to activate your colleagues' agency. Empathy elevates your people in the decision-making process and unlocks the potential for true collaboration. Empathy is, in no small way, the secret sauce of highly effective teams. One company we interviewed for this book gave us clear confirmation of this idea. This global enterprise software company employs a team of organizational psychologists to help in navigate the changing roles of leadership and its workforce, and they told us that among the most pointed changes they have seen in its leadership profile is the rapid adoption of words like *empathy* and *caring* in the job descriptions and performance reviews they have evaluated over the past two years.

Empathy Is Good Business

By embracing empathy as a primary tool of your leadership, you shift the dynamic of your organization. Us (leadership) vs. Them (workers) gives way to the "We" workplace, the foundation of the Human Value Era.

Empathetic leadership puts people first by understanding the needs of workers beyond a paycheck. And that, it turns out, is remarkably good for business at many levels.

Consider the state of the health care industry in the early 2020s. Health care organizations throughout the United States combined had more than a quarter million open job requisitions for certified health care workers, such as pharmacy technicians, certified nursing assistants, and medical records specialists. We surveyed health systems to understand the dynamics of these jobs. Most positions paid well enough, and hiring bonuses often amounted to 15–20% of the worker's starting salary. Still, workers stayed in these jobs for fewer than 12 months. Why? Because the jobs were miserable. Workers report being poorly treated, disrespected, and inadequately trained. In short, their needs were neither well understood nor well received.

Now, imagine a more empathetic approach to this desperate workforce issue. Imagine if those hiring bonuses were used not to entice someone to endure bad working conditions, but to change the working conditions that are the root of the retention problems? What if these organizations provided flexible work hours, childcare, and most importantly, the training and support to build workers' professional credentials? What would happen if an empathetic leader invested time on a nursing ward to understand the daily work environment and endeavor to build a culture of support, understanding, and respect among the many codependent professionals working together? Might that pay dividends?

A team of leadership gurus and researchers wanted to answer that question for themselves. The group, led by author and researcher Tiffani Bova, sifted through three years of employee and financial data provided by a large global retailer and found a clear link between employee satisfaction and revenue. "If an average store could move from the bottom quartile to the top quartile in each of the employee experience metrics we studied, they would increase their revenue by more than 50%, and profits by nearly as much," the researchers reported in the *Harvard Business Review*.[7]

Your empathetic leadership, then, is critical to creating a high-performance working environment, one that nurtures and supports your workforce, empowers distributed decision making, and champions collaborative learning, all centered on the physical and mental well-being of the human beings who show up – virtually or in person – to work every day.

Empathy, Trust, and Compassion: The Trifecta of Superior Leadership

The foundation of such an environment is trust, which must be integrated into every aspect of the business. For example, perks used to mean the little extras that sweetened an employee's compensation package. An espresso machine in the break room, a generous vacation allowance, ergonomic office chairs, an office with a view. Often, the perks of the job came in lieu of pay. (All the free burgers you can eat for a minimum hourly wage and not enough hours to make a decent living. But, hey, burgers!)

Many times, perks bestowed status commensurate with title. (A parking space with your name on it, Employee of the Month!) In almost every instance, perks were earned and meted out as incentives to work harder and harder.

In the new era of human-centered work, perks take on a very different role. They are the symbol of trust. When employees are offered unlimited vacation days, for example the company is saying to the worker, "Take the time you need. We trust that you will get the job done, and you won't leave your collaborators in the lurch." In some organizations, unlimited vacation can turn into no vacation as workers forgo time off, succumbing to social pressure to put in more hours. The best leaders reinforce unlimited time off policies and build trust by ensuring team members do take time away from work to rest and recharge.

It's not enough, though, to pin unlimited time off as a corporate benefit; you have to create a culture that respects and encourages rest and restoration. Analyzing data from over 125,000 employees, the 2017 HR Mythbusters report, conducted by HR software provider Namely, noted that high performers take on average 19 days of vacation and average performers take only 14 days.[8] Still other research has shown that workers who have unlimited vacation time are *less likely* to take time off than those who have work with fixed paid time off policies, and *more likely to work* when they do take time away. A separate Namely study found that people who have the benefit of unlimited time off take an average of 13 days per year, compared to the 15 days taken by those working under traditional vacation plans.[9] In other words, the policies of unlimited vacation must be met with the culture that actually supports that time off because at the end of the day, in the Human Value Era, a rested and recreated human is your best source of value creation.

It turns out, Americans are terrible at vacation. Of the 38 countries that make up the Organization of Economic Cooperation and Development (OECD), the United States is the only country without a paid annual leave policy. Our aversion to vacation hurts our potential, and leaders are starting to realize it – and do something about it. We interviewed the chief strategy officer of a publicly traded biopharmaceutical company who told us that despite her company's pressing mission to develop therapies to treat Covid-19, they forced a mandatory one-week shut down in late 2020, sending all but the most essential personnel home. Why? Because the company knew their people were burnt out and that without a break they would not have the ability to see their products through and meet their customer needs. If this organization can take time during this period of urgency, we can all take some time away throughout the year. We will all be better for it.

The decision making we give to employees about everything from how to do their jobs to when to take vacation is a measure of trust, and trust is the currency of the new workplace. Trust also gives back time as leaders. When you don't trust, you micromanage. When you micromanage, you do your job and theirs. That is highly inefficient, exhausting, and demoralizing to your people. Hire smart people, empower them, trust them, then get out of their way.

The role of the empathetic leader, then, is to create an environment where trust flows multilaterally throughout the organization. We've discussed this in other chapters, but it is worth reiterating here. The building blocks of that trusted environment are:

- Clear and consistent values; a culture that is well articulated, well understood, and well celebrated.

- A foundation of psychological safety that enables risk taking, discovery, learning, and, most importantly, the safety to dissent.

- Unwavering integrity, vulnerability, and empathy that levels relationships between leaders and workers and among workers themselves.

To build this foundation, you need to tap your cognitive and emotional states of empathy. And to firmly cement it and really lead in this new era, you must call upon your compassion. Indeed, empathy without compassion leaves us to wallow in "all the feels" of the people around us, sometimes even clouding our judgment and stifling progress. Compassion drives us to act, and act in the best interest of the collective organization.

Rasmus Hougaard and Jacqueline Carter write clearly about this in *Compassionate Leadership: How to Do Hard Things in a Human Way* (Harvard Business Review Press, 2022). Compassion, they write, is less about doing than about asking, How can I help? "Leadership is not about solving problems for people," they assert. "It is about growing and developing people, so they are empowered to solve their own problems."[10]

By asking your workers what they need, you drive them to consider real solutions to their challenges for themselves, while letting them know that you are supporting them. And while every instinct of a leader is to jump in and solve tough problems, Hougaard and Carter believe it is equally important to back off. "Remember," they write, "that in many instances people do not need your solutions; they need your ear and your caring presence. . . . Taking 'non-action' can often be the most powerful means of helping."[11]

The Power of Listening

Indeed, listening just might be the most important thing you can do as an empathetic leader. Particularly now. Most of us have come through some of the most difficult and disruptive times we've ever known. And many are struggling to deal with it. So much so, in fact, that the US Preventive Services Task Force, a panel of experts in preventative and evidenced-based medicine appointed by the Department of Health and Human Services, issued an advisory in September 2022 calling for doctors to screen adult patients for anxiety.[12]

You come to this step change in leadership at a critical time. No matter what your industry, sector, role, or function, your workforce is empowered. And exhausted. Times like these call for the empathetic leader, one who uses every facet of empathy to build connection and create the conditions to emerge from these most challenging times a better, stronger community of workers.

Welcome to Tomorrow: Leading in Uncertainty

It bears repeating one more time: the Covid-19 pandemic disrupted a workforce desperately in need of that disruption. The old models of employer/employee dynamics are insufficient to accommodate a rapidly changing, rapidly digitizing economy. Where leading companies were on pace to complete their digital transformation in a decade, the pandemic provided a forced reboot. Empowered employees demanded a reset.

We can hope that we don't see a pandemic of the scope and scale of Covid-19 again in our lifetimes, but this pandemic is surely not the last disruption. Climate change, geopolitical conflicts, technology disruptions, housing shortages, labor shortages, inflation, supply chain challenges. These are just a few of the forces that will challenge organizations each and every day from now on.

How do you lead through these challenges? With empathy. With trust. With compassion. Engaging your superpowers to become the best possible leader for these times.

Let's go.

Notes

1. Lewin, Kurt, 1947, "Changing as Three Steps: Unfreezing, Moving, and Freezing," *Human Relations*, available at https://journals.sagepub.com/doi/10.1177/001872674700100103.

2. "Gartner Says U.S. Total Annual Employee Turnover Will Likely Jump by Nearly 20% from the Pre-pandemic Annual Average," Gartner Press Release, April 2022, available at https://www.gartner.com/en/newsroom/04-28-2022-gartner-says-us-total-annual-employee-turnover-will-likely-jump-by-nearly-twenty-percent-from-the-prepandemic-annual-average.

3. Parker, Kim and Menasce Horowitz, Julianna, 2022, "Majority of Workers Who Quit a Job in 2021 Cite Low Pay, No Opportunities for Advancement, Feeling Disrespected," Pew Research, March, available at https://www.pewresearch.org/ft_22-03-09_resignation-featured-image.

4. "The New Geography of Remote Work," Upwork, 2022, available at https://www.upwork.com/research/new-geography-of-remote-work.

5. "State of the Global Workforce Report," Gallup, 2022, available at https://www.gallup.com/workplace/349484/state-of-the-global-workplace-2022-report.aspx.

6. Clifton, Jon, 2022, "The Global Rise of Unhappiness," Gallup, September, available at https://news.gallup.com/opinion/gallup/401216/global-rise-unhappiness.aspx.

7. Gautier, Kate, Bova, Tiffany, Chen, Kexin, and Munasinghe, Lalith, 2022, "Research: How Employee Experience Impacts Your Bottom Line," *Harvard Business Review*, March 22, available at https://hbr.org/2022/03/research-how-employee-experience-impacts-your-bottom-line.

8. "HR Mythbusters: The Reality of Work at Mid-Market Companies Nationwide," Namely, 2017, available at https://cdn2.hubspot.net/hubfs/228948/Namely%20HR%20Mythbusters%20Report.pdf.

9. Bolsu, Rachel, 2018, "How to Implement an Effective Unlimited Vacation Policy," Namely, November 1, available at https://blog.namely.com/unlimited-vacation-policy.

10. Hougaard, Rasmus, Carter, Jacqueline, and Afton, Marissa, 2021, "Connect with Empathy, But Lead with Compassion," *Harvard Business Review*, December 23, available at https://hbr.org/2021/12/connect-with-empathy-but-lead-with-compassion.

11. "Gartner Says U.S. Total Annual Employee Turnover Will Likely Jump by Nearly 20%."

12. "Screening for Anxiety in Adults," U.S. Preventive Services Task Force, September 14, 2022, available at https://www.uspreventiveservicestaskforce.org/uspstf/draft-update-summary/anxiety-adults-screening.

ABOUT THE AUTHORS

Heather E. McGowan and **Chris Shipley** have been thought partners and writing collaborators for nearly a decade. Their first book together, *The Adaptation Advantage: Let Go, Learn Fast, and Thrive in the Future of Work* (Wiley 2020), is a top-rated business book and has been adopted by graduate programs focused on adaptive leadership and learning culture.

A much sought-after speaker, Heather helps leaders prepare their people and organizations for the post-pandemic world of work. Heather gives lucidity to the complex topic of the future of work through her illuminating graphic frameworks and powerful metaphors, all backed by deep research. In 2020, *Forbes* magazine recognized her as one of the world's top 50 female futurists. (https://heathermcgowan.com/ and https://www.linkedin.com/in/heathermcgowan/)

Chris has documented, influenced, and predicted the impact of technology on business and society for more than 30 years. Focusing now on the human, social, and organizational impact of technology and economic disruption, she works with leadership teams of emerging companies as they address the business transformation, cultural alignment, and innovation process challenges. (https://cshipley.com and https://www.linkedin.com/in/cshipley9/)

PRAISE FOR *THE ADAPTATION ADVANTAGE: LET GO, LEARN FAST, AND THRIVE IN THE FUTURE OF WORK*

by Heather McGowan and Chris Shipley

"*The Adaptation Advantage* is the clearest, most compelling, and original examination of the present and future workplace. The big surprise in this book is that it's not about learning to live with more robots but rather learning to become more human. Whether you were born digital or born analog, *The Adaptation Advantage* is an indispensable resource for thriving in a world that is transforming as you read this."

—Jim Kouzes, coauthor of *The Leadership Challenge*,
Executive Fellow, Center for Innovation and Entrepreneurship, Leavey School of Business

"Heather McGowan and Chris Shipley are prophets of the Fourth Industrial Revolution. Their extraordinary insights and tools challenge and empower organizations, leaders, and people across society to thrive in a future marked by exceptional technological and societal change."

—Major General James Johnson, U.S. Air Force (ret.),
former Director of Air Force Integrated Resilience

The Adaptation Advantage is fueled by the power of an elegant idea: our ability to learn and adapt is inseparable from our sense of identity. And as automation driven by machine intelligence remakes our world, the need to continually transform our identities becomes the very foundation of human growth—and how we thrive. McGowan and Shipley have wrapped a vivid and immensely readable narrative around this idea. My advice: read it!"

—Randy Swearer, PhD.
Vice President of Learning Futures, Autodesk

In *The Adaptation Advantage*, McGowan and Shipley deliver a powerful message for corporate leaders about success in the future of work. Learning and identity are not only intertwined but fundamental to any organization's ability to adapt and create value. How exciting to read a book built on the core premise that learning unleashes our human potential while also driving competitive advantage.

—Dr. Sean Gallagher,
Executive Director, Centre for the New Workforce, Swinburne University

The Adaptation Advantage tackles head-on the most critical challenge facing all of us in the near future: Where do we find purpose and prosperity in a world that increasingly feels beyond anyone's control? The extent to which we adapt to a radically shifted concept of "work" will inevitably be determined by our ability to re-think learning – away from a fixed-term preparation for employment, to a continuous way of living. Accordingly, this vital book offers a road map to the oldest question of all: How, then, should we live? Among a growing cadre of dystopians, it's refreshing to hear a much-needed optimistic analysis from McGowen and Shipley.

—David Price, OBE,
Best-selling Author of Open: How We Will Work, Learn, and Live In The Future

McGowan and Shipley's *The Adaptation Advantage* nails it. Adaptive identity requires letting go – letting go of a job or skill set identity in order to thrive in a world of rapidly changing societal norms and technologies. This is required reading for all students of service science, such as myself.

—Dr. Jim Spohrer,
IBM Director, Cognitive Open Technologies

In a world of exponential change, we all need strategies to help us continually adapt. With *The Adaptation Advantage*, Shipley and McGowan have given us the user manual.

—Gary A. Bolles,
Chair for the Future of Work, Singularity University

Twenty years of research have shown me the importance of bringing humans to the forefront of the future of work. By recognizing the centrality of human potential, *The Adaptation Advantage* illuminates the value of resilience, adaptability, and the qualities that make us uniquely human in the future of culture, work, and self.

—Dr. Vivienne Ming
Theoretical Neuroscientist, Founder, Socos Labs

This book is an essential guide for anyone who seeks to understand what it means to be human in the age of intelligent machines. By tapping into our uniquely human capabilities, we can unleash our advantage in the future of work. Heather and Chris urge us to go on an inward journey to uncover who we are and consider how we manifest our passion, character and collaborative spirit as our most enduring and sustainable means of making positive progress as people, leaders and institutions.

—Dov Seidman,
Author of HOW and founder and chairman of LRN and
The HOW Institute for Society

The digital revolution is overturning careers as well as companies. This book will be an essential guide to the future of work for both individuals and organizations.

—Mark Bonchek,
Chief Epiphany Officer, Shift Thinking

Microchips cannot and will not replace relationships. Your next job starts where the robots stop. Learn to embrace that handoff. The best way to do that, Heather and Chris argue, for both individuals and organizations, is through rapid learning, unlearning and adaptation. Heather and Chris' book is an indispensable guide to how navigate this new era in the workplace.

—Thomas L. Friedman,
Foreign Affairs Columnist, The New York Time

INDEX

4 Stages of Psychological Safety, The (Clark), 119

A

Active listening, usage, 179
Adaptation Advantage, The (McGowan/Shipley), 104, 122, 150, 183, 187
Adaptation, learning, 39–40
Ahluwalia, Manak, 75–76, 178
All-gender bathrooms, usage, 25
Allison, David, 118
Anderson, Rob, 147
Anxiety, screening, 197
Apple Together, petition, 136
Aqueduct Technologies, employees (happiness/ listening), 75–76, 178
Aspirational Purpose, 138, 141
Augmented reality, 43
Autonomy, 95
Awareness, power, 173–174

B

Back-to-office mandates, 179
Balance, lifestyle (combination), 142
Banishing Burnout (Leiter), 90
Base camp exit, contents (relinquishment), 154, 156–157
Beating Burnout at Work (Davis), 94
Becker Hospital Review, tracking system (usage), 160–161
Behaviors
  change, 176–177
  culture, relationship, 135, 135f
  shift, 182–183, 183f

Beliefs, culture (relationship), 135, 135f
Belonging. *See* Diversity, Equity, Inclusion, and Belonging
  example, 147–148
  importance, 118, 119f
  loyalty, relationship, 118
  power, unleashing, 117
  sense, 68
Benefits
  culture, relationship, 135, 135f
  identification, 96–97
Bentzen-Mercer, Cynthia, 98, 101–102
Berlin Wall, collapse, 20
Bernstein, Ethan, 110
Bhutan, geopolitical success measure, 93–94
Biden, Joe, 23, 160
Big Mac Index, 64
Bite Ninja (software), 41
Black, Indigenous, and People of Color (BIPOC), workforce, 18
Bleisure, rise, 51, 51f
Bloom, Nicholas, 158
Bloom, Nick, 110
Bosworth, Andrew, 149
Bova, Tiffani, 137
Bowling Alone (Putnam), 47
Bradberry, Travis, 173
Brady, Tom, 96–97
Braham, Jeanne, 147
Brand, Paul, 129
Branson, Richard, 115
Brooks, David, 65
Brown, Brené, 171

Bryant, Katherine, 115
Burnout, 196
    addressing, 95–96
    crisis, 142
    factors, 96
    observation process, 67, 71f
    rates, increase, 111
    reality, 66
Burnout Challenge, The (Maslach/Leiter), 96
Business, phases, 155
Butler, Timothy, 104

C
Candor, power, 174–175
Canteen, The (purpose/belonging), 147–148
Capability, skill, 92
Capacity
    investment, 164
    skill, 92
Capitalism, Socialism, and Democracy
        (Schumpeter), 37
Career accelerant, 143
Career coach, role, 166–167
Caring, term (adoption), 193
Carr, Priyanka B., 117
Carter, Jacqueline, 197
Center for the Edge (Deloitte), 84
Center, shift (work), 45, 45f
Challenger Safety, 120
Change
    management, 89
    norm, 89
Chapek, Bob, 159
Chetty, Raj, 64
Chief human resource officers (CHROs),
        red flags, 95
Childcare infrastructure, inadequacy, 22
Chochinov, Allan, 157
Chouinard, Yvon, 134
Civil Rights Act, Title VII, 25
Clark, Timothy R., 118–120, 156
Cockroach Labs, Inc., 136, 179
Cognitive diversity, usage, 122–123
Cognitive labor, 48
Cohen, Kristin, 185

Collaboration
    in-real-life collaboration, 42
    learning, 38
    location, 43
    organizing, relationship, 122
    virtual collaboration, 42
Collective intelligence (creation), social capital
        (usage), 121–122
Command and control, relinquishment, 156
Community, importance/usage, 96, 101–102
Compassionate Leadership (Hougaard/Carter),
        197
Compassion/empathy/trust,
        combination, 195–197
Compensation, 142
Competence (skill), defining, 92
Competitive landscape, changes, 174
Complex Adaptive Systems, 159
Complexity, leadership (relationship), 86, 87f
Conceptual thinking, usage, 105
Contingency plan, 158
Continual expeditions, 157, 159
Contributor Safety, 120
Coronavirus vaccines, delivery, 159
Corporate America, women
        (underrepresentation), 22
Corporate profits, workforce drain/demands,
        78
Cost of goods sold (COGS), improvement, 85
Counseling, usage, 105
Covid-19 pandemic
    catalyst, 4
    change agent, 34
    fatigue, 88
    genetic sequence, identification, 38
    global status, WHO declaration, 14, 187
    impact, 40, 154
    lessons, 189
    mortality, risk, 160
    navigation, 22
    time, compression, 37, 38f
Creative class, 44
Creative production, impact, 105
Creative projects, usage, 87
Crowley, Mark C., 113, 163, 166, 182

Culture
    beliefs/behaviors/benefits, equation,
        134–135, 135f
    change, 131, 176
    contract, 130
    foundation, 144
    health, trust (impact), 136–137
    intentional culture, 130
    mindful culture, building, 131, 133
    nurturing, dialogue (usage), 132, 132f
    organization operating instructions, 130–131
    shift, 124f
    toxic culture, recognition, 131
Customer dissatisfaction, impact, 10
Cynicism, recovery (difficulty), 67

D
Dao Duy Anh, David, 162
Daring Greatly (Brown), 171
Daszak, Peter, 88
Davis, Paula, 94
Demographics, change, 7–8
DeSantis, Ron, 159
Developmental dyslexia (DD), 115
Dialogue, usage, 132, 132f
Digital disruption, impact, 39
Digital nomads, exploration, 51
Digital payments, usage, 236
Digital transformation, 3–4, 172
Disruptions, frequency (increase), 87–88
Diversity
    embracing, strategic advantage, 114–115
    importance, 27, 115
    leveraging, 28
Diversity, Equity, Inclusion, and Belonging
        (DEIB), 110
    check-the-box concern, cessation, 116
    foundation, establishment, 114
    initiatives, 132
    understanding, 116, 116f
Dyson, Esther, 121

E
Economic Policy Uncertainty Index, 158
Economic trend lines, attention, 158

Edelman Trust Barometer, 30, 137
Edmondson, Amy, 119
Eight-hour workday, artifact, 48
Elliot, Richard, 161
Emotional bleeding, cessation, 163
Emotional Intelligence (Bradberry), 173
Emotional intelligence (EQ)
    levels, 90
    requirement, 174
Emotional Intelligence (Golman), 193
Emotional overload, 110
Emotional pain, attention, 163
Emotional wounds, impact (knowledge), 163
Emotions, management/function, 165
Empathetic leader, role, 196
Empathetic leadership, 192
    flexibility, importance, 98
    importance, 195
Empathic leader, emergence, 187
Empathy, 150
    absence, difficulty, 165
    advantage, 75–76
    business quality, relationship, 194–195
    decrease, 181
    generational empathy, 28, 30
    impact, 196
    importance, 193
    term, adoption, 193
    trust/compassion, combination, 195–197
    understanding, 192–193
Employee-of-the-month programs, usage, 113
Employees
    business treatment, 97
    engagement, reduction, 111
    focus, 98–99
    happiness, 75–76
    preference, prioritization, 137
    stress, 10
Empowered mindset, understanding, 57
Empowered workforce, 44, 96, 151
    enabling, 129
Engagement levels, 137
Enterprise control, 105
Environmental and Social Governance (ESG), 52
Evolving, attribute, 132

Expedition, 188
  continual expeditions, 157, 159
  defining, 154
  enthusiasm, creation, 165–166
Expedition team
  care, 162–163
  composition, 155f
  piloting, 153
  understanding, 155
Expertise, primacy (relinquishment), 154, 156
"Extraneous Factors in Judicial Decisions"
      study, 173–174
Extrinsic rewards, impact, 96

F
Facebook Horizon Workrooms, 43
FaceTime, usage, 36
Fairness, perception, 96
Fearfully and Wonderfully Made (Brand), 129
Fearless Organization, The (Edmondson), 119
Feedback, importance, 178
Ferland, Martine, 68
Flexbility, 142
Florida, Richard, 44
Ford, Henry, 70
Forest fires, fighting, 161
Fosslien, Liz, 27
Four Phases of Psychological Safety, The
      (Clark), 118, 156
Frei, Frances, 165, 167
Friedman Doctrine, impact, 13
Friedman, Milton, 4
Friedman Shareholder Value era, 135
Fuller, Joseph, 6
Fundamentals, focus, 164, 164f

G
Galinsky, Adam D., 123
Gallo, Edoardo, 123
Gender
  identity (X) marker, 8
  markers, irrelevance, 27
  navigation, 25, 26f
  nonbinary gender distinction, 24
Generational empathy, 28, 30
Generation Z, 29, 29f
  burnout, risk, 5
  trauma/uncertainty, 29

workers, workforce percentage, 18
work flexibility/adaptability, importance, 19
workforce entry, 14–15, 28
work preference, 139
Geopolitical success measure, 93–94
Geopolitical trend lines, attention, 158
Germine, Laura T., 19
Gini Coefficient, 2
Global Engagement Survey (Gallup), 9
Global uncertainty, navigation, 158, 158f
Goal, change, 71–72
Godin, Seth, 150
Goffman, Erving, 149
Golman, Daniel, 193
Good Judgment Project, 88
Goodwill, reliance, 122
Google Meet, usage, 36
Gratitude Lunch, 185
Gratitude, practice (building), 185–186
Great Refusal, 190
Great Relocation, 44, 46, 47f, 190–191
Great Resentment, origins, 64, 64f
Great Reset, 57, 191
  impact, 61
Great Reset Opportunity, 142–143, 143f
Great Reshuffle, 190
Great Resignation, 2, 5–7, 52, 58, 190
  cause, 131
  first wave, 167
  impact, 64
  total US nonfarm quits, 7f
Great Retirement, 190
Grenawalt, Lindsay, 137
Gross National Happiness (GNH) Index, 93
Growth IQ (Bova), 137

H
Hagel, John, 84
Harari, Yuval Noah, 149–150
Hartshorne, Joshua K., 19
Healing, 66
Hefernan, Margaret, 88
Herzberg, Frederick, 60, 69, 162–163
Hierarchical reporting structures, impact,
      139
Hierarchy of Engagement (Maslow), 62
Hiring, culture (relationship), 106
Hoffman, Reid, 108

Hougaard, Rasmus, 197
How: Why How We Do Anything Means Everything
    (Siedman), 37
HR Mythbusters report (2017), 195
Human-centered workplace, creation, 50
Human-created intangible value, corporate value
    (relationship), 83
Humanness, power, 181
Human resource leaders, DEIB
    (relationship), 116
Human skills, 183
Human transformation, 36
Human value, 69
Human Value Era, 83, 98–99, 105–106, 196
    beneficiaries list, 135
    challenges, 153
    commitment, 113
    emergence, 189
    foundation, 194
    rise, 83, 84f
    work, connection, 103–104
Human workforce, capitalization, 79
Human work, replacement (modeling), 37
Hurni, Roger, 106, 121
Hybrid work, 179

I
Impression management, 172
Inclusion Safety, 120
Income inequality, measure, 2
Individual/organization
    cumulative shifts, 190–191, 191f
    relationship, understanding, 90–91
Industrial Revolution, workforce (economic
    transformation), 2
Influence, language/ideas (usage), 105
In-office work, 110
In-real-life collaboration, 42
Integrity, impact, 196
Intentional culture, 130
Intrinsic rewards, impact, 96

J
Japan, four-day work week (Microsoft), 49
Jobs
    bias, 107
    control/autonomy, impact, 96

jumping, 69
    rethinking, 104–106, 107, 107f
    satisfaction, 61
    sculpting, 104
    tasks set, 108
    worth, question, 63
Jobs-based work, shift, 87
Jobs, Steve, 149
Joy, Bill, 122
Joy's Law, 122
Justice, perception, 96

K
Kerr, William, 6
Kilduff, Gavin J., 123
Killian, Annalie, 185
Killian, Iola, 185
Killing Time at Work 22 (Qatalog/GitLab
    study), 112
Kindness, act, 140
Kittitas County, communication
    (importance), 161–162
Klotz, Anthony, 58, 95, 190
Knowledge
    absence, power, 172–173
    economy, 48, 156
    work, location (occurrence), 42
Knowledge-based economy, shift, 86
Knowledge-based projects, usage, 87
Knowledge sharing, 121
Korzybski, Alfred, 81

L
Labor shortage, 23
Labor unions, 40-hour work week
    establishment, 70
Leaders
    career coach role, 166–167
    career ladder, climbing, 150
    empathic leader, emergence, 187
    focus, 182
    mindshift, 98
    motivation, 182–183
    resilient leader, becoming, 183
    selection criteria, 182
    traits, value, 182
    work environment, 9–10

Leadership
  approach, 176
  change, 86, 87f
  empathetic leadership, flexibility
      (importance), 98
  empathy/trust/compassion,
      combination, 195–197
  fulfillment, 166
  maps, absence, 98–99
  options, openness, 158
  path, change (preparation), 159–162
  pipeline, 182–183
  profile, change, 182, 183f
  rethinking, 149
  shifts, 176–177, 177f
  skills, management, 182
  uncertainty leadership, 198
Lead from the Heart (Crowley), 163
Learner Safety, 120
Learning
  importance, 143
  respite, 108–109
  rethinking, 91, 93
Learning at scale, conditions (creation), 120–121
Learn Serve Lead 2021, 171
Lee, Sid, 118
Leiter, Michael P., 66, 67, 90–91, 96
Levav, Jonathan, 173–174
Levine, Alison, 153, 159
Lewin, Kurt, 188
Lewis, David, 122, 156
LGBTQ+ couples, online meeting, 43
LGBTQ+ workforce, 24, 26–27
Life
  drivers, 105
  life/work integration, creation, 50, 52–53
  work/life rebalance, 59–60
Life-altering decisions, 174
Lifestyle, balance (combination), 142
Listening
  active listening, usage, 179
  attribute, 132
  care, usage, 89
  performative listening, 179
  power, 177–179, 197
Location-flexible work environments, 48

M
MacFarlane, Alex, 25
Main lab, 136–137
Manufacturing-based economy, shift, 86
Marcario, Rose, 134
Marijuana possession, federal offenses
      (pardoning), 23
Marks, Lawrence E., 115
Martin, Roger, 82, 85, 89, 113, 121, 156
Maslach, Christina, 96
Maslow, Abraham, 62
McCraty, Rollin, 163
McDonald, Calvin, 52
Mead, Margaret, 129–130
Meetings, usage (cessation), 156–157
Mehlman, Ken, 181
Mental distress, rates (increase), 111
Mental health
  importance, 114
  reality, 66
Mental illness, 163
Mentoring, usage, 105
Mercy (leadership), community (usage),
      101–102
Metaverse, 43
Metrics, recalibration, 93–95
Microsoft Japan, productivity (increase),
      157
Microsoft Teams, usage, 36
Millennials, social contract risk, 20
Millennial Survey (Deloitte), 50
Miller, Claire Cain, 110
Mindful culture, building, 131, 133
Mindset
  changes, 176
  empowered mindset, understanding, 57
  shift, 180, 180f
Minimum wage, change (absence), 13
Mixing labs, 136–137
Morriss, Anne, 167
Mothers, caregiving (time/duration), 22–23
Motivation-hygiene theory, 60, 69
Motivation, theory, 162–163
Multigenerational workforce,
      management, 20, 21f
Murthy, Vivek, 114

N

Negative feelings, battling, 163
Net productivity, growth, 81–82
Neurodiversity, usage/types, 114–115
New Way to Think, A (Martin), 85
Nonbinary gender distinction, 24
"No News Is Good News" mantra,
    abandonment, 156
Nonprofit workers, pay sacrifice, 61

O

Obama, Barack, 178
Occupational phenomenon, 67
Office
    return, curation, 111–113
    work, performative aspect, 112
On the Edge (Levine), 153
Operating models, upgrading, 81
Organization
    advantage, 141
    individual, relationship
        (understanding), 90–91
    operating instructions, 130–131
    rethinking, 77–79
Organizing, collaboration (relationship), 122
Out of Office (Peterson/Warzel), 112
Out-of-pocket expenses, 140
Owl Labs (virtual conferencing), 41, 46

P

Pale Rider (Spinney), 3
Pandemic. *See* Covid pandemic
Pan-generational workforce, meeting, 19
Parental Rights in Education Act ("Don't Say
    Gay" bill), controversy, 159
Peers, collaborator role, 123, 124f, 133
Pelley, Scott, 188
People
    focus, 98–99
    management, 105
    self-direction/self-motivation, 180
People-centric activities, focus, 182
"People of the Global Majority" reference, 18
Performance coaches, impact, 176
Performative listening, 179
Personal risk, mitigation, 142

Personal values, ranking, 117
Peterson, Anne Helen, 112
Peterson, Pam, 147
Physical hygiene, 163
Physical object, co-creation, 109
Physical office space, impact, 43
Physical overload, 110
Physical/psychological safety, 142
Physical workplace, 58
Pink tax, 25
Pioneers (business phase), 155
Post-pandemic workplace, business
    adaptation, 178–179
Presentation of Self in Everyday Life
    (Goffman), 149
Productive engagement, 90–91
Project-based organizations, shift
    (importance), 87
Project Starline (Google), 43
Project: Time Off (SHRM), 97
Project work, change, 85, 87
Psychological safety, 172
    foundation, 196
    net, collecting, 119–120
Purpose
    Aspirational Purpose, 138
    competitive advantage, 140–141, 143–144
    example, 147–148
    faces, 138, 139f
    finding, 137, 139–140
    trouble, 144–145
    work reason, 141
Putnam, Robert, 47

Q

QR Codes, usage, 36
Quantitative analysis, usage, 105

R

Rayman, Miriam, 51
Reade, J. James, 123
Relatedness, 95
Relationships
    importance, 68–69, 96
    management, 105
Remote work, impact, 47

Resilient leader, becoming, 183
Restaurants, cloud labor, 41
Résumé mindset, 65
Résumés, usage, 91
Retention levels, 137
Return-to-office (RTO) mandates, 140, 179
Return-to-office (RTO) policies, 8–9, 136
Revelation One, 59
Reynolds, Alison, 122, 156
Rise of the Creative Class (Florida), 44
Rock, Chris, 63
Rockne, Knute, 150
Rossignon, Loic, 147

S
Sales, general, and administrative (SG&A)
        costs, loss, 85
Sapiens (Harari), 149
Schumpeter, Joseph Alois, 37
Self-censor, 120
Self-esteem, protection, 163
Self, healing, 66
Self-worth, premium, 123
Settlers (business phase), 155
Shapiro, Douglas, 21
Shareholder capital doctrine, rejection, 82, 84–85
Shareholder Value Era, 4–5, 83
Sheahan, Peter, 90
Siedman, Dov, 36
Sigelman, Matt, 181
Silard, Anthony, 118
Skills
    gap, closure issue, 92, 93f
    shelf life, 107
    training, 106
Skype, usage, 36
Social acceptance, shifts, 26
Social capital, usage, 121–122
Social dynamics, 91
    people connection, 95
Social Intelligence (Golman), 193
Social intelligence levels, 90
Social Network, The (docudrama), 149
Society for Human Resource Management
        (SHRM), 97
Soft skills, 183

sparks & honey, gratitude (practice), 185–186
Spinelli, Steve, 14
Spinney, Laura, 3
Stakeholders, embracing, 82, 84–85
Starry, Starry Night (Braham, Peterson), 147
State of Employee Empathy, The report
        (BusinessSolvers), 181
State of the Global Workplace (Gallup), 66
State of Workplace Empathy report
        (Businesssolver), 98
Status, premium, 123
Strand, Jacob, 51
Sull, Charles/Donald, 131
Superpowers, embracing, 171
Switching costs (reduction), remote work
        (impact), 47
"Synesthesia on Our Mind" (Marks), 115

T
Talent, work, 180
Tax Cut and Jobs Act, 134
Taylor, Bret, 42
Team
    leaders, work, 47
    work, 180f
Technology
    advances, 172
    application, 105
    embracing, 36
Theory development, usage, 105
"Theory of Human Motivation, A" (Maslow), 62
Thriving, conditions (creation), 103, 113–115
Time, resource, 164
Total US nonfarm quits, 7f
Tour of duty, term (usage), 85, 108–109
Town Planners (business phase), 155
Toxic culture, recognition, 131
Transformational change, 89
Trend Briefing (Future Laboratory), 51
Trust
    building/rebuilding, 165
    empathy/compassion, combination, 195–197
    importance, 136–137, 164, 196
    learning, 36
Trusted environment, building blocks, 196
Turban, Stephen, 110

U

Uncertainty
  continuation, 157, 159
    global uncertainty, navigation, 158, 158f
    leader navigation, approach, 158
    leadership, 198
Unchartered (Hefernan), 88
Unethical behavior, increase, 123
Unleash (Frei/Morriss), 167
Upswing, The (Putnam), 47
US Preventive Services Task Force, anxiety
    advisory, 197

V

Values, 142. *See also* Human value
  alignment, 96
  clarity/consistency, 196
  living, 133–134
VandeHei, Jim, 174–175
Vestergaard, Martin David, 115
Virtual collaboration, 42
Virtual conferencing, 41
Virtual reality, 43
Virtual team meeting, 59
Vulnerability
  impact, 196
  power, 172–173

W

Wahba, Phil, 69
Waldroop, James, 104
Walton, Gregory M., 117
Wardley, Simon, 155
War for Kindness, The (Zaki), 71
Warzel, Charlie, 112
WebEx, usage, 36
Winch, Guy, 163
Women
  educational degrees, earning (increase), 21–22
  underrepresentation, 22
  workforce percentage, 17–18
  workforce presence/majority, 21–24
Woolley, Anita Williams, 22
Work
  approach, change, 60–61
  balanced/purposeful relationship, 66
  bargain, change, 4–5

center, shift, 45, 45f
  changes, 2–3
  Covid, change agent, 3–4
  engagement, hierarchy, 62, 62f
  flexibility/adaptability, importance, 19
  freedom, 5
  future, path (change), 89–90
  gender markers, irrelevance, 27
  Great Relocation, 46, 47f
  human work, replacement (modeling), 237
  hybrid work, 179
  journey, 162
  joy, finding, 124
  life/work integration, creation, 50, 52–53
  location, 40–43, 41f, 109–111
    impact, 48–50
    importance, 44, 47
    necessity, 42
  location-flexible work environments, 48
  new normal, 1
  New Now, 30
  opportunity, 68f, 70
  project work, change, 85, 87
  purpose, finding, 137, 139–140
  reason, 141–143, 143f
  remote work, impact, 47
  rethinking, 91, 93, 107, 107f
  timing, location (impact), 48–50
  tour of duty, 108–109
  value, 63, 65
Work and Well-being Survey (APA), 67
Workers
  adaptation (Covid), 14
  agency
    discovery, 7
    surrender, 189
  attitudes, change, 6
  autonomy, 140
  changes, 36–40
  demographic shifts, impact, 7–8
  employees, social contract (renegotiation),
    181
  empowerment/asset, 40–49
  habits, understanding, 35
  inequity, 82
  self-management, 180
  values, retrenchment, 142

Workforce
    change, 7–9
    diversity, 18, 27
    drain/demands, 78
    economic transformation, 2
    empowered workforce, 44, 96, 129, 151
    human workforce, capitalization, 79
    investment, 181
    LGBTQ+ workforce, 24, 26–27
    loneliness, 114
    meeting, 17
    multidimensionality, 27
    multigenerational workforce,
        management, 20, 21f
    pan-generational workforce, meeting, 19
    rethinking, 13
    women, presence/majority, 21–24
Work from home (WFH), 110
    necessity, 179
Work/life balance, 59
Work/life rebalance, 59–60

Workload, amount/intensity/complexity
    (impact), 96
Workplace
    disruption, 58
    post-pandemic workplace, business
        adaptation, 178–179
    trust, 140
Work Trends Index (Microsoft), 5
Worn Wear program, 134
Worthy, Cassandra, 165–166
Wright, Thomas, 94

Z
Zaki, Jamil, 71
Zedong, Mao, 21
Zoom
    link/email address, 47
    meeting, 192
    usage, 36, 37, 112, 144, 166
Zuckerberg, Mark, 149
Zweig, Ben, 131